Low Mountains or High Tea

Low Mountains or High Tea

Misadventures in Britain's National Parks

STEVE SIEBERSON

University of Nebraska Press • *Lincoln*

Frontispiece appears courtesy Carmelicia Sieberson.

George Orwell's "A Nice Cup of Tea" was first published in the *London Evening Star* (January 12, 1946). Excerpt appears courtesy ESI Media.

J. Norman Collie's obituary was published in the 1943 *Obituary Notices of the Royal Society*. Excerpt appears courtesy the Royal Society, London.

∞

Library of Congress Cataloging-in-Publication Data
Names: Sieberson, Steve, author.
Title: Low mountains or high tea: misadventures in Britain's national parks / Steve Sieberson.
Description: Lincoln: University of Nebraska Press, 2019.
Identifiers: LCCN 2019005321
ISBN 9781496214119 (paperback: alk. paper)
ISBN 9781496216953 (epub)
ISBN 9781496216960 (mobi)
ISBN 9781496216977 (pdf)
Subjects: LCSH: National parks and reserves—Great Britain. | Mountaineering—Great Britain.
Classification: LCC SB484.G7 S54 2019 |
DDC 363.6/80941—dc23 LC record available at https://lccn.loc.gov/2019005321

Set in Minion Pro by E. Cuddy.

For the Italian Woman, of course

THERE WAS CONCERN IN THE British doctor's voice when she pointed out that she had removed only six of the nine sutures. "I'm afraid it isn't as good as we might have hoped," she commented.

"Well," I responded, trying to stay calm, "what do you think is indicated?"

She paused, made a slight *hmmm*, and replied, "Why don't we have a cup of tea."

"You want to go out for tea?"

"Oh no, we'll have it here."

"You want to have tea here in the surgery?"

"Of course, it won't be any trouble at all."

She stepped out and returned several minutes later with three steaming cups on a metal tray of the sort that would ordinarily hold scalpels and sterile dressings. "Now," she said, as if what we were about to do was the most normal thing in the world, "does anyone take milk? Would either of you fancy a biscuit?"

I began to wonder if my brain had somehow slipped out of gear. Was this really happening? After all, we were supposed to be on sabbatical in Italy. What were we doing in England?

Contents

Low Mountains or High Tea

The Best-Laid Plans

NOT LONG AGO, DURING THE intermission of a mountain film festival, I sat at a table outside the screening room to sign copies of my earlier book, *The Naked Mountaineer: Misadventures of an Alpine Traveler*, a memoir of my climbs around the world. A fit-looking man with short-cropped gray hair approached my table. He picked up the book, read the back cover, and said, "Should I buy this?"

"Oh, yes," I responded. "If you like the films, I'm sure you'll enjoy my book."

Taking in a deep breath with a slight pause at the top, the man said, "So . . . have you climbed any of the Fourteeners in Colorado?"

"Yes, seven or eight."

"I've done them all."

"All fifty-four?"

"Fifty-eight actually." Then, having gained the upper hand, he asked, "Have you done any state high points?"

"Let's see, maybe half a dozen. I've never gotten organized about it."

"I've done them all."

"Including Denali?"

"Of course," he sniffed. He almost added, "Hasn't everybody?"

At that point I just wanted him to buy the book, but he was ready for the kill. "Have you done the Seven Summits?"

"No, I haven't had the time or money to try any of them." Okay, I thought, give him his due: "How about you?"

"I've done all but Everest, and I've been on two Everest expeditions that got turned back short of the summit. I'm planning to go back and finish it." After letting that sink in for a moment, he added, "So, have you completed *any* high point lists?"

I should have simply surrendered, but I heard myself saying, "Well, my wife and I recently spent three months touring the national parks in Great Britain, and I did make it to their high points."

"And how high do they get?"

"A little over four thousand feet."

He processed that information for a few seconds. Then, with a *hmmmph*, he set the book down and walked away.

My immediate impulse was to call to him and say: "Wait! There really are mountains in the UK, and they're well worth visiting." I wanted to tell him about my climbs but also about exploring the British countryside and how rocky summits are only part of the picture. Where else in the world can you feel at one moment that you are completely at home and at the next that you are on another planet? Where else can you experience the roots of your own culture but then stumble onto edible hockey pucks and a place where cats' eyes are removed? I wanted to impress on him that we have been to many places in the world and that roaming Britain's back roads was one of our most memorable trips ever.

I wanted to say these things, but it was too late. The man was already at a table where a woman was promoting her indoor climbing gym, and he was asking, "So . . . have you climbed any of the Fourteeners?"

That might have concluded the matter, but I can be stubborn at times and I couldn't let it go. Oh, I didn't really care about Mr. My-List-Is-Bigger-Than-Yours, but I did want to share my stories. If he wasn't receptive, someone would be. So let's proceed. Let me tell you about a summer in the British national parks and how it came about quite by accident.

YES, THAT'S CORRECT. WE HADN'T intended to go to the UK at all, and when my wife and I landed in London on the twenty-seventh of May, we had ninety days on our hands and no plans to speak of. Moreover, we had only the vaguest idea that Britain might have places called national parks. Ancient villages, castles, green fields . . . yes, of course, but preserves of wild country? That was not on our minds.

So, how do two veteran travelers find themselves in a foreign country with a calendar that is essentially blank? No, we didn't get on the wrong flight—it's more complicated than that.

My university in Omaha had granted me a year's sabbatical, and we had decided to spend it in Italy. That was an easy choice because my wife is the daughter of Italian immigrants. She has a distinctive Mediterranean look, she talks with her hands, and she doesn't suffer fools gladly—in my life she is most emphatically the Italian Woman. During our years together she has rather deftly caused me to fall in love with the Italian language, Verdi opera, and exquisitely prepared fresh food. Of course we would go to Italy.

Our first challenge was to agree on the big picture, and my thought was that we explore the Apennine Peninsula end to end. The country is made up of twenty "regions," so we could spend two or three weeks in each. And incidentally, I could tackle each region's highest mountain. My online research suggested that the climbing would be grand—Mont Blanc, Mount Aetna, and many others. Yes, Highpointing the Regions of Italy. Now there's a plan.

Delicately, diplomatically, I floated the idea to the Italian Woman—a red, white, and green trial balloon attached to a bit of climbing rope.

It didn't take her more than five seconds to shoot that one out of the sky. This may not be verbatim, but I think it's a reasonable approximation of her reaction: Are you completely crazy? (She may have dredged up the word *pazzo*.) How would you possibly do those climbs—who would you climb with? (Good question, actually.) Do you have any idea what this would cost? (A lot, come to think of it.) And the clincher: Do you really think I'm going to just tag along and sit around while you disappear for days at a time? (Apparently not.)

"You might be able to do a few climbs with me."

"How many?"

"Maybe two."

"Wonderful."

"It was just an idea."

"Not much of one."

Recovering slightly, I tried, "But if I don't do it now, when will I ever have another chance for something like this?"

"After I'm dead and gone."

"But I'll be ninety-five then."

"Stay healthy."

As the smoke cleared, I picked myself up, and we started considering what might work for both of us. A year in one place such as Rome sounded nice and settled, but shouldn't we see more than that? How about a month each in twelve places? Too much moving, endless logistics. Six places for two months each? Four and three, three and four, two and six? After many weeks of discussion (after all, Rome wasn't built in a day), we settled on a plan that we called "Four Seasons in Italy"—our answer to *A Year in Provence*, with theme music by Vivaldi.

It was a simple but appealing idea. We would spend three months in each of four different places. Summer in the mountainous north. Autumn in a central Italian hill town. Winter in the far south. Spring in Rome. Every season had something to offer: alpine scenery and fresh air in summer (and dare I say, possibly one little climb for me?). The grape harvest in Umbria. The first warm winter of our lives, and on the sea (I thought Sicily sounded good, but the Italian Woman is of the firm belief that Sicily is Not Italy, and that is why the toe of Italy's boot appears to be kicking the island toward North Africa). And to cap it off, a lovely spring in the Eternal City, ground zero for everything Italian. We had a plan, and our first step was to find our summer home. An internet search yielded an apartment in a British-run hostel in the Dolomites north of Venice. We happily paid a hefty deposit and began dreaming of rock pinnacles soaring over green meadows filled with wildflowers and romping lambs.

Now, in order to set the stage for what happened next, I need to mention that our planning for Italy took place during the spring, in Madrid, where I was teaching on a faculty exchange. Based on advice from my host university, we had entered Spain on tourist visas, and the personnel department had assured me that when the semester ended, we could move on to any EU country. They were dead wrong. In early May, when we visited the Italian embassy in Madrid to sort out a few details, we learned that (1) an American tourist in Spain or any of the other Continental countries (the "Schengen Area") is allowed to stay for ninety days only; (2) after ninety days we would have to leave Europe for three months before returning for a new ninety-day period; and (3) we had already been in Spain for 120 days and were thus Illegal Aliens. Under the circumstances our only hope of moving directly to Italy was to apply to the Italian government for a long-term visa. Also, because we were American citizens based in Omaha, we had to present this application at the Italian consulate in Chicago.

In desperation I contacted a professor friend in Rome, she called a colleague at the University of Perugia, and that person quickly issued an invitation for me to spend the academic year as a visiting professor. The Italian Woman and I then prepared our applications and paid a second visit to the Italian embassy. The sympathetic official reviewed our documents and pronounced that we would have no difficulty getting a one-year visa from the consulate in Chicago.

During our final days in Madrid we had the uneasy feeling that the Spanish deportation police were lurking in every subway tunnel, and at times we hesitated leaving our apartment for fear of being recognized as scofflaws. In mid-May, just as soon as my semester in Spain had ended, we left the Schengen Area—fortunately not in handcuffs. We flew to Omaha and then immediately to Chicago, where we had an appointment to present our applications. We had every expectation that a week later we would be winging our way to the Italian Alps, visas in hand, for the first of our Four Seasons.

AT THE ITALIAN CONSULATE ON North Michigan Avenue there was one woman, the Processor, reviewing applications from behind a bullet-proof glass partition. A tinny-sounding speaker amplified every word spoken by the Processor to each trembling applicant. There were four appointments ahead of us—a woman from Thailand, a young man from China, an overweight American family, and a ponytailed American musician. Apparently, they were all imbeciles because nothing in their papers was remotely close to what the Italian government required, and it was beyond the Processor's comprehension that they could have so badly misinterpreted the clear instructions on the consulate's website.

Each and every one of the people ahead of us was summarily rejected, and with each successive *arrivederci*, my jet lag weighed a little heavier on my shoulders. Nevertheless, I thought we would provide a ray of sunshine in the Processor's dreary day because we had done a dry run with her counterpart, the Processadora, at the embassy in Madrid. Also, my wife's appearance screams "I'm one of you!"

As we approached the counter, the other people in the waiting room drew an audible, collective breath.

"Good morning," I said cheerily into the thick glass.

"What are you applying for?"

"A research visa for myself and a spousal visa for my wife. Here are our two applications." I slid the papers down and under the glass.

The Processor took our documents, flipped through them quickly, and without looking up said, "No." A slight pause, and she added, "No . . . No . . . No."

Apparently, we were imbeciles too, and we had produced nothing to justify sullying the Processor's homeland with our stinking presence during the coming year. I mentioned that we had had these papers reviewed in Madrid, and the Processor responded, "I cannot comment on how they do things in Spain." She pronounced *Spain* with a distinct hiss at the beginning, as if it were a profanity. She continued, saying that this was Chicago and the rules here were clear enough. I pointed out that the University of Perugia was expecting me, and the Processor responded that the university should have known that their letter of invitation was laughably insufficient. I reminded her that I had proof of insurance, salary, and money in the bank, plus a printed screenshot showing that on Facebook I had "liked" Silvio Berlusconi's tanning salon. The woman raised a hand as if to call for someone offstage to snare me with a hook and drag me away.

Meanwhile, my wife was standing beside me in a state of shock. Her lip was quivering with either rage or anguish— sometimes it's hard to tell. I pleaded with the Processor, "Isn't there *anything* we would qualify for?"

Sullenly, she took another look at my application and said: "Well, you are a law professor. Instead of research, you could go for study, yes?"

"Yes," I responded eagerly. "I will study the Italian constitution, the European Union, and international law. Further study is part of my job as a professor." As is the ability to think on my feet and dispense hooey at a moment's notice.

The Processor studied our papers again, looked up, and with the slightest hint of pleasantness, responded, "Okay then, you have enough here to qualify for a study visa—not research but study. I can process your application for twelve months of study."

My wife and I were smiling now. I gave her a little one-armed hug, and I wanted to lean forward and kiss the glass barrier.

"Oh," said the Processor, "there's just one thing."

"Okay," I responded. "What is it?"

"Your wife can't go with you."

The sobs this elicited from the woman on my side of the glass could have melted the marble heart of a Bernini statue, but the Processor was evidently made of titanium. My wife and I left empty-handed, thoroughly deflated, now certain that Italy was the last place we would ever want to visit.

IT WASN'T UNTIL WE WERE sitting at Midway Airport for our flight back to Omaha that either of us uttered a word about what to do next. There was nothing for us in Omaha. I had no work there during the coming year, and we had no home either—in a fit of reducing our carbon footprint we had sold our house and most of our furniture before moving to Spain. And even more, we had declared ourselves nonresidents for U.S. tax purposes for the year, so we couldn't stay in the States for more than a few weeks without incurring an enormous tax bill. With Europe out of the picture and our own country off-limits, where could we go? Four Seasons in Ecuador? Do they even have seasons in Ecuador? We kicked around a number of possibilities, then settled back into a gloomy silence.

At that dark moment I heard someone speaking softly into my ear. I recognized the silky voice—it was either Prince Charles or Camilla, and it said: "Come to England, old chap. We British aren't part of that silly Schengen thing. We don't use the euro. Come to think of it, overlooking a bit of Saxon blood, we're hardly European at all. You can have a jolly good summer here, and as soon as you arrive, we'll sit down and have some tea and chips."

A few days later we were on our way to Britain. Fifteen national parks and their high points were waiting for us—we just didn't know it yet.

2

Multifarious Puddings

THE ITALIAN WOMAN AND I had made brief visits to England in the past and had seen all the major attractions, but we had never considered going there for a long stay. For one thing, we were attracted to the "otherness" of Continental cultures and their languages, and it seemed a bit lame to follow in the footsteps of so many Americans whose most daring foray abroad is a trip to Britain. For another, when your hometown is Seattle, where the Italian Woman and I had spent most of our lives, you don't find it too appealing to go somewhere else where it rains all the time. And really, why invest much time in a nation whose seminal event in history was a successful invasion by the French and whose signature food is, coincidentally, French fries?

Yet we had to face facts: the British Isles were available to us, while Italy was not. I took encouragement from a *Monty Python* sketch in which a would-be bank robber, played by John Cleese, was stunned to discover that he was holding up a lingerie shop instead of a bank. After being informed that there were no piles of cash on hand, he paused and said: "Adopt, adapt, and improve . . . Just a pair of knickers then, please."

BEFORE LEAVING THE UNITED STATES we had taken care of a few necessary details. First, having been burned once, I researched the UK visa requirements and confirmed that with no paperwork an American can enter as a tourist and stay for six months. Then, with some trepidation, I called Collett's Mountain Holidays, owners of the apartment we had rented in the Dolomites, to explain that we would not be coming to Italy. When I asked for a refund, they told me that their policy was to return only half the deposit. But then, after I pleaded for mercy, they offered to refund half and credit the rest toward a stay in one of their other lodges. How about northern Spain? No, we can't go back to the Continent. The French Pyrenees? No, same continent. Well, how about their nice B&B in the Yorkshire Dales? Where's that? Northern England. Okay, I'll call you from London, and we'll get directions from there.

Collett's made it clear that we would need a rental car to get to them and that any exploration outside London and the main tourist areas would be nearly impossible without our own vehicle. I said this would not be a problem, but that was just bravado. The thought of a British road trip was daunting. I had driven in England—and every American should do it once, just for bragging rights—but I was certain that I had used up my life's allotment of driving on the left and returning in one piece. The next time I sat behind a misplaced steering wheel, I would surely meet my Maker.

To give us a passing chance at survival, I thought it might be safer if we would take a train out of London and rent a car in a less congested part of the country. And so I phoned the widow of an old acquaintance in the West Midlands, which I knew to be north of London and thus in the general direction of Collett's lodge. The woman and I had never met, but we had spoken on the phone several years earlier. She was surprised to hear from me but happy to help, and she agreed to reserve us a car at a rental agency in nearby Worcester.

ON OUR ARRIVAL IN LONDON we checked into a hotel, and I immediately set out to purchase SIM cards for our mobile phones and iPads. At a nearby shop a helpful young man named Jason outfitted us with UK phone numbers and 3G data plans. He explained things so clearly that I was certain we would have no problems with technology during our time in Britain. Spain had been a challenge, as I had tried to articulate concepts like "¡mierda! ¡no mas minutos!" Now, in the land of my mother tongue, I was confident that our life in the wireless world would be a breeze.

Our first dinner in England was serviceable fish and chips, washed down with a sensational pint of ale. The next morning we began our reacquaintance with the "full English breakfast." Fried eggs, fried tomatoes, and fried mushrooms—no problem, rather tasty in fact. But the fried sausages were ghastly—shiny with grease on the outside, pasty and gray on the inside—and the fried bacon looked like a piece of evidence from CSI: Miami. (I see that I have just used the word *fried* five times.) Most peculiar was the puddle of baked beans, exactly like the canned pork and beans we eat at picnics in the United States. Beans with eggs seemed like a serious mismatch, akin to eating pizza with a bowl of cornflakes.

Arriving by train in Worcester, we were greeted by pouring rain, a taxi driver who refused to get out and assist with our bags, and a fifteenth-century hotel whose tilted floors caused us to lurch around like inebriates. At one point I leaned over so far that I hit my head against a sconce.

Once I had achieved equilibrium, I called our car rental agency, and that is when I had my first experience with what proved to be all too common in the UK, namely, that the people who answer the phone aren't necessarily British and, whoever they are, they certainly spice up the conduct of business. I inquired about the car we had reserved, and the voice responded, "Can you give me the blah blah of er blah blah blah?" I couldn't understand him. After several repetitions, first at normal speed and then more slowly, I asked him to spell the first word. It was *details*. Okay. Now let's work on the next one. Normal speed, then slowly. Finally, a plea for him to spell it, and it came out as *credit*. I then summoned all of my life's experience and guessed that the third word was *card*. The fellow on the other end of the line must have shuddered to think that he was entrusting one of his automobiles to such a dimwit.

The next morning it was relatively easy to pick up our Vauxhall, but as expected, it was white-knuckle time, especially on the first few roundabouts. Once we were on the M5, it was a bit easier, except for the fact that people kept trying to pass us on the right. Traffic was heavy, and every truck in England was heading north with us. Finally, an hour beyond Manchester, we exited at Kendal and drove east into Yorkshire.

I had heard of Yorkshire pudding, a blob of batter cooked in meat drippings—obviously somebody's idea of a joke. I hadn't thought much about an actual place called Yorkshire, and the Yorkshire Dales sounded like a bad lounge act on a cruise ship. "Hellooooo! I'm Dale, and this is Dale. We're from Yorkshire, and we call ourselves the Yorkshire Dales. We want this to be your best vacation ever, so we're going to sing some of your very Favorite songs just for You!"

OUR MAP INDICATED THAT A mile or two east of the M6 we would be entering the Yorkshire Dales National Park. This was an exciting prospect because when Americans hear the words *national parks*, we envision spectacular wilderness preserved intact, places where visitors can sample nature's finest vistas and get close to geysers, waterfalls, and wildlife. We think of the enduring symbols of our parks, the rangers in their loden green uniforms and campaign hats, and of course their mascot, Smokey Bear. And so, as we left the motorway, I expected to find a park entrance station where we would pay a fee and an avuncular fellow with a white mustache would hand us a map and litterbag. I anticipated large billboards telling us to "mind the wildlife." There was none of that. If there was so much as a sign indicating the park boundary, we didn't notice it. Instead, we just proceeded eastward on a small two-lane highway, the A684. The village of Sedbergh was supposed to have a National Park Centre, but we missed that as well. Beyond the village we drove through hills and dales (ahhh, Dales!), winding this way and that, steadily climbing into country where sheep and cows grazed in pastures enclosed by hedgerows and stone walls. There were no forests, no waterfalls, and no bears.

It turns out that a national park in the UK is quite a different beast than the American variety. Britain has little true wilderness, so its parks must accommodate both scenery and human activity. Land is designated as a park for protection of its flora and fauna but also its cultural heritage, and it is managed to allow agriculture and commercial activity. Thus, every preserve has natural beauty but is also crisscrossed by roads and dotted with towns and farms, and since it sports little signage, it is most easily identified as a colored blob on the map. Also, while the American National Park Service is a federal agency with an organizational hierarchy, the British parks are separately managed by local councils. Overall, the closest American equivalent is New York's Adirondack Park, which is managed not by the federal government but by a state agency and is home to 130,000 permanent residents and more than a hundred towns and villages.

It was a lovely late afternoon as we traversed the verdant landscape, crossing from west to east with the sun behind us. Unfortunately, I wasn't in the right frame of mind to fully appreciate the experience. I was tired from jet lag, unsure of what the summer would bring, and petrified every time we met an oncoming car or truck along a narrow road on which everyone was driving down the middle. At one point I pulled onto a scenic turnout, not to admire the view but just to compose myself. The Italian Woman wasn't feeling much better; she evidently found it highly unnerving to be sitting in the left front seat with no steering wheel to hang onto. I noticed that on every curve, her feet were compulsively probing for a phantom brake pedal.

THE TOWN OF LEYBURN WOULD be largely ignored if it weren't located just at the eastern edge of the national park. It does provide a base for exploring the eastern Dales, but the town itself offers only the basic amenities—a few pubs and restaurants, two outdoor shops, a supermarket, that sort of thing. We were disappointed that our first home in the UK wasn't a picture postcard village, but thanks to our arrangement with Collett's, we would stay in Leyburn for two weeks.

What was perfect was Eastfield Lodge, a first-rate B & B. It had only eight sleeping rooms, a cozy living room that they called the "lounge," and a cheery dining room with a view across the valley to a row of green hills. Vic, the long-haired manager who bore a comforting resemblance to a pop culture Jesus, told us that there were two things that would make our stay memorable. First, his breakfasts. He showed us the list of the available dishes, all of which were made with local, organic ingredients. Eggs, tomatoes, mushrooms, sausage . . . wait a minute, what was this? Vic sensed our skepticism but assured us that his morning meal was superior to any other.

Vic's other point of pride was that we were at ground zero for the finest country walking in all of England. He took us into a library room where there was an array of guidebooks and maps, any of which we could borrow. He also said he would help us plan our walks every day. The Italian Woman and I were enthusiastic about this prospect, ready to get some fresh air after five months of subways and nightlife in Madrid.

Before turning in, we walked into the village center to Saffron, a Bangladeshi restaurant. It sounded like an improvement over fish and chips, and it was. I'll never remember the name of what we ordered, but the mix of spices was so complex and exotic that it felt like eating a symphonic production of *Sheherazade*.

This being a Wednesday evening and still in May, Saffron was nearly empty. As a result, we could eavesdrop on the two English couples at the next table. We gleaned that they were from somewhere south of Yorkshire, here on a brief getaway. They were all retired from something or other, and their chief activity seemed to be gardening. Their conversation was rather subdued until one of the women suddenly perked up.

Woman: Oh, Roger, do tell them what happened last week.

Roger: Really, most remarkable, what.

Woman: You simply cahn't *imagine* what he saw.

Roger: I was in the wood behind our house, and there it was!

Woman: The most *extraordinary* thing.

Roger: Are you ready for this? A *green* woodpecker.

Other woman: You must be *joking*.

Other man: I've never heard of such a thing in those parts, much less seen one.

Roger: I still cahn't believe it myself.

Woman: Wasn't I right? The most *extraordinary* thing.

In the scheme of things, what I just described may not seem of much consequence. To most of us, it is a bit silly to think that a person could get excited about seeing a bird, and the lives of Roger and his companions sounded rather dull. And yet the interchange was highly significant. You see, we had understood every word.

In all of our travels and living abroad, communication had been a constant challenge—one that we had voluntarily taken on, but a challenge nevertheless. We had always tried to learn enough of a country's language to accomplish basic tasks, but the exchange of ideas with locals was invariably elementary, often accomplished with one or two words and a variety of improvised gestures. Also, we could never know whether the person we were talking with was sophisticated or crude, sincere or dismissive. We existed in a nuance vacuum. Even if we were modestly fluent—as with my fading Dutch and my wife's rusty Italian—or if we found a local who had mastered English as a second language, there was still a noticeable lack of depth in our exchanges. It was comforting from time to time to bump into an American or other native English speaker, but we didn't journey abroad to interact with our own kind, and we didn't seek them out.

At Saffron it struck me that our three-month tour of Britain would be unlike our visits to other places. The summer would offer us the opportunity to understand more than a few phrases and to more deeply grasp the subtleties of what was being said. There are real cultural differences between the United States and the United Kingdom, but the way we organize our thoughts and express ourselves is largely the same. Language is identity, and in a linguistic sense we had come home.

VIC WAS CORRECT ABOUT HIS breakfast. Every single item was fresh and flavorful, but to us it was still the Full English and heavier than we really wanted. To liven things up a bit, Vic suggested two items we had never tried—black pudding and white pudding. Rather than explain their composition, he coyly suggested we just try one of each. The Italian Woman politely declined.

I, however, took the bait, and I quickly discovered that they weren't puddings as we Americans use the word—no resemblance to custard or crème caramel. Now this wasn't a complete surprise because of my previous knowledge of the Yorkshire pudding. *Pudding* seems to be a catchall word used by the British to describe anything they can't remember the name of, like *whatchamacallit* or *whatsit*. "I say, Love, whilst you are in the garridge, kindly fetch me the sixteen-millimeter pudding so I can mend the perambulator."

Vic's puddings were discs of some sort of organic material that had been fried to the consistency of a Presto log. The "white" one resembled an ordinary sausage patty, the black one a hockey puck. I took a bite of each and went no further but, instead, fired up my iPad to discern what mischief was afoot. That is how I learned that the black one is oatmeal bound together by pork blood that has congealed, aged, oxidized, and putrefied. The white one uses pork fat and suet to cement the oatmeal into any shape your heartburn desires. Back in the day when Scotland had a Death Row, they offered white pudding and chips as a last meal and then let nature take its course. Later I thanked Vic for schooling me in the dark arts.

IT WAS RAINING LIGHTLY, BUT we decided to take a short hike. Vic gave us a guide for "Walk Number 4, the Shawl Way," which runs west from the center of Leyburn along a ridge and then down to the hamlet of Preston-under-Scar, or Preston for short. England has these town names that are more like phrases, and there seems to be no rhyme or reason as to which word predominates. Kingston upon Hull is commonly referred to as Hull, while Stratford-upon-Avon (notice the hyphens) is of course Stratford and not Avon. Henley-on-Thames, site of the rowing competition, is known simply as "on." Incidentally, the town of Stratford-*upon*-Avon is located in the district of Stratford-*on*-Avon, just to keep things perfectly muddled.

Back to Preston: it sounds a bit creepy, doesn't it, to be living under a scar, as if you once received inadequate first aid for a laceration on top of your head. As it turns out, a "scar" is a geographical feature, a cliff or exposed hillside, undoubtedly related to its larger cousin, the escarpment. As to the Shawl Way, the name refers to a legend in which Mary, Queen of Scots, was fleeing from imprisonment in nearby Bolton Castle and, upon arriving in Leyburn, discovered that she had dropped her shawl.

Despite Vic's excellent pamphlet, we quickly lost our way. The map seemed clear enough, but we later determined that the written descriptions should have been taken metaphorically rather than literally. In any event, within twenty minutes we had no clue where we were. We wandered over fields of wet grass, through stiles and gates, and along narrow roads lined with stone walls that nearly prevented us from stepping aside for the whizzing traffic. Luckily, it had stopped raining.

We somehow ended up in the village of Wensley and were delighted to find a pub called the Three Horseshoes. It was just before 3:00 p.m., and we were desperate for lunch. Unhappily, the bartender said he was closing in seven minutes, so no food, but we could order a beer if we would drink it quickly. We slammed down a couple of half-pints. The only other patron, a woman named Jewel who was well into her third glass of wine, asked me an incoherent question about the laptop computer on her table. Hoping to avoid being drawn into a conversation, I glanced at the screen and suggested, "Just reboot, and it will be fine." This evidently struck her as a brilliant solution, and in gratitude she offered us a lift back to Leyburn. While under way, she apologized for the rather pungent smell of her car, saying that she cleaned horse blankets for a living and had to transport them around in her back seat, where the Italian Woman sat with a desperate look that translated as "I need air!"

In Leyburn we realized that its pubs would be closed as well, and so we made for a tearoom called the Posthorn. The fragrance of freshly baked scones nearly knocked us over, and I eagerly asked the host if they were serving high tea.

"We're serving *afternoon* tea," he replied. "Would you like to sit over there at the window?"

I took his slight stress on *afternoon* as an indication that I had committed some sort of faux pas but that he had been too polite to say, "Welcome to England, where we invite you to learn our language and customs." It was like having someone correct you on the pronunciation of their name simply by repeating it differently than you have said it: Are you Mr. Turtle? Yes, I'm Tur-TELL. Later I learned that *high tea* is generally regarded as an Americanism. Historically, the late-afternoon consumption of small sandwiches, scones, and cakes was known among the upper crust as "low tea" because they ate from low tables while lounging on settees. Among the working class a heartier version of the meal was their supper, and they sat at ordinary high wooden tables—thus "high" tea. These days the appropriate way to avoid classism is to call the event "full tea" or "afternoon tea." My miscue notwithstanding, I wish to note that at the Posthorn we did sit tall at our table for two.

Our food was served on a three-tiered platter that suggested an elegance otherwise lacking in the somewhat Spartan dining room. We ate with gusto, and at one point the Italian Woman remarked: "Now Stevie, this is what England is all about. We need to do this every day."

"Great idea," I responded, reaching for my second scone, "but we're in a national park. There must be a lot to see. Don't you agree that we should take a long walk every day to earn our calories?"

"Not if it's raining like today. I prefer to stay dry. And I'll thank you never to accept another ride with a horse blanket woman."

Meanwhile, at an adjacent table a man sat alone, drinking coffee from a French press. He was staring at a small, well-worn book of mathematical formulas. Occasionally, he would write something in tiny letters along the edge of a large manila envelope, just below the return address. Then he would pick up a pocket-size transistor radio, hold it aloft, and rotate it slowly as if to improve its reception. It wasn't producing any sound whatsoever, and it didn't appear to be turned on. After that the man would set the radio down and return to studying his little book. He repeated this cycle precisely every ten minutes during the hour we were having our tea. At some point it dawned on me that he was writing, "There is a stranger at the next table, watching me, trying to figure out what I am doing. I'm on to his little game."

3

Baby Steps and Buttertubs

THE NEXT DAY, ON VIC'S recommendation we drove to Jervaulx, described in a brochure as the "atmospheric ruins of a great Cistercian abbey." I didn't feel much atmosphere, but "ruins" was an apt label for piles of rubble and sections of wall that remained from an earlier collection of chapels, kitchens, and flagellation chambers. Fortunately, someone had planted grass throughout the complex, and that offered a cheery contrast to the sad, gray stone. After a quick walk-through, we couldn't think of anything else to do, so we chose a stone bench in a sunny spot and sat down to a pleasant lunch of Stilton cheese on currant buns. If not for the man on the riding lawn mower, the scene would have been completely peaceful and relaxing.

After our picnic we attempted to follow the directions for "Walk 14, Jervaulx Abbey and East Witton." We were promised "a gently undulating ramble through parkland, pastures, and plantations," culminating in "a delightful 1¾-mile riverside stroll." What we experienced were multiple gates to choose from, where the guide described only one, stiles and ladders where the description said "no ladder—stiles," and ultimately the conviction that there was no river in the vicinity. All of this occurred despite the fact that after the Shawl Way fiasco, I was determined to interpret the guide with a measure of artistic license, rather than to follow its directions too slavishly. Come to think of it, we might have gotten lost precisely because of my new organic method. In any event we fortunately found our way back to the abbey and our car, none the worse for wear. It was a dry and sunny day, and that was enough to make us happy.

That evening, at the end of a pub dinner, we were introduced to the beloved English dessert called "spotted dick." It's somewhat like an American brown bread set in a blob of vanilla custard. There were efforts a few years back to change the name to Spotted Richard, but those were derisively rejected as political correctness run amok. Also cast aside were Spotted Mr. Happy, Spotted Master of Ceremonies, and Spotted Bill Clinton. The traditional name endures, and those visitors who are too prim to order it are missing the boat.

ACROSS THE VALLEY FROM EASTFIELD Lodge rose a flat-topped mound that dominated the view from our dining room. Vic identified it as Pen Hill, at 1,726 feet the highest mountain in the area. He said it was a good walk, somewhat more vigorous than our first two outings. The Italian Woman said she was game, so on our third day in Leyburn we set out on our first uphill hike—a climb if you will. In my knapsack I carried a meat pie and fruit tarts we had bought that morning at one of the local bakeries. Actually, we purchased two meat pastries, but they smelled so good that we had eaten one just outside the shop.

From the nearby village of West Witton we drove up onto the moors and found our trailhead next to a cattle guard. The path began as an old road but soon turned into a field of heather. The musical *Brigadoon* has a sweet little song about wandering through "the heather on the hill," and a stroll like that had always sounded romantic. The Pen Hill heather, as it turned out, was knee-high, dense, and difficult to pass through. Also, the ground was boggy in places, and we had to step carefully. Eventually, a slight trail appeared, and on it we made our way to the base of the mountain. From there the path went straight up, alongside a stone wall. When we reached a horizontal wall halfway to the top, we traversed beneath it to a gap, passed through the opening, and found the upper slopes.

The final section was a zigzagging path. It was a sunny day, and in the lee of the mountain, with no breeze, it was actually hot. I had never, ever felt warm in England before this, and for the Italian Woman the heat was withering. A true Seattle native, she tends to wilt when the temperature rises above seventy. At one point she groaned: "I'll never make it. Just leave me here and send someone to get me." We paused for water, and she revived enough to carry on. When we finally topped out, the cool wind returned. We sat beside a square cairn that the map identified as a "pile of stones" and ate our remaining pastries. The Italian Woman began warbling with happiness at the expansive views and the tasty pies.

As we relaxed, a local man named Walter arrived with his two cocker spaniels, which he said were hunting dogs. Together we looked back toward the trailhead, and Walter pointed out that just adjacent to our heather bog lay a series of walled pastures with grazing sheep. Through the grass ran a well-defined dirt path. Walter had come up that way, and he said it was far easier than the route we had taken. The Italian Woman glared at me, but I took shelter in the fact that we had simply been following the directions—literally, this time—from Vic's guidebook.

Walter told us that the sheep in that area are "hefted." I nodded understandingly, thinking that this was a variant on *hefty*, and shouldn't all sheep be plump? Actually, as the man explained, *hefting* refers to attachment, or bonding, to a particular section of land. Being hefted, these sheep would not be happy anywhere else. When hoof-and-mouth disease decimated the local flocks some years earlier, it had taken several succeeding generations—and a good deal of psychotherapy—to achieve hefting among the replacements. The human counterpart to hefting can be found practically anywhere. Many people are deeply bonded to their neighborhood, city, or region, while wanderers like my wife and me are often seen as having some sort of attachment deficiency syndrome.

The Italian Woman and I strolled along the summit plateau at the upper edge of a cliff, and we located the Beacon, a circle of rocks where, according to our guidebook, locals traditionally lit signal fires to warn of attacks. The book also mentioned a centuries-old ritual in West Witton, where every year on August 24 the villagers reenact the "burning of the Bartle." The original event, so the story goes, was the fiery execution of a sheep thief named Bartle, who had been driven down from the mountain into the village. These days a straw-stuffed effigy is burned while the people chant:

In Pen Hill Crags he tore his rags
At Hunter's Thorn he blew his horn
At Capplebank Stee he brock his knee
At Grisgill Beck he brock his neck
At Wadham's End he couldn't fend
At Grisgill End we'll mek his end
   Shout lads Shout!

Thirty years before our climb of Pen Hill, I had witnessed a burning man ritual on the south coast of Crete, and I will never forget the primal feeling of it. But when I think of Bartle and everything else he had gone through on his final day, the unfortunate chap might have welcomed the flames as an end to his misery.

Our descent through the sheep pastures was quick and easy. Our first climb in the Yorkshire Dales National Park had taken an hour to get up and only half that long to return to the car. When I congratulated my partner on her success, she thanked me and immediately declared the next day, coincidentally a Sunday, to be a day of rest.

THE NEXT MORNING THE ITALIAN Woman found a motoring guide to the "Herriot Trail," and we were reminded that for the past forty years the Yorkshire Dales have largely been known as the setting for *All Creatures Great and Small.* My wife had read the books and seen the television programs, so the drive appealed to her. I had somehow missed the phenomenon, but I was game, and it was, after all, my partner's turn to choose the itinerary.

Veterinarian Alf Wight was fifty when he began to write about the Yorkshire folk and their animals. He took the pen name James Herriot from a football goalkeeper, because in the 1960s any self-generated publicity was considered unseemly for a professional person. How different it is today, at least in the United States, where the airwaves are saturated with ads for lawyers, doctors, and drugs that will cure dry mouth, restless legs, and other diseases you have never heard of but now realize you might have. Wight's practice was in the town of Thirsk, but for his stories he created the fictional hamlet of Darrowby. The forty-nine *All Creatures* television episodes were filmed in Thirsk and throughout the nearby valleys of Swaledale and Wensleydale—a church here, a pub there, a village green somewhere else.

Our brochure directed us through a dozen hamlets and across several moors. At one point we drove through a stream, the same one Herriot fords in the opening sequence of the TV programs. Actually, I did it several times so the Italian Woman could get a photo with the water splashing properly, as a group of nearby campers stared at us in wonderment. We traversed the adorably named Buttertubs Pass, located the Red Lion pub in Langthwaite, and stopped for tea in Askrigg. With its open landscapes and villages of gray stone, Yorkshire had a character all its own, different from other parts of England we had seen. I enjoyed the excursion so much that back at Eastfield Lodge, I insisted that we watch a few episodes of *All Creatures* on a DVD, and I started reading the first book. A bit late to the party, I had become a Herriot fan.

THAT EVENING, IN THE LOUNGE, we had an earnest discussion about the summer ahead. After a flurry of activity in Madrid and Chicago, we had diverted to England and were now settled in Leyburn. We had switched over to porridge and fruit for breakfast. We had done some country walking. Now that we had a routine of sorts, it was time for a bigger perspective.

It started with the Italian Woman asking, "Stevie, what exactly are we doing here?"

"Well, we're using our Collett's credits because we can't go to Italy."

"Yes, but what is this summer going to be? What's the plan?"

Compared to the Four Seasons in Italy, which was a grand plan for an entire year, we had landed in England without an itinerary. Spontaneity sounds appealing, but the truth was that we were already feeling the need for some sort of agenda.

I said that I had always wanted to climb the highest mountains in England, Scotland, and Wales. That would be Snowdon in Wales, Scotland's Ben Nevis, and Scafell Pike in the Lake District of England, and as far as I knew, all of them were walkups. After Pen Hill I was confident that the Italian Woman could take several more conditioning hikes here in the Dales and then we could do the Big Three together.

"Three walks isn't much of a summer," she observed. "We need more than that."

That spurred us to get on the internet and start surfing for ideas. I looked for information on country walking, and eventually I stumbled onto a website with a map of Britain showing all of its national parks—ten in England, two in Scotland, and three in Wales. The site also included a list of the high points of each park.

"Hey, look at this," I said. "There are fifteen of these national parks. Maybe we could drive to all of them—they're spread all over the country."

"Well," she responded, "I love the Yorkshire Dales, and I've always wanted to see Scotland, so sure, let's go to the national parks. I never need to go back to Stonehenge or the Tower of London."

I suggested that we could spend roughly a week in each of the parks and hike to their high points—a scenic road trip with some fine exercise.

"Wait a minute. Didn't we have this conversation when we were planning for Italy?"

"Oh, you mean highpointing the twenty regions?"

"Yes, I thought we agreed that was a bad idea."

"But that was different. Britain will be so much easier. Nothing is more than a few thousand feet high, and you'll be able to climb them all . . . here, look at the list."

"First of all, I'm not a climber, and besides, if they're not very impressive, why would you want to go up a bunch of low mountains?"

"Well . . . umm . . . because they're *there*."

"I've never understood that. Do you know how nerdy it sounds?"

"How could it be *nerdy*? We're talking about mountains."

"But highpointing sounds so silly. Who really cares if something is highest or second highest or tenth highest? What are you looking for—some sort of certificate of achievement?"

I had no logical answer—how do you explain the mystical lure of the peaks? I had to cut my losses. What was clear enough was that we both wanted to see a lot more of Britain, but neither of us wanted a museum and cathedral tour. So, we would set out on a road trip to the fifteen national parks, primarily to enjoy the British countryside. We would take driving tours like the Herriot Trail, and along the way we would stop in pubs and tearooms. My mate would consider a few walks here and there, but only if the weather was perfect, the trail was easy, and she was in the mood. I shouldn't expect anything more ambitious than that, and I would kindly keep my climbing ambitions to myself.

VIC HAD LEFT ON VACATION, and filling in for him at the B&B was Jen, a Vancouver native now living near Nottingham. She was rail thin; had short, spiky, bleached hair; and was so trim that when she walked into the breakfast room, all of the guests instantly felt dumpy and ashamed. Jen—even her name was lean—was training to be a professional walking guide and trek leader, and she looked as if she could hike for days without ever stopping for so much as a sip of water. Her appearance was intimidating, but she quickly disarmed us with her attentiveness.

With Jen's help I located a map for the unnamed mountain across the valley, adjacent to Pen Hill. This looked like another good conditioning walk, and it was another blue-sky day. When I proposed the hike to the Italian Woman, avoiding the word *climb*, she agreed to give it a go.

The path started in the hamlet of Caldbergh, but we almost didn't make it that far. On a road so narrow that both of our side mirrors were practically touching the hedges, we met a FedEx truck. I couldn't imagine that anybody in such an isolated setting had even heard of FedEx, but here we were, nose to nose with one of its delivery vans. I wasn't sure of the protocol when two vehicles meet like this with no hope of passing by each other, and I considered sobbing to demonstrate my helplessness. Fortunately, the FedEx man started backing up, and he kept on until he was able to maneuver into a driveway. With profound gratitude I rolled down my window and offered him my wallet.

Once again, our walk map was hopelessly imprecise. I had expected better, because this one was a highly detailed Ordnance Survey topographic map rather than a hand-drawn amateur guide. Only fifty yards from the car we had to choose one of two dirt roads, and a quarter-mile farther along, the one we selected ran dead into a farmyard. The other alternative proved better but still not what the map showed. The track traversed a slope, and below us lay a walled pasture in which a farmer was trying to herd sheep with a mud-caked Range Rover. Each time he stopped to crank his steering wheel, the sheep just laughed at him and returned to where they had been. The man was persistent but, as far as we could see, wholly unsuccessful. We wondered whether his border collie had run off.

Eventually, the red dirt track gave way to low heather and tundra grass. We walked easily uphill, and along the way we saw open metal boxes filled with some sort of pellets. At the mountain's flat, grassy top we found a wooden wall maybe six feet tall and four feet wide, with a bench next to it. Puzzled, we sat down and ate our lunch. Later I was told—by someone who was probably pulling my leg—that the boxes contained food for grouse, and sheep won't touch it. The wall and bench were a hunter's blind, where sporting fellows could relax out of the wind while waiting for an unsuspecting bird to begin a tasty meal, then take aim and show the little bastard who's boss.

On our return from Caldbergh, we stopped at Middleham, boyhood home of Richard III, supposedly the last English king to die in battle. His remains were discovered in 2012, more than five centuries after his demise, and DNA testing has now established that his death was caused by a black pudding served at his final breakfast. In any event we threw caution to the wind and ordered lunch at the Richard III Pub. While eating cottage pie at an outside table, we noticed dozens of horses and riders passing by, and the waitress explained that just beyond the village is one of England's most famous training centers for professional jockeys. It's called "The Gallops," and those trainees who don't cut the mustard are sent to a second-tier facility known as "The Trots."

That evening we visited with Jen and a guest named Barry, and we mentioned the idea of touring the national parks. They had never heard of anyone traveling to all fifteen, but they felt it was doable since we had the whole summer. When I delicately raised the matter of the parks' high points, the two said they didn't have much information, but they assumed that all of the fifteen would be walk-ups. As for the Yorkshire Dales, neither of them had climbed its highest mountain, a peak called Whernside, but they had heard it was a straightforward hike on a good path. They also felt that given the Italian Woman's success to that point, she was ready, and incidentally, she should understand that the British don't really refer to their hiking as mountain climbing. They use the term *hill walking*.

Clearly outnumbered, the Italian Woman said she was amenable to more "hill walking." She would go with me to Whernside, and if the good weather held, we could do it the next day just to be done with it. Later she reminded me that she didn't give a farthing about making it to the top of something just because it was higher than something else, but she would come along to humor me.

4

The Hard Way Down

ONE THING ABOUT STAYING AT a B&B is that breakfast is served within a fairly short time window. You must be in the dining room at the appointed hour, or you will miss your black pudding. For the Italian Woman and me, the 8:00 to 9:00 a.m. hour at Eastfield Lodge was always pushing things a bit, and we generally made an appearance at five minutes before nine. As a result, on the day we would attempt to reach the highest point in Yorkshire Dales National Park, we left the lodge at ten fifteen. That's far too late for a real climb, but I was satisfied that this was just going to be a stroll of four or five hours. As we were getting into the car, Jen came out and told us that her husband was arriving that afternoon. She wanted us to meet, so she would prepare a special dinner for the four of us.

We drove west from Leyburn to Hawes, then south to a junction called Ribblehead, where our trail began at a large roadside car park at 968 feet in elevation. The drive had been around thirty miles but had taken more than an hour because of narrow roads and my reluctance to play chicken with every car we met.

Whernside, at 2,415 feet, sits at the western edge of the national park, as the crow flies only twelve miles east of the M6 and thirty miles from Lancaster on the Irish Sea. Two other prominent peaks, Ingleborough Hill (2,372) and Pen-y-ghent (2,277), stand nearby. They are actually more impressive looking, but the broad and whale-shaped Whernside is highest. With three mountains in the same neighborhood, there is, of course, a marathon called the "Yorkshire Three Peaks Challenge." First accomplished in 1887, it has drawn the stout of heart ever since. The length of the full loop varies by the route taken but generally measures at around twenty-five miles, and the climbs add up to 5,249 feet of elevation gain. If you complete the circuit in twelve hours, you are entitled to join the Three Peaks of Yorkshire Club, which is simply a list kept at a local café. Runners have accomplished the task in two and a half hours, not even enough time to get hungry.

A snack truck stood in the car park, and we thought it would be a welcome oasis after our hike. We waved to the attendant and set out at eleven forty-five, each with an adjustable trekking pole in hand. It was sunny and warm, most un-English. Our walk would take us northward up a shallow valley, with Whernside on our left. At the north end of the valley we would veer left and onto the north end of the mountain's sloping summit ridge, then south, climbing gradually to the summit marker midway along the ridge. From the monument we would continue heading south, dropping to a point at which we could turn left again and descend from the ridge back into the valley. In short, we would do a counterclockwise oval loop of six miles, with an elevation gain of 1,447 feet. The Italian Woman hadn't done anything this ambitious in more than twenty years, but with perfect weather and many hours of daylight, we could take things slow and easy.

The most interesting feature of the Whernside loop is actually man-made. Not far from the trailhead we found ourselves walking along the base of the massive, twenty-four-arch Ribblehead Viaduct, one of England's grandest. Built in the 1870s of local limestone, it stands more than a hundred feet high, has foundations sunk twenty-five feet into the ground, and extends for a quarter-mile. It continues to serve the Settle-Carlisle Railway. As we passed, a group of spelunkers in red suits and helmets emerged from beyond one of the openings in the viaduct. This part of the Dales is known for its scenic caverns, and our map showed many "shake holes," or sink-holes, where the earth has collapsed into a subterranean chamber. In this area the local mountain rescue groups are actually called "cave and mountain rescue." I was once a member of Seattle Mountain Rescue, but I am far too claustrophobic to even think of a mission into a place that is dark, dank, confined, stifling . . . your skin is clammy, hands reach out to grab your throat, you can't breathe . . . and then your headlamp fizzles out.

HAPPILY STAYING ON THE EARTH's surface, we walked northward, parallel to the railroad track. The path was firm and dry, and in places it consisted of rock slabs that had been laboriously laid to offer smooth passage while protecting the surrounding vegetation. Our walk description told of remnants of shantytowns created by the "navvies" (navigators, or navigation engineers) whose labor built the nearby Bleamoor Tunnel. We looked around but saw only sheep.

Nearly two miles up the valley our path angled left, over the railroad tracks on a stone aqueduct. There, eight other walkers were having lunch. I thought it would be interesting to stop and visit, and I asked the Italian Woman if she would like to take a break. She was not feeling social, and she insisted that we carry on.

The path began to rise steadily—the next mile and a half would present most of our elevation gain. On our left we saw an impressive waterfall called Force Gill, one of a series that tumble down from Whernside's northeastern side. I had never seen the word *force* used to describe a waterfall, but I later discovered that it comes from the Norse *foss*, or *fors*, a consequence of Yorkshire's occupation by Danish Vikings late in the first millennium. *Gill* was also an old Norse word, meaning "stream" or "ravine."

The path now alternated between well-packed dirt, rock slabs across boggy areas, and stone steps on the more angled slopes.

The Italian Woman was slowing down, clearly not enjoying herself. At several points I suggested that we take a break and eat something, but she ignored me and kept walking. The final section before Whernside's summit ridge was the steepest yet, and we were essentially climbing a long stone staircase. The Italian Woman was obviously fatigued, and again I proposed a rest. She refused and growled, "You'd better enjoy this, because I'm never going to do it again."

When we reached the summit ridge, I said: "Look, we've done most of our climbing. It's time for lunch." Not waiting for a reply, I took off my pack, sat on a rock, and started pulling out food and water bottles. This time the Italian Woman couldn't argue—I had put the food where she could see it. She sat next to me, and we started eating.

From our perch we had an expansive view of our entire route so far, all the way to the car park. Directly below us were two large tarns. The breeze was strong, but it felt good. As we ate, a number of people came from below and walked by. Except for a man wearing earplugs and swaying to his music, everyone said hello as they passed. At one point an old man approached, moving with no apparent energy or enthusiasm. I was surprised he had made it this far. I asked him how he was, and he rasped, "Nearly done with the second one." He was attempting the Three Peaks that day.

One couple stopped for a short chat. They were Nigel and Debbie from Manchester. Nigel said he was a retired policeman, while Debbie was between jobs. I guessed that they were in their late forties, and both were very fit. They told us they had a cottage in the area, and they were on a series of conditioning walks to prepare for a summer in the Alps. Today they were accompanied by Talisker and Arran, a pair of lively border terriers named for two of Scotland's renowned single malt whiskeys.

Nigel was particularly keen to suggest other walks for us, and he rattled off one idea after the next, as I scribbled on my notepad. Then the couple moved on, and soon we, too, started along the summit ridge. I was surprised to discover that a rock wall ran the length of the ridge. Our path was on one side, and on the other a tractor was pulling a plow across a huge field. Highest point in Yorkshire Dales National Park, and here was a farmer working the land. The Italian Woman immediately commented that the fellow had obviously arrived at this place by a much easier route than ours, and she wondered how I could have believed that she would enjoy the longer approach. Scenery be damned, she just wanted to get up and down as quickly as possible.

Our path was dry and well-worn, and the final half-mile to the top rose gently another 250 feet. A dozen people were spread around the summit area, which we reached at two twenty-five. I expected the Italian Woman to be happy, as she had been on Pen Hill and our other walks. Instead, she was sullen. She refused to step through the wall to the summit monument— which in the UK is called a "trig point"—where Debbie and Nigel were sitting. I prevailed on her to pause for a photo on the path, but that was it. Less than five minutes after arriving, we were heading down.

After half a mile of gentle descent along the summit ridge, the path veered left and onto an irregular staircase that dropped steeply into the valley below. Here I lengthened our walking sticks and reminded the Italian Woman to reach down ahead of her, plant the pole, and use it for balance on the next step or two. I stressed that there was no hurry on this section. She wasn't interested in a tutorial. She simply wanted to keep moving and get off the mountain.

DESCENDING IS NEVER SMOOTH, AND we both stepped carefully to maintain our balance. The Italian Woman led the way, and from behind I thought she was doing well. Several hundred feet below the ridge we stepped aside as Debbie and Nigel and their dogs passed us. I watched them for a few seconds, then looked up the hill to see if anyone else was about to overtake us. When I turned back toward the Italian Woman, I was surprised to see that she was lying sideways across the path just below me. I hadn't heard her go down. I quickly called ahead to Debbie and Nigel: "Hey! Can you come back up?" As they returned, I knelt next to my wife and asked if she was okay. She said yes, but she didn't know what had caused her to fall. I didn't immediately see any injuries or blood, but I was afraid she might have hit her head on a rock.

Nigel, too, did a quick exam, and we agreed that we could move the Italian Woman to a patch of grass next to the path. We carefully sat her down and helped her lie back on the slope with her head on a small foam sit pad. Then I started to look her over more carefully. Her eyes were tracking normally, her pulse was strong, and her breathing was normal. She was fully communicative and said she had no pain. There was a momentary fright when I saw a spot of blood on the foam pad, but a closer inspection indicated that it hadn't come from her head. When I finally got to her legs, I saw blood on her left boot. I pulled her pant leg up for a closer look and found myself staring into a gash just to the outside of her shinbone, the tibia. In the opening I could see the long muscle, the tibialis anterior. It seemed intact, and there were no signs the bone was broken, but this was a nasty wound. Remarkably, there was little blood. Whatever sharp rock the Italian Woman had fallen against, it hadn't severed any major vessels.

"Sweetie, you've cut your leg. Nigel, can you look at this?"

The former city cop remained calm as he examined the wound. "Let's wrap it," he said. From his first aid kit he removed a large sterile pad and a long bandage. In mine I found an elastic bandage and some tape. I then pinched the sides of the wound together and applied the pad as Nigel began to wrap the area, first with the bandage, then the elastic, then some tape to hold everything in place. A few minutes later we were finished. Amazingly, the Italian Woman said it still didn't hurt, and she wanted to continue down the trail. The rest of us immediately vetoed that. Two-thirds of the descent remained, and we were certain that any walking would aggravate the injury. The wound hadn't bled much, and we wanted to keep it that way.

The breeze was cool, so we helped the patient into her sweater and jacket, and we elevated her leg on my knapsack. Then Debbie sat next to her, and the dogs lay on either side of her head, nuzzling her cheeks. Meanwhile, Nigel was attempting to reach mountain rescue on Debbie's mobile phone. The 999 dispatcher kept trying to put him through to the police or fire department, and he became irritated, demanding that he be connected to the rescue group. Eventually, the call went through. Nigel described our position and the fact that the Italian Woman would need to be carried out. I checked my watch; it was 3:35 p.m.

At just past four we saw a car pull into a farm pasture far below, at the bottom of the mountain. A single person got out and started jogging up the trail. Yes, jogging. At four thirty he arrived in a T-shirt and running shorts, carrying nothing but a small fanny pack and a radio. His name was Martin Holroyd, and he was from the Cave Rescue Organisation (CRO) in the nearby town of Clapham. After learning that Nigel was a former policeman and that I had been in a mountain rescue group, Martin took a very quick look at the Italian Woman, then got on the radio and instructed someone to bring the litter for a carry-out. The patient's condition did not merit a helicopter evacuation. Meanwhile, several more cars had arrived, and other people were already moving up the path.

Martin conducted a more thorough exam of the patient and had me fill out an accident report. Things were moving very quickly, and by five fifteen a dozen other team members had arrived with blankets, two halves of a litter, and other equipment. Think of it—in less than two hours from

Nigel's call, thirteen men had dropped what they were doing, driven to the mountain, and climbed more than half a mile uphill. On the scene they didn't waste much time either. They assembled the litter, placed the Italian Woman into it, took up their positions, and started down with her. Interestingly, they didn't carry the stretcher. It had skids underneath, and the team simply slid it down the grassy slopes, controlling it with short pieces of rope. This was infinitely easier than it would have been to lift the apparatus and maneuver it down the rough steps of the path. In Seattle Mountain Rescue we had used a litter with a wheel underneath—it was designed for trails. Skids would have been useless in our world because, unlike the Yorkshire Dales, the slopes of the North Cascades have very little grass.

Nigel, Debbie, and I started down the path carrying some unneeded CRO gear. I proceeded very carefully, using both of the walking sticks. I had been on rescues before, but the shock of seeing the gash in my wife's leg had me stressed out, and I was afraid of taking a tumble myself. Nigel seemed to sense this. In twenty-five years on the Manchester police force he had responded to countless casualties, and he knew the maxim "If you witness an accident, you are also a victim." He stayed close to me, and from time to time he asked how I was doing.

THE COW PASTURE NEAR THE hamlet of Bruntscar had turned into a parking lot. A dozen cars, an ambulance, and a support truck were scattered about when Nigel, Debbie, and I arrived. We talked to the ambulance attendants, and they said they would take the Italian Woman to the Royal Infirmary in Lancaster. They showed me a map, and I learned that we would be heading even farther away from Leyburn.

The Italian Woman and her rescuers arrived at five thirty. It had taken the rescue party only ninety minutes to get up the mountain and back off again. They loaded their patient into the ambulance, spent a few minutes accepting my profuse thanks, and then jumped into their cars to get home for supper. Here is the matter-of-fact official report from the Cave Rescue Organisation:

Incident 30/2013–Jun 04 Tue 15.38 Whernside, North Yorkshire— Mountain Rescue: A walker from the USA (f, 68) sustained a deep 4-inch long gash to her lower leg after slipping on the descent from the summit ridge towards Chapel-le-Dale. Following treatment by CRO the casualty was stretchered down off the hill and transferred to a road ambulance at Bruntscar. Volunteer hours: 47.

A woman named Mali drove me in the emergency support truck to our car and then led me to a village, where we waited for the ambulance. From that point the ambulance driver told me to just follow them to the hospital in Lancaster, an hour's drive southwest. To keep up, I ran at least one red light and ignored proper etiquette at several roundabouts. This was highly unnerving, but I took comfort from the fact that, like the pope and the U.S. president, I had an ambulance close at hand. At one point I lost sight of the vehicle, only to find it pulled over and waiting for me.

We arrived at the Royal Lancaster Infirmary at 6:45 p.m. I parked in a staff-only lot and scurried into the emergency room. The Italian Woman lay calmly on a gurney in the hallway, her jacket and boots stuffed next to her. The two ambulance attendants came to say goodbye and wish us luck. The patient had bonded with them and was sorry to see them leave. We continued waiting, and at one point I remembered to call Jen at our lodge to tell her we wouldn't make it for dinner.

An hour later a treatment room opened up, and there a nurse removed our field dressing from the Italian Woman's leg. She complimented me on how professionally we had wrapped the injury, then left to find the doctor. His name was Asim, and I took him to be Pakistani. He examined the gash and immediately said that the muscle hadn't been cut, and therefore surgery wasn't necessary. Instead, he cleaned the wound and then closed it with nine sutures approximately half an inch apart. Meanwhile, the patient, in keeping with her surroundings, maintained a stiff upper lip.

At 9:00 p.m. the Italian Woman was released, but to our surprise, at no point had anyone asked us for a payment. I mentioned this to the attending nurse, and she responded, "As long as you are in Britain, you are guests of the National Health System." The patient's name and date of birth would be sufficient for their records. With a teasing smile the woman added that any meaningful tour of the UK should involve a visit to the NHS — didn't I agree? I warned her that if she traveled to the United States and needed medical attention, she was on her own.

ONCE THE ITALIAN WOMAN AND I were in the car, I asked if I could do anything for her. She replied, "I'm hungry," and I realized that it had been seven hours since our lunch just below the summit of Whernside. With directions from a hospital security guard, we found a convenience store, where I bought sandwiches and sodas. From there we wound our way through the center of Lancaster to the M6.

Near Kendal we exited onto the A684 and began to retrace our original route to Leyburn. I was mentally wrung out, and as a result, in the village of Sedbergh I made a wrong turn. Instead of heading east to Hawes and Leyburn, I turned north. I didn't realize my mistake for half an hour, when I commented to the Italian Woman: "The sunset should be behind us, not on our left. I think we're heading north." A bit later I said: "Look at all those wagons and caravans. They weren't here six days ago."

The highway was lined with encampments of Travelers, England's own Gypsies. Of course, they might have recently moved in, but somehow the scene was different. When I saw a sign for Kirkby Stephen, I pulled over and studied the map. We were well off route, and at that point it made sense to go a bit farther north to the A66, a four-lane road ("dual carriageway") running east. We could make good time on that road, and near its terminus we could turn south and approach Leyburn from the north. I hated having to do this, but it seemed the most efficient way to get us back to the lodge.

Kirkby Stephen was a battle zone. Wagons and horses were everywhere, and the streets were strewn with beer bottles, manure, and human bodies. The men still standing were either singing or arguing. Some of the hotels had posted handwritten signs that said, "Pub open to hotel guests only." Most of the ordinary pubs had closed, and those that hadn't were under siege. We were only too happy to pass through the village without running anyone over or having a bottle thrown through our windshield.

On and on we drove, into the darkness. At one point directly north of Leyburn, I decided to try a shortcut south on a country road. We passed along one-lane roads through the hamlets of Brignall, Barningham, and Newsham before emerging, as it developed, back onto the A66. Now I just wanted to park the car and go to sleep. The Italian Woman was also weary, but she was more composed than I was. She said everything would be okay, and we carried on. Finally, at eleven thirty, after a two-and-a-half-hour road trip, we arrived at our lodge. Jen and her husband helped us settle into the lounge, plied us with red wine, and had us recount the day's events. They were kind and understanding, and they reminded us that a gash requiring sutures was unfortunate, but a tumble down a mountainside could have been so much worse.

AFTER HELPING THE ITALIAN WOMAN with a sponge bath, I tucked her into bed. She was asleep in thirty seconds. I showered and sent an email to Nigel and Debbie before turning in. Then I lay awake for more than an hour, feeling enormous guilt. I replayed the mountain scene over and over in my mind. I couldn't stop looking into my wife's open wound, staring at her pulsating muscle. I should never have talked her into climbing.

I should have accepted the fact that our time in Britain should be a village and pub affair, with no more than occasional glances upward to the surrounding hills. How could I have been so stupid and selfish?

It was our ninth day in the United Kingdom, and it was just as well that our plans for the summer were still rather vague—after Whernside everything had changed.

5

Searching for Urra Moor

THE FIRST DAY AFTER WHERNSIDE was a time to decompress. I served the patient breakfast in bed, resisting the temptation to slip a black pudding onto her tray, and then we spent quiet hours reading and napping. Later I ran out for pizza and beer, and we watched three episodes of *All Creatures Great and Small*.

The following morning the Italian Woman came downstairs, slowly, to breakfast and an outpouring of sympathy from the other guests. They made suggestions about non-strenuous activities in the area, and Jen showed us a rack of brochures in the map room. There we learned that Yorkshire is indeed more than a walking venue. Do you fancy the York Dungeon Wax Museum? Or perhaps the Dracula Experience in Whitby, where Bram Stoker lived? Why not visit Mother Shipton's Cave—England's oldest visitor attraction, open since 1630—and learn about the prophetess who predicted the defeat of the Spanish Armada. My personal favorite was the Forbidden Corner—Strangest Place in the World! It sounded like one of those mystery spots that permeate the American West, advertising shrunken heads, six-legged pigs, and "gravity gone wild," where a leering, unshaven man in a sleeveless undershirt takes you into a dimly lit room, releases a rubber ball onto a tilted floor, and then grunts as the ball miraculously seems to roll uphill.

Later, as I scurried about doing laundry, the Italian Woman sat in the lounge surfing the internet. She found the Cave Rescue Organisation's write-up of her own incident. There were also grim descriptions of fatalities and serious injuries requiring emergency helicopter evacuation. Also among the reports was this one:

Incident 27/2013–May 17 Fri 09.00 Meal Bank Quarry, Ingleton, North Yorkshire—Animal Rescue: On Thursday evening a sheep and three lambs were reported to be stuck on a ledge in Meal Bank Quarry; on Friday morning a small CRO team successfully hauled all four animals to the quarry top, and freedom. Volunteer hours: 20.

The posting included a photo of a helmeted climber dangling from a rope and making eye contact with a rather wary-looking lamb. We had a good laugh, and we started to gain a bit of objectivity about her accident. Mountain walking will always involve some risk, even if you are a grazing sheep.

We began to discuss what to do when it was time to leave Collett's lodge the following week. I suggested we could abandon the national parks altogether and simply spend the next three months in London doing city things. That was not my preference, but at that point my guilt would have led me to do whatever the Italian Woman wanted. Interestingly, she wasn't ready to give up seeing Scotland, Wales, and more of England, so we considered how we might travel around for the next month and then perhaps settle in London. I immediately dove into my maps and discovered three nearby national parks: North York Moors, Northumberland, and the Lake District. A counterclockwise circuit through those places would not entail any long days in the car. This appealed to the Italian Woman, and to my great surprise she said that it was okay with her if I wanted to do a few more climbs along the way, provided they didn't take too much time. I did not protest.

THE NEXT MORNING I CHANGED the dressing on the Italian Woman's leg. This was our first look at the wound since Lancaster, and it wasn't a pretty sight. It was swollen and red, warm to the touch. I had asked the doctor in Lancaster if he would give her antibiotics, but he had said no, that standard practice in the UK was to avoid such drugs until absolutely necessary. I had observed something like this many years earlier in the Netherlands, when a friend was in the hospital and practically at death's door from a laceration on her hand before her physician would prescribe the amoxicillin that had her back on her feet in a few days. It was obvious that my wife was going to have to fight the infection with no more than clean bandages and her own white blood cells.

Surprisingly, the good weather in England was holding, and even more unexpectedly, the Italian Woman suggested that I just go out and do a hike on my own. If I wanted to drive to another national park and find its highest point—silly as the concept was to her—she would not object. She wanted another day in the lodge, and it was evident that she was already tired of my fawning ministrations. I asked her if she was certain that she didn't need me hovering over her the entire day, and she said no, she could take care of herself.

Now I faced something of a dilemma—I was somewhat hesitant to set foot onto another trail. It seemed a foregone conclusion that I would fall to my death, leaving the Italian Woman injured, alone, and far from home. After Whernside the idea of climbing to Britain's high points now sounded foolhardy. And besides, with my companion out of commission, we would probably not have the time to visit all fifteen national parks, and achieving only part of the list didn't make much sense. On the other hand, it wasn't every day that the Italian Woman suggested that I head for the hills. Of course I would go.

My road atlas showed that North York Moors National Park was a short drive east from Leyburn, but I needed a trail map. Unfortunately, Vic's library collection had nothing on the Moors. I dashed into the village to the tourist office and both outdoor shops, and they not only lacked information; they couldn't understand why I would leave the Dales to visit that other place. Someone suggested that I drive to the village of Stokesley, thirty miles away and at the edge of the Moors. It was a large town, gateway to the national park, and I should easily be able to purchase a map there. To avoid starting completely blind, back at the lodge I got onto the internet and scraped together a few facts and figures.

It was obvious that the Moors play the shy and homely cousin, always second fiddle to the more vivacious and beautiful Dales. Where the Dales have dramatic hills, even mountains, the Moors have, well, moors. Their landscape is more gently contoured. The claim to fame of the Moors is undoubtedly its twenty-five mile stretch of North Sea coast, home to mysterious-sounding places like Ravenscar, Robin Hood's Bay, and Dracula's own Whitby. Nobody pays much attention to the elevation of the Moors National Park, as I soon discovered firsthand.

The highest summit of the Moors is rather appropriately called Round Hill, whose 1,490 feet give it the rank of twelfth among the fifteen national park high points. The uplift is sometimes referred to more colorfully as Urra Moor, which is technically the name of the larger moor on which the hill is located. The path across Round Hill happens to be an overlapping segment of several major walking routes, including the Cleveland Way, a hundred-mile trail that circles around the western, northern, and coastal edges of the national park. If it weren't for its location on these popular paths, Round Hill might be even more obscure, if that is possible. A website called The Walking Englishman drily suggests that many people reach the apex of the North York Moors National Park "without realising it." The description adds, "When there, dwell in pride." All right, the climb of Round Hill didn't sound too difficult. I just had to find it.

LEAVING LEYBURN ON THE A684, I drove east through Bedale and then into the larger community of Northallerton. I was supposed to continue on the A684 through the town and then another six or seven miles northeast, to connect with other roads leading to Stokesley. That was the plan, in any event. The reality, I discovered, was that Northallerton had been laid out by an engineer on LSD. Something like ten roads converged in the town, and I quickly found myself in a vortex from which I nearly didn't escape. The problem was all those roundabouts.

I understood the Roundabout Theorem, but putting it into practice was daunting. After some initial fits and starts, I established a pattern of entering each circle cautiously and then driving around multiple times in hopes of seeing directions to the A684 or the villages of Brompton or Ellerbeck. The good thing about actually being in a roundabout is that at that moment you are King of the Castle, and you have absolute priority over all of the commoners waiting at the edges. Also, if you drive around fast enough, nobody has time to venture in, and traffic begins to back up on all the entering roadways. If this had been Italy, everyone would have been laying on their horns, but the long-suffering Yorkshire folk just gritted their teeth and said, "Tut tut."

Eventually, of course, I had to exit the merry-go-round and slingshot myself onto a new street. I tried to use the position of the sun to guide me, but when you are driving in circles, that's not easy. Nevertheless, I told myself that I was making progress. Then, just as I started feeling confident, I came to my first ever double roundabout.

A large road sign displayed what appeared to be a pair of old-fashioned spectacles. Each round lens had little tentacles fanning out in all directions, while a thicker stem connected the two circles. There was so much information on this sign that I couldn't absorb it in the two seconds available, so I simply charged ahead and entered the first circle, Lens 1. On my second or third time around, not having seen a logical exit, I spotted what I took to be the second roundabout, moved toward it, and was soon careening around Lens 2. It didn't take long before I concluded that none of its tentacles looked good either, so I returned to Lens 1. I repeated this process a couple of times, and while I felt that I was now the world's leading expert on these conjoined traffic circles, I knew that it was time to take my leave. I did so, and I hadn't gone more than a few hundred yards when I realized that I was not only in a dead-end hospital car park, but I had actually pulled into one of the slots.

I stepped out of the car and stretched my arms, trying to appear nonchalant, as if I had just arrived from London and needed only to retrieve a bunch of flowers from the back seat and head into the postsurgical ward to see Aunt Lily. I was actually looking around desperately, wondering how to get the hell out of there. I thought I should go into the building to ask someone how to return to the A684, but then to my left I saw the sign that said PARK AND PAY. I turned to my right and saw an even larger sign that said HALT AND HAND OVER YOUR MONEY. Neither display mentioned any grace period, so I knew that I would either have to feed the machine or be handcuffed and forced to watch as my Vauxhall was towed away. Meekly, I walked to the first pay station and dug into my pocket for some coins, when a voice in my head said: "Stephen, this place is not meant for you. Return calmly to your vehicle, back out slowly, and drive away. Do not look back."

The thought occurred to me that the man in the car rental agency had been right when he told me I would need a GPS. Perhaps I had been too cocky when I assured him that a map and my own common sense would be sufficient. What I hadn't said was that I was too cheap to pay ten pounds extra per day for an electronic device that I didn't know how to use.

I returned to the double roundabout, then back to the hospital, then back again. I had now passed the Northallerton Public Safety building four times. Police officers were standing near all of the entrances, smoking and fiddling with their billy clubs, but there was no place for me to pull over and ask for guidance. I decided to throw caution to the wind and exit the roundabout in a direction that I felt was completely wrong. This I did, and I somehow got onto a road leaving that cursed town. I really didn't care where I was headed. I would just drive to the next village, locate it on my map, and proceed from there.

REMARKABLY, I WAS SOON RUMBLING into Stokesley, a pleasant market town on the northwest edge of North York Moors National Park. From the village I could see a range of hills to the south, and I assumed that one of them was my destination. Unlike Northallerton, Stokesley was rather straightforward. Its center was a quarter-mile-long collection of shops and restaurants on either side of an elongated town square called the Plain. Probably due to some ancient dispute or an acute lack of civic imagination, the streets on either side of the square were both called High Street. ("Oh, you don't want *this* High Street. You want *that* one.")

It was market day, and the Plain was filled with people crowding around to buy vegetables, tea towels, and pirated CDs. Because of the congestion, I had to drive slowly, looking for a place to stop. The car park at the far end of the center had an opening, and there I was surprised to learn that it was a park and pay affair. In the United States most small towns want to encourage commerce, and free parking is an essential draw. In England you pay for the privilege of stopping to spend your money, and it's not cheap—several pounds for an hour or two.

Having dutifully paid, I set out to find the tourist information office. The first thing I spied was a travel agency, and I popped in to ask for directions. Sorry, sir, but we have no tourist office in Stokesley. Okay, where could I purchase a map of the national park? Hmmm, interesting question. Why don't you try the Martins News Agency at the far end of High Street? I walked the length of the town center and found Martins, which sold everything but maps. They suggested I try Browns News Agency on the other end of the Plain and, as it turned out, practically next door to the travel office where I had started. Alas, Browns had no maps either, but they helpfully suggested the Yorkshire Shop, near Martins: "That shop sells lots of local items, and they will surely have maps and information." Back I went, my third pass through the center, and by now I was quite familiar with Stokesley. I was also starting to feel that this was turning into the pedestrian version of my roundabout-to-hospital circuit back in Northallerton.

The Yorkshire Shop was a delightful place, filled with ceramics, sweaters, and other handicrafts, all locally made. The ladies in the shop unfortunately had no brochures and no maps. They suggested Martins and Browns, but when I explained I had already tried those places, they cheerfully recommended that I drive to another town somewhere north of London and south of Scotland, but before I left, wouldn't I like to buy a blanket made of finest Yorkshire wool?

As I stepped back outside, I saw a bicycle shop across the way. Aha! The people there will be intimately familiar with the countryside, and they will undoubtedly have maps. I was greeted by an anemic young clerk and told him I was looking for any information about Round Hill and the national park. In a heavy Yorkshire accent he replied that they sold bicycles, not maps. "And yes, well, I don't really know the hills around here. You'll be wanting to see Jerry over there. He's a serious walker, he is."

When Jerry finished an hour-long phone call, I explained that I hadn't been able to find a map, but could he perhaps tell me how to find the trailhead for Round Hill?

"Ah, now," he began, apparently trying to retrieve something from his brain. "Round Hill, you say . . . well . . . in this area they're all quite round, aren't they? Can you be more specific?"

"No, it's actually called Round Hill, and it's just outside Stokesley. It's on something called 'Urra Moor.'"

"Hmmm . . . Round Hill on Urra Moor. No, I haven't heard of that one."

"But it's the highest mountain in the national park. I think it's a popular walk."

"Yes, that is the national park out there," he said, gesturing toward the rear of the shop.

"Okay, well, thanks," I responded. Then I added: "Look, I think Round Hill is just outside Carlton-in-Cleveland. Maybe I should go there and inquire."

"Yes," Jerry replied, "I suppose that's a good plan." He looked pleased that he had been able to help me on my way.

A FEW MILES FROM STOKESLEY lay the tiny hamlet of Carlton-in-Cleveland, which on my road map appeared to be within the boundaries of the national park. Carlton (or was it Cleveland?) had only one establishment, a bar-restaurant. There I asked the waiter for help, and he took me into the kitchen to talk to Geoff, "a local man who knows these things." Geoff was indeed local, but he had never heard of Round Hill or Urra Moor. I mentioned that Round Hill was the highest point in the national park.

"Oh, it is now, is it? How about that."

I asked him if he would look at my road map with me. He willingly abandoned something that was bubbling on the stove, and we stepped outside to my car. I laid my road atlas on the hood and pointed to where a red footpath crossed a yellow highway, the B1257.

"Oh, that'll be the Cleveland Way," he said. I now recalled that Round Hill was on the long-distance path, but in the excitement of traversing the town center four times, I had not mentioned the path to anyone back in Stokesley.

"Yes," I said, "I want to be on the Cleveland Way."

"Well, if you're sure that your round hill is on that footpath, then I'll tell you how to get to where it crosses the highway."

Geoff directed me to the nearby village of Kirby, where a small arrow at a street corner pointed to the B1257. The road immediately started climbing into the hills. After a few miles I arrived at a large car park called Clay Bank, and I remembered the name from one of my online sources. Clay Bank didn't appear on my road map, but I was certain that this was one possible starting point for the Round Hill climb.

Without a more sophisticated plan I decided to don my knapsack and start walking farther up the road. I knew that the Cleveland Way crossed the highway near there, and I hadn't seen anything before Clay Bank, so logically I should just continue along the road on foot until I found the trailhead. This was not the way I wanted to start a climb, and in fact the entire afternoon had felt like a Marx Brothers movie, but at this point I either had to start walking or just give up and go home. I made a vow never to get into this predicament again. I would immediately buy a printer so that if I couldn't find a proper map, I could at least print map segments and route descriptions from the internet.

As I was locking my car, a man and woman walked into the parking lot and dropped their knapsacks next to one of the other vehicles. I scurried over and asked if they knew where the Cleveland Way was. Indeed they did, and in fact they had just returned from it. The man pulled a large Ordnance Survey map from his pack, spread it out on top of his car, and showed me the lay of the land. They had just come from the Cleveland Way segment west of the highway, but there, just to the east, stood Round Hill. All I had to do was follow the road a hundred yards, and on my left I would find the path. Nearly two and a half hours after leaving Leyburn, I started my walk.

AS THE MAP HAD SHOWN, a wooden signpost on the left pointed to the Cleveland Way. "Well, let's do this," I said to myself. I was immediately greeted by a path made of flagstones set in grass. The way ran along the edge of a pasture, beside a stone wall. At the far end of the field the path rose more steeply a few hundred feet in a series of Whernside-like steps. Twenty minutes from the car I reached the top of the steps, at one end of what proved to be Round Hill's summit plateau. In the distance, perhaps a mile away, lay a slight bulge that might be the summit, but I wasn't really sure. What I did know was that the path ahead of me was wide and nearly level. I realized that Round Hill was no challenge at all, and I laughed at myself for having been concerned back in Leyburn.

I walked quickly toward the rise in the plateau. The air was warm, and the breeze was soft. I had expected rain here on the

Moor, so this was remarkably pleasant. As I neared the high section of the ridge, I came across a three-foot stone pillar next to the path. Well, I thought, maybe this is the summit monument. No, the path still seemed to be going slightly uphill, so this was just a teaser. I passed several more of these pillars, not knowing what they were. Then, off to the left, I saw a larger monument perched on a hummock of grass that rose ever so slightly from the surrounding heather. I followed a narrow track through the heather and thus conquered the summit of Round Hill. From the car it had taken me all of forty-five minutes.

I took off my knapsack and sat in the grass to eat a sandwich. A bird soared above me, making a cry that sounded like "cur-LEE, cur-LEE." It was a curlew, and it was telling me that I was trespassing on its territory, but it soon tired and flew off. I took out my phone and tried to call the Italian Woman. She didn't answer, so I reclined in the grass, thinking: "It's a beautiful day, and I've got this lonely summit to myself. Life is good." At that very moment a tractor drove by, pulling a manure wagon and kicking up a cloud of dust. The Cleveland Way across Round Hill was a farm road.

My descent took slightly less time than the walk up. Partway down I met two people, either a seventyish father and his doting daughter or a spectacularly lucky old man and his trophy wife. In response to my cheery hello, they both just grunted, so I didn't learn whether they were there to walk the Cleveland Way or just climb Round Hill. On the final staircase section I moved very carefully, using both walking sticks to maintain balance. I may have looked awkward, but I didn't care. I didn't trust these Yorkshire steps, which had nearly done in my wife, and I wanted to get down in one piece.

Back at Clay Bank I discovered that there was an excellent view up the valley to another mountain, Roseberry Topping, which sounds like something to drizzle over ice cream. If not that, then what is a roseberry? I'm no gardening expert, but I don't think roses actually have berries. Hips, yes, but no elbows and no berries. I later learned that the word is actually derived from Viking words for Odin's Hill. Odin, or Woden, was the tough-guy father of Thor and other Norse gods, and he must be mortified that his hill's name has morphed into something as sissified as *roseberry*. *Topping* is more easily recognized as a derivative of *top*, as in *mountaintop*.

Roseberry Topping is a rugged-looking peak with a summit plateau that comes to something of a point above a steep cliff on one side. At 1,050 feet it is barely two-thirds as high as Round Hill, but it is far more prominent. In ancient times it was believed to be the highest mountain in the Moors. The peak holds a modest place in history, because at its feet lies the village of Great Ayton, childhood home of the renowned navigator James Cook. As a boy, Cook often climbed the mountain, and on a clear day he could see coal ships sailing in the distant North Sea.

Drawn to the seafaring life, Cook joined the Royal Navy, where he rose to the rank of master and went on to circumnavigate the globe. On his third major voyage to the Pacific, in 1779, he and his crew were the first Europeans to visit Hawaii, and it was there that the captain was killed in a skirmish with the natives. Somewhere between Round Hill and Roseberry Topping stands a prominent stone tower, Captain Cook's Monument. I wasn't able to see it from Clay Bank because of an intervening ridge, and I didn't feel the need to drive to it. I wanted to get back to Leyburn.

My return to Eastfield Lodge was remarkably uneventful. The roundabout gods allowed me swift passage through Northallerton, and my drive took just an hour. When I walked into our room, the Italian Woman's first words were, "You must have had a good climb because you look so happy."

And then it was her turn. She declared herself ready for an excursion, and we drove to Harrogate, a spa town and favorite haunt of James Herriot and his wife. Our destination was Bettys Café Tea Rooms, founded nearly a century earlier by a Swiss immigrant but widely known as the quintessential English tea experience. The name Bettys is a complete mystery, and apparently it is not *Betty's* with the apostrophe missing. We joined the long queue under a Victorian wrought iron and glass marquee, patiently (and for my wife's part, painfully) waiting to be ushered into the Holy of Holies. Once inside, we gratefully sat for shrimp sandwiches, tea (of course), and the house specialty, an oversized scone called the "Fat Rascal." After ten days in a farm town, the Italian Woman reveled in this more cosmopolitan experience. Now in her element, and momentarily forgetting her injured leg, she reminisced about the elegant ladies of her Seattle youth who would gather for small meals and gossip on the fifth floor of the Frederick & Nelson department store. She reminded me that a national park high point is one thing, but a well-laid table is everything.

6

Joke-a-Fone

UNTIL QUITE RECENTLY, EXPLORERS PREPARED for an expedition by going to the library to study books and maps, and when I started seeing the world in the 1970s, that is how I did it. The twenty-first century is an entirely different ball game. The internet and search engines are accessible across the globe, and wherever you are, if you can get online, you have at your fingertips far more information than you could possibly use. But it is even more amazing than that, because smartphones and tablets now offer wireless access to the internet, and GPS can map your location and surroundings nearly anywhere on the planet. With the world's largest library in your pocket, you can deftly make and change plans on the fly.

I am hesitant about offering the preceding paragraph because in a short time the technologies and terminology will have changed and the descriptions will seem laughably dated. However, I am going farther out on this limb to report that during our summer in Britain we traveled with two smartphones, two iPads, a laptop, a printer, and an Apple TV. What wonderful tools they were—when they worked, of course, and there's the rub.

As we roamed from place to place, it was my job to get the electronic devices functioning in every apartment, hotel, or B&B. I assumed this role because the Italian Woman simply cannot bear watching those little gears going round and round on a screen as something is loading or connecting. If it doesn't work immediately for her, forget it. In a way it's like me with food. I would rather reach for a box of cereal and a bottle of milk than try to figure out how to cook a meal. So, the two of us had a rather successful symbiotic relationship as we moved about. In every new location—and there were many of them—the Italian Woman organized the kitchen, and I set up the office.

Where this is headed is that I am going to pause in our chronological narrative and tell you a horror story from the realm of electronic gadgetry. There are many such stories from our time in the UK—tales of settings, passwords, and apps; Wi-Fi and AirPrint; cables, charging stations, and plug adapters. The internet alone would provide a semester's worth of lectures. Nevertheless, I am going to keep it fairly simple, because our deepest fears often arise from the most basic elements, like fire and water. I am going to tell you about our cell phones.

A DECADE EARLIER WE HAD spent eight months in Slovakia and had gotten along with just a landline. As we were settling in, several people told us that we should get mobile phones (which is what Europeans call their cell phones), and everyone seemed to have a preference on which plan to subscribe to. We had had cell phones in the United States, so we were willing to give it a go, but as it turned out, we couldn't find a phone store in Bratislava where anyone could explain their services—day-to-day usage was evidently a matter of "feel," and we had no feel for what the Slovaks were about—so we dropped the idea altogether.

There were a few moments in which we regretted that decision. I recall standing at a pay phone in Banská Bystrica in central Slovakia trying to call some friends who lived in the area. I was responding to each message in Slovak by inserting more coins, and then we ended up taking a taxi to a mountain village, where we wandered the streets knocking on doors until someone recognized the name of our friends and directed us to their house. A cell phone would have saved us a lot of grief.

By the time we moved to Europe, in 2013, we had caught up with our children and were totally dependent on our smartphones for everything from email and texting to news and weather reports. Oh yes, and phone calls. Even a brief separation from these devices left us with a hollow feeling. Fortunately, in Spain our host had put us onto his plan, and we used our new European phones with relative ease. I assumed that in the UK, where I could actually understand the recorded instructions and messages, it would be even easier. I was mistaken.

DURING OUR BRIEF STOPOVER IN London we had purchased SIM cards and data plans for our cell phones and iPads. This took place at an establishment I will call Joke-a-Fone, but before you set this book down and do a Google search, let me tell you that discretion suggests that I not use the firm's real name, and besides, I wouldn't want my experiences with a particular company to suggest that one is appreciably worse than the others. The bastards are all alike.

Because we would be in Britain only three months, we could not have a monthly service contract with Joke-a-Fone. Instead, it would be pay-as-you-go, a system with a charge per minute for phone time and a charge per megabyte of cellular data on our various devices. In addition, we added a special service that would permit us to inexpensively make international calls. Interestingly, it would cost us twenty-five pence per minute for a local call but only seven pence per minute to phone the United States. At that initial session I had put twenty pounds onto each device. Should we use all our minutes or data, we could simply purchase more—"top up"—at any supermarket or tobacco shop. One more thing: we could call customer service at *151, but all calls from pay-as-you-go customers would be charged at twenty-five pence per call. I didn't think that made sense, but I was satisfied that I understood how everything worked, and I assumed I would never have to call for assistance.

Two days later I was calling our banker in Seattle, presumably at seven pence per minute, when I was cut off. It was late at night, and the next morning on the Italian Woman's phone

I called *151 for Joke-a-Fone customer service, only to be told that I had used up the twenty pounds on my own phone. But how could that be? I had made three local calls the day before, and I hadn't spent more than ten minutes calling the States. As it turned out, the sales clerk in London had somehow failed to actually put us onto the international plan, and the call to Seattle was eating my credits at the rate of two pounds per minute. Customer service apologized and said they would restore the twenty pounds. Then they recommended a different program. Instead of pay-as-you-go, I should try their Unshackled Plan, which offered three hundred minutes for a flat fee of twenty pounds. It sounded cheaper than pay-as-you-go, so I agreed to try it. We would leave the Italian Woman on pay-as-you-go, and once again, I felt relieved to know exactly what we had.

The next morning, while checking email on my iPad, I received a pop-up message that all of my data was used up. This was curious because I had only used the tablet on the Wi-Fi system of our B&B in Leyburn. I shouldn't have used any cellular data at all. I tried calling *151 on my phone, only to receive a message that I had no credits available. Once again, I used the Italian Woman's phone to call for help.

After a long wait, in which I received several recorded reminders that the call was going to cost twenty-five pence, the helpful Joke-a-Fone representative told me:

> First, on my Unshackled Plan I could not call *151 because my minutes cost only six or seven pence, and they wanted twenty-five pence to help me. What I should do is buy extra pay-as-you-go credits for the purpose of calling customer service at twenty-five pence per call. In the alternative I could continue to use the Italian Woman's pay-as-you-go credits to call for assistance.
>
> Second, I could not make international calls on my phone because that is not a feature of the Unshackled Plan. If I wanted to call abroad, I would have to purchase pay-as-you-go credits. In the alternative I could use the Italian Woman's phone

for international calls because, yes, the previous customer service rep had indeed put her onto the international calling plan.

Third, both the Italian Woman's iPad and mine had all of their data left. The pop-up message was in error.

I suggested that it wasn't fair to be charged twenty-five pence to call customer service in response to an erroneous message from the phone company. After checking several levels of management, the representative agreed to reverse the service charge for that call. Although I had just spent an hour of my life sorting things out, I felt satisfied that I had gotten something out of Joke-a-Fone.

ONE WEEK LATER, STILL IN Leyburn, I wanted to purchase a printer, and an internet search suggested that the closest seller was a Tesco department store between Leyburn and Richmond. I thought I would phone ahead to be sure they had what I wanted, but when I placed the call, I received a message that I had no phone credits available. I had hardly used the phone at all since joining the Unshackled Plan, so I assumed that I had most of my three hundred minutes left. Once again, I used the Italian Woman's phone to call *151.

Before speaking to the representative, I was forced to endure a long wait, during which I heard the following message every thirty seconds: "Thank you for calling Joke-a-Fone. Your business is important to us, so kindly sit there and give us your undivided attention as we try to find someone who can stop playing video games long enough to help you." Eventually, a live person answered, but he was in the security department and he wanted to know my maternal grandmother's maiden name. Luckily, I remembered, and he was glad, but before transferring me to customer service there was a second question—namely, when was the last time I had topped up. I explained that I had been a customer for only one week, so buying extra credits had not been necessary. That was not the answer he was looking for, and eventually a second agent came on the line. I gave her my entire Joke-a-Fone history, including the difficulties of the previous week. After a few *hmmm*s the agent said that I had passed the security test and she would transfer me to a customer assistance representative. As she did so, I was cut off.

I called back, and after an endless wait with the same recorded message, I was connected to another security agent. After I told my story, he asked for my grandfather's maiden name, and I said, "Well, now . . . which grandfather?" With a chuckle he responded, "Correct answer!" and he said he would put me through to the help desk. I told him what had happened on my previous call, and I implored him to stay on the line until the transfer was successful.

In the loving embrace of a real customer assistance rep—this one with a rather thick Scottish accent—I asked why I couldn't use my phone. After some checking, the man informed me that the person who had set up my Unshackled Plan a week earlier had done it all wrong. He would immediately clear things up. When he announced that everything was in order, I mentioned that I had made several calls to *151, and that my wife suspected that I was receiving shoddy service and false error messages just so Joke-a-Fone could charge me twenty-five pence to call for help.

"Oh no, sirrr, that's nawt how we operrrate. We wud neverrr do thaht."

"Well, can you do something about all of the *151 charges?"

"Oh, yes, sirrr, we can rrrectify this by rrrefunding yerrr charrrges on those calls."

"Great, now can I use my phone?"

"Ye'd best give it an hourrr beforrrr ye trrry, just te make sherrr that the Unshackled Plan is worrrrkin."

An hour later I tried to call Tesco, and I received the same message—that I had no credits available. Back to the Italian Woman's phone, *151, another long wait, and a security interrogation ("Who was the mother of your first pet?"). This time, in response to the question of when I had most recently topped up, I tried a new tack and said I had done it two hours earlier. I hadn't, but my answer satisfied the security person, and I was transferred to customer assistance. The woman there clicked away at her keyboard for several minutes before telling me that my account was in order. She had a pronounced Yorkshire accent, and I found it a bit difficult to understand her, but I needed to soldier on. I asked why I was receiving the message that I had no credits to make the call to Tesco.

After thinking on the matter, the woman asked me what number I was trying to reach. I gave her the Tesco number, and she immediately responded that the prefix was 0845. Yes, I said, that's what I just told you. Well, any number beginning with 0845 is a "premium number" used by a call center, and with my Unshackled Plan I couldn't connect to such a number. I had all of my Unshackled credits left, but when trying to reach a premium number, I was shackled, so to speak.

This kicked off a discussion on what numbers I could and couldn't call on my phone as opposed to my wife's. She didn't know because, you see, she was a pay-as-you-go representative and my phone was on the Unshackled Plan. She suggested that she transfer me to an Unshackled person.

The new representative in the Unshackled department said hello, but before I could explain the situation, he said, "My computer doesn't recognize the phone number you are calling from." I mentioned that it was my wife's phone, and she was pay-as-you go. "Ah," he responded. "Then I'm afraid I can't help you because I'm Unshackled. I will transfer you to pay-as-you-go." I tried to stop him, but I was cut off. A recorded message said: "Thank you for calling Joke-a-Fone customer service. We hope we have resolved your issues. Goodbye."

The Italian Woman, of course, would have quit long ago, and she would have been in the kitchen polishing off a nice three-course dinner. I, on the other hand, wasn't finished. I called again, and during the security screening ("What was the phase of the moon on the day you started kindergarten?"), I said that I had topped up my phone one minute earlier. I was put through to another pay-as-you-go person, and amazingly, he had previously been Unshackled, and he was able to understand the cosmic complexity of my situation. He told me that any number beginning with 08 or 09 was a premium number. "Most" other numbers are ordinary numbers, including those starting with 07, although not with 070, which is premium, if I caught his drift. To call premium numbers I could purchase pay-as-you-go credits on top of my Unshackled Plan or use the Italian Woman's phone.

That led to the obvious question of how much it costs to call a premium number using pay-as-you-go credits. The man said it varied, depending on the contract the receiving company has with Joke-a-Fone, but it could be as much as one pound per minute, roughly fourteen times the rate to call someone in Singapore on the international plan. I asked if I would be charged for each minute at the accelerated rate if I called Tesco and was put on hold while I was being routed through its system. The answer was yes. Joke-a-Fone had a tough enough time keeping its own system opaque and burdensome. It could not be responsible for the inefficiencies of some other company.

I vowed that I would never use my phone or the Italian Woman's ever again.

DURING THE NEXT FOUR WEEKS we received daily messages on our phones and iPads that our credits had expired. We ignored them. Violating my earlier vow, I did in fact make one or two brief calls on my phone as part of our trip planning, but I did my best to horde my Unshackled minutes, thinking I would never again pay another farthing to Joke-a-Fone. Then one day I couldn't place a call, and I was forced to call *151 on the Italian Woman's phone. It had been several weeks since I had spoken to customer service, and it was like reconnecting with an old friend. I breezed through the security check ("On what side does Aunt Tilly wear her nipple ring?"), and soon I was live with a Scottish woman, who checked my account.

The woman sweetly reported that my Unshackled minutes had expired at the end of the thirty-day period since I had purchased them. I responded that nobody had ever told me that my three hundred minutes were good for only one month. She was sorry for any misapprehension I had been under. So, what should I do? "Go to your nearest tobacconist and purchase another month's worth of Unshackled. Remember, you will have three hundred minutes at a bargain rate."

And that's when it finally dawned on me: somewhere in a ruined abbey on the misty moors of Yorkshire, land of multifarious puddings and roseberry topping, quite by accident and completely unawares, we had fallen down the rabbit hole.

7

Stare-Down on a Lonely Road

NORTHUMBRIA SOUNDS LIKE AN OUTPOST established by an explorer from one of the hill towns of central Italy. It is not, and if you are looking for Montefalco wine or *porchetta*, you have come to the wrong place. It turns out that Northumbria took its name as the land north of the Humber River and, English spelling being the precise art that it is, a double *h* to make *Northhumbria* just didn't fly. All the more credit, then, to the crafty pair that managed to sneak into *withhold*. Now then, to add just slightly to the confusion, Northumbria and Northumberland are not the same thing. Northumbria was an ancient kingdom that included parts of what are now Yorkshire, Lancashire, and even southeast Scotland. Modern Northumberland is a remnant of that kingdom, and it sits along the Scottish border as England's northernmost county.

Why would anyone make the effort to visit Northumberland? Well, it's only a stone's throw from Edinburgh, which is a fine city indeed. But as for Northumberland itself, it has no cities at all and thus claims England's lowest population density. It does have its share of castles, so that's something. There are a couple of north-south highways, in case you like driving north or south, and if you fancy a long row of stones, you can visit Hadrian's Wall. The county's eastern edge is a stretch of seacoast, but then again, Britain has plenty of that. All in all this out-of-the-way corner wouldn't seem to be much of a draw, but for me it had one compelling feature—a national park with an impressive range of hills. If the Italian Woman would permit me another climb, Northumberland was logically our next destination.

WE FOLLOWED THE A1/M1 NORTH out of Yorkshire, past Newcastle upon Tyne, and into Northumberland. Our destination was the sleepy village of Belford, best known for a cylindrical stone tower whose purpose has been lost in the mists of time but whose name—the Spindlestone Ducket—suggests that it was a place where rocks were spun into gold coins. The Italian Woman had booked a country cottage just outside the village, and she reported that the place was described as "self-catering." We both thought it sounded autoerotic, as if the cottage were alive, capable of dimming the lights and satisfying its own desires. Actually, the term refers to a furnished house or apartment where guests do their own cooking and cleaning.

The government inspectors had just left, and the owners, a retired professional couple, were giddy from the news that their bungalow would again receive the coveted four-star gold rating. And it was a lovely little house . . . if you could ignore the fact that its back wall was literally at the edge of the A1. The owners had insulated and sealed the structure like a hyperbaric chamber, and you really didn't hear the enormous trucks passing by every five seconds. But you felt them. Again, the furnishings and appointments were first-rate, so the proper frame of mind was to accept the place as one large, four-star vibrating bed. It worked for the Italian Woman, and she spent the afternoon napping.

The next morning my companion was in pain, and she couldn't do more than make it downstairs to the couch. Compounding her misery, she had lain awake half the night waiting for a truck to come crashing through the bedroom wall. I had tossed and turned as well, but I had been obsessing over Whernside. Now I volunteered to spend the day tending to her, but to my surprise, she declined, saying that it would be better for me to get another climb out of the way immediately. Then

I would be available to do things with her when she was able to move around.

Communications between spouses are always saturated with nuance, so I couldn't be sure if my wife really wanted me to stay home that day or not. There is the added challenge that she is a Seattle native, and people from that city are notoriously reluctant to say anything disagreeable. Like the "Japanese Yes," which means only "I understand," the "Seattle No" refers to someone saying "Maybe" or "I'll think about it" or "That's an interesting idea," when they actually mean "Do I look that dumb, or are you out of your freakin' mind?" That morning in Northumberland I chose to take the Italian Woman at her word, loaded my knapsack, and drove off.

JUST WEST OF BELFORD LIES Northumberland National Park, a rugged preserve that sits on the English side of the country's border with Scotland. Straddling the line are the Cheviot Hills, desolate highlands that in ancient times were the scene of many cross-border skirmishes. Most famous of these was the 1388 Battle of Otterburn, between forces of the Earl of Douglas, a Scot, and the English Earl of Northumberland. A fifteenth-century narrative poem tells of Northumberland leading a hunting party onto a "chase"—a hunting ground—on the Scottish side of the border, only to be attacked by Douglas. Using a variation of the upland's name, the poem is titled "The Ballad of Chevy Chase." In due course the name made its way to a town in Maryland and also to an American boy whose formal name was Cornelius Crane Chase. His grandmother had descended from Clan Douglas, and she gave her grandson the nickname Chevy. Later, as a faux news anchor on the first season of *Saturday Night Live*, he began his reports with the iconic line, "I'm Chevy Chase, and you're not."

On leaving the vibrating cottage, I found myself on a country lane, the B6349. Then it got worse. The deeper you get into the British highway alphabet and the more numbers that are assigned, the narrower the road gets. At one point I was on the D438772, which meant that my wheels were running on either side of an abandoned sheep track. I had thought that driving in Yorkshire was unnerving, but here among the hedgerows I could see nothing but a twenty-foot section of road immediately ahead. At one point I met an oncoming car, screamed, and slammed on the brakes. That made me angry. A few minutes later, when I saw a pastoral scene of alfalfa being harvested, I couldn't appreciate it. "There's too much hay on that wagon," I said balefully.

After driving half an hour into the Heart of Darkness, I unexpectedly popped out into a town where human beings were milling about and actual commerce was being conducted. This was Wooler, which evidently lies midway between Wool and Woolest. I needed to pass through and connect with a spur road leaving the other end of the village, so I pulled into a car park with the intention of asking for directions. Amazingly, there stood the Cheviot Centre, a tourist information office. I fed the greedy park and pay machine—information doesn't come cheap, even in Northumberland—and went inside.

A prim but agreeable woman sold me a topographic map and pointed out how I could get from Wooler to a trailhead at Langleeford, which appeared to be a hamlet at road's end. She described the standard route to the national park's high point, a hulking plateau called The Cheviot. "You see, you first ascend Scald Hill, then drop a bit and climb to the higher summit. From there, take the scenic loop by carrying on to Cairn Hill and then dropping down into the valley to return to Langleeford." I said that I wasn't much interested in the three-peak circuit, but that I just wanted to get to the high point and back in the most direct way possible. The tilt of her head and the lift of an eyebrow suggested that perhaps my slam-bam approach to her magnificent hills did not meet her approval.

Following small, faded signs that pointed to Langleeford, I ventured onto country lanes that were even narrower than the ones east of Wooler, and these were punctuated with potholes. It seemed as if not many people came to this neck of the woods. I prayed fervently that I would not meet another car or, heaven forbid, a FedEx truck. Eventually, I was moving up a shallow valley where, right on cue, the sky clouded over and began turning blacker by the minute. I had the increasingly uncomfortable feeling that I was traveling between Nowhere and Beyond.

Nearly an hour from our cottage, I drove past a single car parked on a grassy patch above a small river. There was also a sign that said, "Limit of access land—No parking beyond this point." Now I was confused; I thought I would be stopping in a village called Langleeford. I continued for a few hundred yards, until I came to a gate and a second sign that said, "PRIVATE ROAD—Estate vehicles only." There wasn't a hamlet or a single building in sight. I looked around, and fortunately I spotted a small footpath sign pointing up the hill to the right. It said "Permissive Footpath—Scald Hill 1½." I turned around and drove back to the grassy car park. There, I was just lacing my boots when another vehicle arrived. Hoping for some companions who knew what they were doing, I approached the car. The occupants were an older couple who had come for birdwatching; they had no intention of climbing anything.

IT WAS NOON WHEN I set out. I walked briskly back to the estate entrance and turned up the Scald Hill path. It initially took me through a fenced cow pasture and onto an open meadow, with moorland beyond. The track then followed a wire fence straight up the hill, through grass and heather. The way was firm at first, with soft spots here and there. All in all an easy stroll, and I was happy that I knew where I was.

After I had settled into a rhythm, I began to pay closer attention to the weather. Sinister clouds hovered all around. Fortunately, they sat well above the hilltops, but their lower edges looked like wispy stalactites—a sure sign of rain. Halfway up Scald Hill I was certain that at any moment I was going to get soaked. Then again, I had rain clothing in my knapsack, so even if there was a downpour I could keep walking as long as there was no . . . That's when I heard a low rumbling in the distance. Thunder. I prepared to dash back down the hill, but first I peered intently in all directions, looking for lightning. I didn't see any, but the booming continued. Then it struck me that the sounds were too regular and uniform to be natural. I decided it must be a quarry or construction project. I later learned that the noises came from the nearby Otterburn Army Training Estate, home to the UK's largest firing range.

Thunder or no thunder, it was dark and bleak, and I began to have serious doubts about what I was doing. Highly skeptical that I could actually make it to the high points of fifteen widely scattered national parks, I wondered why I was bothering with this one. Who in their right mind would be here slogging alone in the gloom up an increasingly muddy slope? There were no trees, no flowers, no wildlife. What fun was this? Shouldn't I be planning a round of golf at St. Andrews? Shouldn't we buy a National Trust card and visit the cultural gems of Britain? Why not a theater binge in the West End? What kind of person would invest time and energy into walking up a series of round hills?

There, that felt better. A few minutes of grumbling was sufficient, and I returned to the business at hand. I came to a rock pile that from below appeared to be the summit, but it wasn't. Then another and another, and I finally arrived at the actual top of Scald Hill, forty minutes under way. This was 1,801 feet in elevation, and I had gained nearly 1,100 feet since leaving the car. Now, exposed to the other side of the mountain, I was struck by a stiff, cold breeze. I put on my ear band, took a drink of water, and moved on.

Ahead of me rose The Cheviot. Its summit was nearly nine hundred feet higher, and the sky around it was even darker. I was ready to climb on, but first, I had to descend slightly to a broad saddle. It proved to be a bog. Rocks and planks had been laid in the muddiest sections, but in spots I sank nearly to my ankles. Once onto the slope of The Cheviot, conditions were similar to the walk up Scald Hill—dry path, then grass, then mud, then rocks. I tried to pick the best route to avoid the muck but was not always successful. I pushed myself hard, hoping to get to the top and on the way down before the rain hit.

Forty minutes after leaving the top of Scald Hill, I arrived at the front edge of The Cheviot's summit plateau, at 2,625 feet. Ahead lay an extensive peat bog that is said to be as much as six feet deep in places, but luckily, someone had laid stone slabs end to end to protect the vegetation and prevent people from disappearing into the quagmire. On what was essentially a sidewalk, I jogged the final third of a mile to the summit marker in five minutes. I moved as fast as I could, because I was again buffeted by the cold wind and I had to keep moving to stay warm.

As I neared the nine-foot stone monument at the 2,674-foot high point, I saw a man standing with his back to me. I called out, not wanting to frighten him by suddenly showing up at his side. He turned and saw me as I approached. I introduced myself, and he responded: "I should tell you at the outset that I'm not much of a conversationalist. When I do have something to say, I tend to keep it rather basic. Frankly, I'm not much given to subjects, predicates, and subordinate clauses." Of course, that isn't what he really said. All that came out was "Graham."

Graham had a ruddy face, a salt-and-pepper mustache, and wisps of white hair protruding from a black baseball cap that he wore backward. He seemed vaguely familiar, and it eventually occurred to me that he was a dead ringer for Captain Kangaroo. I assumed he was older than me, probably in his seventies. He appeared ready to leave the summit, and I suggested that we descend together. He thought for a moment and said, "Okay." Then with a gesture he added, "Going by way of Cairn Hill." This meant that he was going to take the scenic loop recommended by the woman in Wooler. I didn't really want to put in the extra miles, but I decided that on such a dreary day the companionship, such as it was, would be preferable to a solo return over Scald Hill. Graham generously waited five minutes while I wolfed down a cheese sandwich, and then we were under way, with him in the lead. As we left, a few raindrops hit us, and I braced myself for a deluge. Fortunately, the cloudburst never happened.

THE PATH FROM THE CHEVIOT to Cairn Hill was a spur off Britain's most famous long-distance trail, the Pennine Way. That track runs 267 miles from the Peak District near Manchester, north through the Yorkshire Dales, passing very near Whernside, and then into the Cheviot Hills. It ends in Scotland not far from where we were walking. We moved into the wind, walking on slabs across the summit plateau, then down to a shallow saddle and back up to the top of Cairn Hill, at 2,459 feet. Like The Cheviot, this summit was essentially flat. A signpost had one arrow pointing west toward the Pennine Way, one back toward The Cheviot, and a third into the valley, to Langleeford.

As we started to descend, my right knee began to ache, and I knew immediately that my iliotibial band was acting up. ITB syndrome is an inflammation caused by the rubbing of a sheath of tissue around the knee, and it is painful. I had had my first bout many years earlier, on a nineteen-mile hike out of Washington's North Cascades. I was in agony, but not knowing the cause, I assumed I had trashed my knee and would be crippled for life. Instead, the doctor gave me an anti-inflammatory and a set of stretching exercises that allowed me to continue walking and climbing. In the Cheviot Hills it dawned on me that I had neglected my ITB for many months, and I was paying the price.

I sat down, rolled onto my back, lay my right foot across my left thigh, and pulled my legs toward me. In yoga this is called an inverted pigeon, or figure 4. Graham was startled at my contortions, and when I said, "Pigeon," he reacted as if I had just called on my accomplices to emerge from the shadows and relieve him of his valuables. After a few minutes the pain subsided, and we moved on. I stopped a few more times to repeat my stretching, and each time Graham glanced about warily.

Around 350 feet below the summit of Cairn Hill, we reached what the map identified as Scotsman's Knowe, a variant on the word *knoll*. We saw nothing resembling a mound, but we did find the beginning of a stream called Harthope Burn—*burn* being a Scottish term for "brook." That told us we were at the head of the Langleeford valley. The trail from that point was elusive, and we tried following sheep tracks through heather and tall grass, now and then stepping through bogs, and crossing and recrossing the stream. It was tedious, but the brook filled the air with a soothing sound. The gray sky was growing lighter as well, so all in all it was cheerier down there than on the hilltops. At one point I saw what I thought was a shiny black strip of electrical tape on the ground and wondered why anyone would have dropped it there. As I bent over to pick it up, it moved, and I realized that the thing was a slimy slug.

Despite my best efforts to engage in conversation whenever we paused for a breather, I still couldn't coax much out of Graham. Eventually, I gave up and just followed him silently. He struggled with route finding, but I knew that I couldn't have done any better.

Harthope Burn was growing larger as rivulets poured in from the slopes on either side. We passed through a little vale with trees and the world's loveliest double waterfall, called Harthope Linn. In short order the valley flattened out, the stream now a small river. The path turned into a wide track and then a rough dirt road. Along the way we passed several stone circles, identified on my map as sheepfolds. Finally, we reached a farmstead that had been hidden from the access road. This was the elusive Langleeford. From there it was half a mile down a gravel road to the cars. The return from Cairn Hill, just short of four miles, had taken two hours.

Back at the car park I said goodbye to Graham, and unexpectedly, with his door open and one foot inside the car, he started chatting. He said he gets out hill walking at least once a week, and he had driven four hours from Leeds that morning just to climb The Cheviot. I complimented him on his fitness, thinking he was a decade my elder. He said he was sixty-one, and if he was surprised to learn that I was sixty-four, he didn't show it—no doubt he was picturing me on the ground holding my right knee like a professional footballer.

Graham said he was a retired airline engineer, and suddenly everything made sense. As I had observed back in Seattle, aerospace professionals are a taciturn and inexpressive lot, and that's a good thing when you think about it. You don't want the people designing your airplanes to be wild and crazy guys. If ever there is a place for total focus, it's in the aerodynamics laboratory. There's a famous tale of a Boeing engineer who is insulted by someone, and he says, "Now you've hurt my feeling." Exhausted from all the sharing, Graham said goodbye and drove away. After draining my water bottle, I left a minute later.

Less than a mile down the one-lane road, I was traversing a hillside with a steep drop-off to my right, and it was there that I came nose to nose with another car. It was a taxi, actually, and I immediately determined that the pig-faced driver had no empathy. A hundred feet behind him was a wide spot where we could pass each other, but he gave no indication that he was willing to move. Instead, he took a drink from his liter of Coke and turned to his passenger to continue their conversation.

I just sat and looked at the other car, not knowing what to do. I thought of getting out and asking the fellow to back up, but he appeared so unpleasant that I didn't dare. He had the better of me, because his meter was running and he was in no hurry whatsoever. I, on the other hand, was sweaty and tired and anxious to get home. As a result, I blinked first and started backing up very slowly, trying to avoid the edge. I could hear bushes rustling against the side of the car on the uphill slope, but my eyes were riveted on the chasm just below my window. Once, I glanced up and saw the driver laughing and gesturing toward me with his soda bottle. Several times I thought I would just quit, but I knew I would again lose the stare-down. When I finally came to a place where the taxi could get by, the driver rewarded my troubles with a scornful smirk, and as he passed, I was certain that he discharged a snort.

On my return trip I drove through Wooler and then into the hamlet of Chatton. There I followed a sign left to Belford. At the next intersection Belford was another left. Two more of those, and I was back in Chatton. I tried a different route and found a sign that indicated BELFORD 4. I followed it, and several miles down the road, at the next intersection, a sign read BELFORD 7. You've got to love those Northumbrians and their playful sense of humor. For a moment I considered calling the taxi driver to lead me home.

THE ITALIAN WOMAN WAS RELIEVED to see me; the gray skies had concerned her, and she was wondering whether I had gotten drenched. She herself was feeling better. A day of reading and napping had restored her spirits, and her leg was less painful. We finished the day with shepherd's pie and a bottle of French red, a Pigassou that was soft and smooth with a slight afternote of bacon. As we ate, I described the day's events in detail, including my encounters with Graham and the man in the taxi. Despite the doubts I had felt on the way up Scald Hill, I realized what a satisfying climb it had been. If every mountain outing and every homecoming could be as good as this, well, then, Whernside would fade away.

8

No Trace of Janet Leigh

WE HAD BOOKED FOUR NIGHTS at the vibrating cottage, leaving two full days after my climb to explore Northumberland. On the first morning the tide chart showed that Lindisfarne, the Holy Island, would be accessible from 8:55 a.m. until 4:10 p.m. That was a perfect window of opportunity for us to visit the historic offshore site, which was a mere nine miles from our perch along the A1.

Lindisfarne was where, in AD 793, Vikings emerged from the mists of the North Sea and made what is regarded as their first significant assault on Britain. The event presaged a two hundred–year period of occupation instigated by a fellow named Ivar the Boneless, who evidently produced no offspring. Perhaps because of my many Norwegian friends, I have always been fascinated by their seafaring ancestors. Several years earlier we had visited the Viking Ship Museum in Oslo and its counterpart in Roskilde, Denmark. I had researched Scandinavian history and had watched the 1958 movie *The Vikings*, whose all-Nordic cast included Kirk Douglasson and Janet Leighsdottir. I was eager to visit the scene of the crime.

During low tide you can drive to Lindisfarne on a causeway that is lined with placards warning you not to even think about returning when the road is covered with water. Then, on the island itself, additional signs directed us into a large park and pay lot, with the admonition that parking in the village is for residents and overnight guests only. At one edge of the car park stood a National Trust welcome wagon, where a cheerful volunteer informed us that it was a quarter-mile to the village and a similar distance from there to Lindisfarne Castle, where I assumed the Viking raid had taken place. When I informed the man of my wife's injury, he said I should just drive her to the castle and then return and park. I did this, and during my solo walk I discovered that I was still gimpy from my ITB episode the previous day. In any event, twenty-five slightly painful minutes later, I joined the Italian Woman on a bench just below the rocky promontory on which the castle stood. Nearby a lone bagpiper was playing the theme from Dvorak's *New World* Symphony, which as far as I know has no connection whatsoever to Northumberland or Kirk Douglas.

Once inside the fortress, we learned that it was actually built around 1550, more than 750 years after the Viking raid. It was designed as a small military installation to protect the seacoast and was never a home to royals or nobles. The current look of the interior dates back only a hundred years, when architect Edwin Lutyens did an Extreme Makeover, Castle Edition, in the Arts and Crafts style. We enjoyed touring the place, and the views from its parapets were impressive, but overall it was disappointing that there wasn't so much as a hint of anything Viking. I asked one of the docents about the great raid, and she directed us to the priory in the village.

The priory turned out to be another of those ruins that the British seem to treasure more than life itself. The UK is filled with places like this, and after seeing a number of them, I have reached several quite logical conclusions: First, the priories and abbeys of Britain are in ruins because all the nuns and monks have died off. Second, they perished because their vows permitted them to eat nothing but black and white pudding. Third, the only abbey still standing is Westminster Abbey, where everybody is buried.

In Lindisfarne we learned that the priory's ruins stand on the very spot where legendary clerics Saint Aidan and Saint Cuthbert lived, and there a monk named Eadfrith had crafted the illustrated Lindisfarne Gospels, one of the world's great artistic treasures. And indeed, this was where the Viking raid had occurred. There was only one catch, and that was that the pink stone rubble visible today is what remains of a church built in 1150. In fact, on the entire island there isn't anything left of the Vikings except a short documentary film at the Heritage Centre. Even the Lindisfarne Gospels are gone, kept in the British Museum in London, although that summer they were temporarily on display in Durham. A three-month event in that city included a stage play titled *A Funny Thing Happened on the Way to Durham*, described as a "ninety-minute romp though fourteen hundred years of Northumbrian, Scottish, and English history." The festival brochure also invited you to download "Lindisfarne Gospels Durham Deals."

In my disappointment of the moment I still had the movie to fall back on. Now there's some real action. Kirk Douglas has his eye plucked out by a falcon. His half-brother, Tony Curtis, has his hand hacked off. They both vie for Janet Leigh, who is their half-sister or something like that, and you just know that Curtis will win and he and Leigh will produce a leggy daughter, and then Leigh will be slashed to death in a shower. The boys' father is Ernest Borgnine, who shouts, "Marty!" and jumps into a pit of ravenous wolves. Finally, Curtis kills Douglas in a duel and then solemnly intones, "Prepare a funeral for a Viking." Douglas's body is cast adrift on a Viking ship that is bombarded with flaming arrows. It's a whale of a tale, and they just don't make them like that anymore. Lindisfarne today is pale by comparison.

As we returned to the car, we chatted with the National Trust worker, who was closing up his trailer and preparing to pull it off the island ahead of the incoming tide. I told him I was disappointed about the lack of Viking ruins but that we had enjoyed the ambience of Lindisfarne. It might be a nice place to come and relax for a week or two. "Oh, no, you don't want to do that," he responded with a shudder. "Once the tide rolls in and the island is cut off, the shops and restaurants close and the locals come out from their homes. You remember the film *Deliverance*, don't you? That's what this place becomes."

THAT EVENING I SET UP my work station in the cottage, firing up our new printer. After my no-map follies on Urra Moor, I had decided that I needed the capacity to print guides and route descriptions from the internet, even if that meant hauling another piece of equipment with us for the remainder of the summer. I had also bought a power strip, so that at any given moment I could operate my laptop and the printer while charging our other devices.

International travel demands that you arm yourself with an array of plug adapters, and by now I have quite a collection. I have also come to believe that a country's plugs, like its shoes, are a reflection of its overall sense of style. The thin, flat prongs of an American plug are the flimsiest, like a pair of flip-flops. The two round tines on the Continent are elegant, like Manolo Blahnik stilettos. Italy, land of Prada and Ferragamo, has tried to improve on its neighbors by adding a third prong in line with the first two, but the result is something that resembles a toothbrush. And then you have the British, whose triangular, three-tine devices are so heavy and clunky that in the field of pluggery, they are the orthopedic shoes. During their years of membership in the European Union, the British never bothered redesigning their cumbersome plugs, nor did they ever consider driving on the right side of the road.

Why do they drive on the left? During my first two weeks in England I had struggled with my road orientation. I was grateful that our Vauxhall's steering wheel was on the right, because it served as constant reminder of where I was. I have heard that if you spend enough time upside down in a yoga headstand, your brain eventually tells you that things look normal. Well, by the time we reached Northumberland, I was finally getting comfortable, even going so far as telling myself that it seemed natural to be on the left because that's where everyone else was.

Then again, this is wrong, wrong, wrong. In Latin the left side is *sinistris*, meaning "sinister," while the right side is *dextra*, which gives us "dexterous." Even the English word *right* means "correct," while *left* suggests something unwanted, as in *leftover* or *left behind*. Don't those things speak for themselves? Why do the British thumb their noses at their Continental neighbors and most of the rest of world? I remember vividly the television footage on September 3, 1967, when the Swedes crossed over to the right. Ja, sure, there were some initial challenges, but if Sweden could do it, why not the United Kingdom?

Navigating down an English road, there are times when I just want to scream: "Enough! Let me demonstrate how the civilized world is supposed to work." Then I have a fleeting and terrifying vision of moving into the right lane just to prove my point. Of course, that puts me directly into oncoming traffic, and my demonstration and I are short-lived. These thoughts leave me with a death grip on the steering wheel, breathing rapidly and perspiring. During one such episode the Italian Woman looked at me in alarm and asked if I was all right. I replied in terms that I hoped would avoid any further discussion: "I'm having a hot flash." She was not amused, and she was right, of course. I had momentarily forgotten that no man will ever appreciate what women go through.

Now I ask, are these just the ravings of one solitary American tourist who can't go with the flow? Or does everybody from the United States and the Continent feel like this when they drive in the UK? But then consider that on any given day in America there must be thousands of demented British visitors behind the wheel, muttering, "I've got to show these Yanks how it's done!"

WE HAD BEEN TOLD THAT we should stop in the town of Alnwick, three of whose seven letters, as it turns out, are silent. That leaves only *Anik*. This is an obvious echo of the Norman

Conquest and the French language, in which consonants are thrown randomly into words with no intention that they ever be pronounced. Even the words for "good words"—*bons mots*—come out as "bo-mo." Well, the thought occurred to me that since Alnwick's *l*, *w*, and *c* are merely visual decorations, they could be placed anywhere with no consequences. Thus, the spelling could be *Walnick* or *Clanwik* or *Anwilck,* and the pronunciation would still be *Anik.* This is one of those phenomena that sends me to my knees in gratitude that I didn't have to learn English as a second language.

In size and in ambience Alnwick was a cut above Leyburn, indeed worth a visit. We stopped for coffee at a homey little café called the Art Shop, which displayed a collection of delightfully quirky drawings and prints. My favorite was a parody of a famous Japanese piece, Hokusai's 1830 wood-block print *The Great Wave off Kanagawa.* It shows a giant wave curling over several small fishing boats, with Mount Fuji in the background. From a distance the Alnwick version looked just like the original, but closer inspection revealed that the wave was made entirely of white rabbits.

Alnwick has a well-preserved castle that appears in the *Harry Potter* films. We drove to it and saw crowds of children queuing up, waving their magic wands. The fortress is one of Northumberland's major tourist attractions, but the Italian Woman wasn't interested, and I was equally content to bypass the whole Hogwarts thing. I had read the first Potter book when our children were caught up in Pottermania, and although in many ways I have not matured past the age of fourteen, I just couldn't get into it. I had been spoiled by the artistry of Tolkien and Lewis, and it was disappointing that the new series had little of that. Obviously, many others disagreed, and Ms. Rowling did manage to sell a few of her books.

The Italian Woman had a craving for fish and chips, so we made our way up the coast to a surfside village that is aptly called Seahouses. We found the object of our desires at a popular place called Neptune, and the food was good enough to please my companion. Yet it was pale in comparison to the ginger ice cream that we ate on a bench overlooking the tiny, sheltered harbor. Next to us sat a man who had purchased two of the ice cream cones—one for himself and the other for his dog.

Seahouses was full of references to a local woman named Grace Darling, who at the age of twenty-two had participated in a dramatic offshore rescue in 1838. In dreadful weather she and her father rowed a boat to retrieve the victims of a shipwreck, and young Grace went on to be the subject of songs, paintings, and even a Wordsworth poem. A government rescue boat stationed in the marina today is named in her honor.

While in the village, we stopped at a pharmacy. We had used all the extra bandages and dressings given to us at the Royal Lancaster Infirmary, and we needed a fresh supply. I described what we were looking for, and I also asked for a tube of antibiotic cream, because my partner's wound was still red and warm and had not fully closed. Instead of supplies, I received a stern rebuke from a pompous man behind the counter. Of course I couldn't purchase bandages—if I so much as looked at the wound, I would be practicing medicine without a license. Of course I couldn't purchase antibiotic cream—it was a controlled substance. He and I would both land in jail and be assigned to the same cell, and then he would have to lecture me all day long for fifteen years. All we could do was drive back to Wanlick, to the medical clinic, and have a proper professional change the dressing. And they surely wouldn't use antibiotics in any form, even if it meant saving the planet from the Microbe That Would Destroy All Civilization. Now, if I could just step aside for the next person in line . . .

THE FOLLOWING MORNING WE LEFT our cottage to make our way to North West England. This, however, was to be more than just a transit across the tiny waistline of the UK—we had decided that en route we would visit Hadrian's Wall. The previous summer our daughter and her husband had walked the entire eighty-four-mile Hadrian's Wall Path in a six-day downpour, and somehow they were not bitter about the experience. They recommended that we at least take a look. Our approach would be what is affectionately known as the "Italian Woman's Basic Tour": drive to it, jump out for a photo, and drive on.

On our beloved A1 we drove south to Tyne, then west on the A69. When we had left the city well behind, we exited at Corbridge, drove north on the A68, and turned west onto the B6318, a modest little road that appeared on the map to closely follow the famous wall. We drove and looked and drove and looked some more. At one point I said: "Here's a stone wall on my side of the road. This has to be it."

"Stevie, don't you see the identical thing on my side? And notice how similar they are to the ones running up and down the hills in all directions? These look just like every other stone wall in England."

"Well, maybe the Romans had such a good idea that people copied it everywhere."

"We need to keep looking."

There were tantalizing little brown signs here and there that said, HADRIAN'S WALL, but we just couldn't find it. At one point we saw a row of grassy mounds, and my companion suggested that maybe the wall had gotten covered over during the past two thousand years, like a lost temple in Egypt. Now it was my turn to doubt.

We saw a low escarpment with a vertical cliff running its entire length. This time we both thought we were onto something, so we drove toward it on a dirt lane. It surely looked like a wall, but on closer inspection it obviously wasn't man-made, and the entire feature was only half a mile long. That couldn't be it.

A sign directed us to Chester's Fort, a Roman stronghold built into a section of the wall. We were too cheap to pay the entrance fee, but the ranger on duty told us to keep going west to a car park at Steel Rigg. We did that, but all we found was another escarpment. Maybe that was the wall after all. We drove on to another car park with a view of another escarpment, but there, on the outside of a toilet building, was a picture of a hand-crafted stone structure. We looked in all directions, and at last we were gazing at it, the real deal—Hadrian's Wall. Immediately, we both said, "How could that possibly keep the Scots out?" Really, unless the ancient Celts were two feet tall, they could have walked up to this glorified curb, had a good laugh, and just scrambled over it.

Our final deed before departing Northumberland was a slow-down through the village of Haltwhistle, which claims to be the "centre of Britain." A bit of on-the-fly internet research informed us that the town has nothing to do with halting or whistling, and neither is it at the precise geographical center of the country. I think a good municipal slogan would be "Come to Halt-whistle, where nothing we tell you is the truth." Of course, that creates a conundrum. If it is true that nothing they say is true, then they have actually told you the truth, in which case the slogan would be false. With those thoughts to chew on, we left Northumberland, possibly forever.

9

Of Daffodils and the Silent W

WHEN AMERICANS PLAN A VACATION in England, we tend to focus on its historical places in or near London. We scurry about to visit Stonehenge, Bath, and the Tower of London, and when we have tired of listening to tour guides dressed as gin bottles, a few of us might linger an extra day or two and go walking in the Cotswold Hills, because that's what everyone tells us we ought to do, and then it is "Thank you very much, let's move on to France and Holland." It takes a bit more time and dedication to visit England's northwesternmost county, Cumbria.

The heart of Cumbria has another name, one that is familiar to anyone who has studied English poetry—the Lake District. I first learned of the region in the fall of 1964, when I was a junior at my Iowa high school. That September I began a literature class with Mr. Vanden Bosch, who until then I had known only as my basketball coach. The combination of my lack of athletic talent and his wooden communication skills in the gym had made our association rather unsatisfactory, and as a result, I was not pleased when I was assigned to his section of eleventh grade English. But then, as if two new people had pushed us aside and taken over our relationship, Coach began to speak passionately about Shelley, Keats, Coleridge, and Wordsworth, and I found myself hanging on his every word.

The movement called Romanticism was a reaction against the intellectualism of the Enlightenment, with the Romantics rejecting science and celebrating nature, emotion, and beauty. Let's be clear that we are not talking about today's concept of romance with a small *r*—the treacle that permeates popular music ("Tonight I Celebrate My Love for You"), Lifetime movies (*How I Married My High School Crush*), and Harlequin books (*Second Chance with Her Soldier*). No, the nineteenth-century poets were ardent in their beliefs and serious about what they were doing. They also possessed artistic talent. I had always planned on being a scientist, but at the age of sixteen I saw a new path for my life: I would be a writer. The fact that I have spent most of my adult years in the legal profession represents a detour for which I am now trying to make amends.

Words-worth. Could there be a more perfect name for a poet?

I wandered lonely as a cloud

Like any sensitive adolescent, I felt alone; I was certain that nobody understood me. My parents were clueless, my friends often witless, and the elders in my Dutch Reformed church were on another planet entirely.

That floats on high o'er vales and hills

I used to lie on the grass behind my Iowa home and watch the white clouds drift by, wishing I could move on with them. I wanted to escape my strict Calvinist community. I wanted to travel to faraway places and learn other languages. I wanted to live in the mountains and climb them.

And then my heart with pleasure fills,
And dances with the daffodils.

A grown man talking not about politics or the price of corn, but flowers! Not about theological purity, but a dancing heart. Just when I needed it so badly, I heard the good news that my dreams were not crazy after all.

Nearly half a century after that literature class, I readily admit that reading poetry is less entertaining than watching a film by the Coen brothers. And really, the starry-eyed Romantics are best taken in small doses about once every ten years. Nevertheless, I am not so jaded as to have forgotten what it meant to be touched for the first time by their appreciation for the beauty of our world and their way with the English language. So, a twenty-first-century adult can still feel a thrill on approaching the very place where William Wordsworth and the others had drawn their inspiration. I had never been to the Lake District, but part of me—the same part that longed for mountains as a boy and even today watches Hallmark movies with my wife— was coming home.

WE HAD BOOKED AN APARTMENT in the northern section of the Lake District National Park, in the town of Keswick, which we of course assumed would be pronounced *Kess-wick* or *Kezz-wick*. Not so. Like its Northumbrian cousin, Alnwick, the Cumbrian town mysteriously strangles the *w* and calls itself "Kezzik." What the *c* might have sounded like at one time is anybody's guess, but the *ck* combination with a single *k* sound (technically, an endocentric digraph, in case you are interested, and while we're at it—I'm sorry to digress even further—you might ask yourself whether it is indeed the *c* or the *k* that is silent) is something we are used to. A silent *w* seems such a waste of perfectly good ink. In any event, in writing the narrative that follows, I was tempted to use the phonetic spelling for *Kezzik*, but that seemed too paternal. If the people of Keswick are content to live a lie, then I decline to interfere.

Once in Keswick, we set out on foot to find a supermarket and at once came face to face with the town's outdoor vibe. The pedestrian-only streets were filled with holidaymakers, but unlike Aspen and St. Moritz, where the beautiful people parade about in thousand-dollar sequined ski suits and furry mukluks, the look here was all North Face and Helly Hansen. Municipal law in Keswick apparently mandates that you carry a knapsack at all times. Also required are stout walking shoes with yellow laces and, because it was drizzling, a hooded blue rain jacket. Actually, the town's market square looked just like Seattle on . . .

well, nearly any day of the year, and to a Seattle person, dancing around puddles is part of life's rhythm. All we needed to complete the picture was a Starbucks latte in a double cup.

Whether by magisterial decree or a deep instinctual need, nearly every human in Keswick was being towed by a canine. The Italian Woman immediately got misty over the fact that we had left our own lovable Lucy—coincidentally, an Old English sheepdog—back in the States. We had to do it, but it was tough for my mate to part with her constant companion. Even I had to admit that I missed those little morning walks, standing around with a plastic mitt on my hand, watching the backside of an animal and waiting for the previous evening's dinner to crown, blossom, and fall steaming and gleaming to the earth.

There is something about living with a dog that changes your perspective. Even if you already enjoy the companionship you need from another human, the addition of a dog alters the landscape. First of all, it takes you down from your high horse. How can you maintain your dignity when out dog walking? Everyone who sees you knows that soon you'll be bending over to pick up some droppings, and then you'll carry the baggie, and it will sway back and forth as you continue on. Also, doesn't your dog's curiosity arouse your own? Just what is it that's so interesting down there? Shouldn't you get onto your knees and take a whiff? Whatever the dog is sniffing, it must smell good. Imagine how we would behave if a spot of grass evoked Chanel No. 5. And over here is a patch of fresh ground coffee. And wait! Next to this tree I detect baking bread! Ooh, ooh, ooh—let me drag you toward that streetlight and see what we can find. And that stranger down the way—shouldn't you run to him and inspect his pant leg? What are we missing by walking with our heads five or six feet above the ground?

Back in Keswick, I'm guessing that most of the animals in the market square were well mannered back in the city, but something in the country air of the Lake District had turned them into raucous beasts. The town square was a cacophony of barking and yelping, and a good many hours were spent untangling dogs and humans from intertwined leashes. Much as we felt the absence of Lucy, Keswick was fortunate that she was not with us. She is the world's most manic herder, and given enough rope, she would quickly have had the entire population trussed up like Thanksgiving turkeys.

It appeared that every second shop in Keswick was an outdoor equipment store. The town boasts more such establishments than any other community in Britain and proudly calls itself the "Outdoor Retailer of the UK, if not Europe!" Here I should mention that I am a notoriously reluctant shopper—I decide what I need before entering a store and then, never looking left or right, go directly to that item, grab it, pay for it, and leave in haste. Maybe it's just that I'm cheap, but I cannot bear being confronted by colorful displays of things I don't need, and I am afraid something is going to leap into my arms and coo, "Buy me, big boy." There are two exceptions to my officinaphobia— yes, that's a thing. One is outdoor shops. I would posit that the world's greatest cathedral, surpassing even St. Peter's and Notre Dame, is the imposing glass and timber REI flagship store in downtown Seattle. Bless me, Father, for I have lusted after expedition-tested microfiber.

The other exception is, naturally, bookstores. I thank the Almighty for Omaha's cheery Bookworm, Seattle's peerless Elliott Bay Book Company, and the host of independent sellers who have not yet succumbed to Barnes & Noble, which itself has not yet succumbed to that online juggernaut whose name escapes me. Keswick has two indies of note, the musty and utterly inviting secondhand shop with the unremarkable name of Keswick Bookshop, and the tourist-focused Bookends, which offers every conceivable walking guide to the Lake District.

And so, with all of that gear and all of those books singing their siren songs, Keswick had my number.

AT A SMALL BUTCHER SHOP we decided to purchase some lamb chops, and a handwritten sign in the meat cooler proudly announced that it was local Herdwick lamb. Not knowing what that meant, I asked the butcher, "Is there something different about Herdick lamb?"

"What's that you say?"

"Herdick lamb. Is it different from ordinary lamb?"

"What kind of lamb?"

"Herdick. What it says on the little sign here."

He picked up the card, looked at it, and said, "Oh, you mean *Herdwick* lamb."

"You pronounce the *w*?"

"Of course, that's why it's there."

NOT WISHING TO PRESS MY luck with the Italian Woman, I knew it would be prudent to begin our week in the Lake District behaving like tourists, giving no thought to climbing any mountains. In any event the UK national weather service, which has the oddly bland name of "Met Office," stated on its website that the weekend would be wet . . . so amazingly wet that all of the blue-jacketed hill walkers were advised to spend their time indoors, spending money at Keswick's fine array of shops.

It was indeed raining buckets on Saturday morning, and I was tempted to lie around and mope. On the other hand, I had sold my wife on the many attractions of the Lake District, so I rose and cheerily banged some pans together, proclaiming, "Let's Get Out and Do Something!" This was met with considerable resistance, because the Italian Woman does not appreciate being woken up, and furthermore, one should never propose any activities until she has showered and had a cup of strong coffee. Once the caffeine had taken effect, she grudgingly reviewed a stack of brochures, and we agreed to seek out a cottage of some renown.

Heading south from Keswick into the heart of the national park, we passed a lake with the Tolkienesque name of Thirlmere. Then came the village of Grasmere and a lake of the same name, then Rydal and a lake called Rydal Water. You may sense the beginning of a pattern here, but let me jump right to it: As countless writers have noted, in the vaunted Lake District there is only one feature actually called a "lake," and that is the tongue-twisting Bassenthwaite Lake (say it several times and it comes out *bath-and-sweat*). Every other body of water is a "mere" or "tarn" or simply "water." You will find Windermere, Buttermere, Stickle Tarn, Seathwaite Tarn, Crummock Water, and my personal favorite, Wast Water, which sounds like the dumping station at an RV park.

Maybe the fact that it has only one is why the area is called the Lake District and not the *Lakes* District. You've got to admire the mathematical precision of those who selected the singular form of the word, but really, a solitary lake does not a district make. I'd like to suggest renaming it the Mere District. Its official slogan: "Well, at least it's something."

10

Bad Mice and Blind Cats

IF BEATRIX POTTER HADN'T CREATED her retreat there, nobody but nobody would ever make their way to Near Sawrey or its neighbors Far Sawrey, Hawkshead, and High Wray. All of them are isolated by tortuous roads and are located on the wrong side of the Lake District's largest body of water, Windermere. The story goes that when Miss Potter was house hunting, she fell in love with Hill Top Farm at Near Sawrey, but she had an alternate property in mind near High Wray. When negotiations with the seller of Hill Top came to an impasse over price, the street-smart young woman uttered those legendary words, "It's my way or the High Wray." The seller caved, and Hill Top ultimately became one of the most beloved shrines in England.

And what's not to like? If you survive the journey to Hill Top, you are so grateful for a few more hours of life that you would relish a ruined abbey where they serve black pudding, let alone a rustic cottage and Mr. McGregor's garden. The National Trust, which owns and operates Potter's longtime home, has things well under control without making every guest feel like a thief or terrorist. To avoid overcrowding, you are given an entry time, and so the Italian Woman and I strolled about the garden for fifteen minutes before being ushered into the house.

Hill Top has low ceilings and rather small rooms, but it overflows with character. Most of the furniture on display was actually used by Potter and her husband, William Heelis. Of particular charm were the reproductions of her artwork and correspondence left lying about for visitors to examine. It's as if you had dropped in for tea with Beatrix herself and, as she fussed about, you picked up a drawing from the table and said, "Hmmm, a bunny with an artist's beret, do you really think that's going to work?"

The docents on duty were particularly well informed and happy to explain how this teakettle or that chair had made its way into the children's books. One of the hosts commented that they receive many visitors from Japan, whose people love to attribute human characteristics to animals. She added that an exact replica of Hill Top has been built near Tokyo and that Beatrix Potter and Walt Disney have been canonized as Shinto saints.

The Italian Woman and I were in a small room upstairs, and a cheerful fellow was just starting to talk about a doll's house and how it was the setting for *Two Bad Mice*, when out in the garden there arose such a clatter that I sprang to the window to see what was the matter. I tore open the shutters and threw up the sash (I had inadvertently swallowed a sash at lunch), and what to my wondering eyes did appear but an enormous bus disgorging a stream of people dressed in navy-blue golf jackets and cream-colored slip-on shoes. No waiting required for this crowd—they breezed past the queue and flowed directly into the cottage. We were soon exchanging hip bumps with forty-two of our newest, most intimate friends.

The Italian Woman quickly became nervous that someone was going to brush against her leg, so the two of us wiggled our way back downstairs and out to the garden. We sat on a bench and took in the fresh air. Eventually, the tour group must have received a "time's up" signal from their guide, because they poured en masse from the house and made for the parking lot. That is, all but one fellow, who diverted into the garden for a few last photos. His wife tried to dissuade him, and with a desperate look in her eyes she pleaded, "Kazu, for the love of sushi, we need to get back to the others."

Kazu responded, "Yes, dear," but he was thinking: "I've had it up to here with the herd mentality. I swear, one of these days I'm gonna chuck the whole thing and hightail it to Montana, gonna buy me a pickup truck and a little haying operation and never take orders from nobody ever again, and then you'll be sorry." A few minutes later he was politely awaiting his turn to climb onto the bus, but he was thinking, "You'll be sorry, you'll . . ."

It turned out that Hill Top had no in-and-out privileges, and by leaving the cottage we had terminated our brief tenancy. Once outside the compound we bought ice cream bars and talked about Beatrix Potter, the woman who had made this day possible. My biggest surprise was that she did not, in fact, look like Renée Zellweger, who had portrayed her in the film *Miss Potter*. More a combination of Queen Victoria and Eleanor Roosevelt, to be frank. The Italian Woman was impressed that Potter in her later years had become one of Cumbria's leading experts on those adorable Herdwick sheep with the black bodies and white faces. I noted that she had married her lawyer, Mr. Heelis, and I reflected on the fact that after twenty-seven years of law practice in Seattle, I couldn't recall a single instance of a client throwing herself at me. Of course, most of my clients were Alaska fishermen and Norwegian bankers, so there wasn't much of a pool of eligible hotties out there.

NOT FAR FROM HILL TOP, on our return to Keswick, we came upon a road resurfacing project. A large red sign with white letters proclaimed, CATS EYES REMOVED.

Still feeling the animal love from Beatrix Potter and her many fans in Tokyo, the Italian Woman gasped and said, "Oh, how could they?"

I responded, "I'm no cat lover, but that does seem a bit excessive."

I would like to leave it there, but I feel I should reassure you that the British are not a race of animal abusers. Cats' eyes are those reflective highway lane markers that are particularly helpful at night or when the road is wet. They were developed in 1933 by one Percy Shaw of West Yorkshire, and they are otherwise known as reflecting roadstuds (and what a wonderful word is *roadstud*). Without them, British highways would be even more dangerous. Interestingly, cats' eyes are a source of national pride, which suggests that the UK is somewhat short on inventors.

It took a bit of research to unearth the rather mundane truth about cats' eyes. A few days later we saw a similar sign and stopped to take a picture of it. That evening we emailed the photo without comment to some cat-owning friends in Minnesota.

THE RAIN CONTINUED ON SUNDAY, so we attended St. John Church in Keswick, a Church of England parish. The Italian Woman and I self-identify as Episcopalians, Anglicans, or whatever the regional label is. We are drawn to the comforting fussiness of the services and the inspired prose of the Book of Common Prayer. While so many churches—at least the ones we were raised in—treat their members like toddlers who only understand the word *no*, the Anglican fellowship is refreshingly inclusive and positive. Bishops, priests, and parishioners can be single or married, male or female, straight or homosexual—or any combination of these. Work on that just a bit, and you'll find that what the previous sentence lacks in technical precision, it makes up in general spirit. When a visitor asked an Episcopal cleric whether it was proper to stand, sit, or kneel during the Eucharistic prayer, his answer was yes. This is the denomination that is described as having Seven Commandments and Three Suggestions, and U Pick. "You'll find a warm welcome here at All Saints à la Carte."

While in Leyburn, we had attended the village church, but the small crowd had been a disappointment, if not a complete surprise. We would see similar turnouts in other places, where everyone in attendance had already been measured for a space in the churchyard, and in another year at most the last member would be padlocking the door for the last time. Strange it was to show up on a Sunday morning and find that we were a quarter of the crowd that day. But nothing would top our experience at the Anglican church in Curaçao in 1999, where one of the four old women in attendance (there was no one else) proudly showed us to our pew but asked us not to sit until she had dusted it off. She then handed us the guestbook to sign. During the service I looked up and saw blue sky through gaps in the roof. A pigeon sat in the rafters cooing "All Things Bright and Beautiful." Two years later we were back on the island and returned to the church. It was the same routine with the same four ladies, and when we were handed the guestbook, we discovered that the most recent entry was our own.

Compared to Leyburn and Curaçao, St. John in Keswick was abuzz. Some forty people were worshipping that morning, and the sheer size of the crowd suggested that "this is the place." St. John even had a choir of five women and three men. Most novel, at least to us, was the children's play area on one side of the sanctuary—not off in an anteroom or adjacent church hall, mind you, but in the nave itself. On this festive Sunday morn two preschoolers were occupying the little enclave along with a grandmotherly attendant. If we factor in the children's parents, there were exactly four people under the age of sixty attending the service. Even so, the energy in the church was palpable, especially when the little nippers started a contest of I Can Bang the Wooden Block on the Table Louder than You. The Italian Woman and I couldn't help but stare in wonderment, but no one else seemed to notice.

We later learned that the archbishop of Canterbury had decreed that every Anglican church demonstrate its generational inclusiveness by positioning a crèche smack in the worship space, in hopes that somewhere in the UK a family might consider attending services, as one had indeed done in Keswick. The mandate applied in every bishopric (there, I said it) in Britain, along with the admonition that if you cannot tolerate block banging, then you should turn off your hearing aids. Of the several churches we were to visit during our summer travels, all of them had a play area, but this was the only one in use.

Lest I sound like an unsatisfied customer, let me hasten to add that our several visits to St. John during our time in Keswick were in fact the social highlight of our summer. Foreign travelers are lucky to engage in even a fleeting conversation with someone on a train or at a restaurant or market. At the lovely old church in the Lake District, we actually got to know people, and everyone we visited with made us feel as if they were happy to see us. Let me illustrate.

After the service, nobody left. Instead, some folks scurried about setting up tables and folding chairs, while others brought out food for the monthly parish lunch. One man noticed us and invited us to stay. After we exchanged names—his was Gordon—he said, "And what part of America are you from?" All right, there must be something in the way I say "Steve" that screams: "I'm from your breakaway colonies, the United States of America. Have at me." I responded that we were from Seattle by way of Omaha.

"Well, obviously you're not a typical American."

"Oh? Why not?"

"You're not typical because your trousers aren't too short."

I didn't know whether to thank him for recognizing my sartorial good sense or demand an apology for his backhanded insult to my fellow countrymen. If I had been on my toes, I might have complimented him for having learned to speak with a mouth full of marbles, but I just chuckled, "Heh, heh."

When lunch began, we sat with Gordon Trousers and his wife, Priscilla, and on closer inspection found them to be of good cheer. They and others at St. John that day wanted us to know that they appreciate American visitors, feel a strong affinity for the States, and have enjoyed their trips to the far side of the Atlantic. No one could resist adding just one little observation as to which aspect of American culture baffles them—that we eat breakfast beans only at picnics, that we fail to appreciate the good qualities of that purple-pissing lunatic George III, and the like—but overlooking our peccadilloes and armadilloes, they just *love* us. And to that, let me add that throughout the summer, no matter how we may have struggled to fully understand the British and no matter what amusement we took from them, we loved them back.

11

A View to Five Lands

THE LAKE DISTRICT IS A national park, and of course I wanted to climb its tallest mountain, which also happens to be the highest point in all of England. Very few foreigners have even heard of Scafell Pike, a mound of rock tucked out of sight in a jumble of other peaks. I was aware of it because of my interest in the history of climbing, a sport more or less invented by the British. Over the years they used their relatively gentle highlands as training grounds for more challenging ranges, and they ventured forth to achieve first ascents of the Matterhorn, Mount Everest, and countless other peaks around the world. Throughout the nineteenth and twentieth centuries the hills of northwestern England enjoyed a certain cachet in alpine circles, not for their technical difficulty but for the climbing celebrities who frequented them. Edward Whymper, George Leigh Mallory, Chris Bonington, and many other members of the mountaineering pantheon had at one time or another honed their skills in Cumbria.

Early Monday morning it was gray but not actually raining, so I gently nudged the Italian Woman and suggested that it might be a good day for me to get some exercise. She was ready for a few more hours in bed, so she grunted her assent, rolled over, and burrowed under the covers.

With Keswick as the starting point, there are two primary ways to approach Scafell Pike. The shortest and most frequented path to the summit is from Wasdale Head, west of the peak and near the infamous Wast Water, where you should not stop to fill your canteen. Despite the western route's popularity, the trailhead is a ninety-minute drive from Keswick on what the guidebook describes as a "long and twisty" road. Given my experience navigating to Hill Top Farm, I take such descriptions very seriously. The principal alternative is to travel to the mountain from the north. What you get is a hike that is four miles longer than the Wasdale route, but the drive is only twenty minutes. Under the circumstances it was an easy choice: I know what my legs can do; British country roads are a crapshoot.

The B5289–obviously not a major thoroughfare—took me south of Keswick into a valley called Borrowdale. This proved to be a scenic drive along the edge of Keswick's own lake, Derwent Water. I skirted the villages of Grange and Rosthwaite and after eight miles entered the hamlet of Seatoller, where I turned onto a country lane. In the space of another mile I passed through Low Stile Wood, then over Seathwaite Bridge, and finally to a dead end at Seathwaite Farm. There was parking along one side of the road and on the other sat a pasture occupied by several soggy-looking bivouac tents. It was now drizzling slightly, and I knew I would soon get wet, but I was glad I didn't have to start my climb by crawling out from a dripping tent into sodden grass. In the shelter of my car I slipped on my rain jacket and hat and draped a waterproof cover over my knapsack. Stepping out into the mist, I extended both of my walking poles. I normally use them only on the descent, but they would be helpful if the ascending trail was slippery.

A van and two cars had arrived ahead of me, and eight hikers were huddled together in a discussion. They were a guided party, and the leader told me they would climb Scafell Pike by Grains Gill to Esk Hause and then, continuing in a clockwise loop, descend by the Corridor. I had planned on doing just the opposite. I was tempted to ask if I could tag along for the company and, frankly, the route-finding help, but I realized that I had no business horning in on a professionally led group. I told the guide my own plans, and we said we would meet up on the mountain when our routes intersected.

I set out at 7:20 a.m., just ahead of the guided party. I nearly fell as I passed through the farmyard and discovered that if you want skating rink conditions in midsummer, try rounded cobblestones coated with manure and rain. Then, if you are the farmer, make yourself a cup of coffee and sit at the kitchen window to enjoy the spectacle as day-trippers go sliding by.

The path began with a mile-long bridleway to Stockley Bridge, an arched stone structure spanning the stream called Grains Gill. Here I crossed over and began to ascend a path along a second stream, Styhead Gill. As I climbed, I turned back and saw the guided party continuing up Grains Gill. We waved to each other, and I immediately felt very alone. I thought of running back to them, falling on my knees, and offering to pay any price to join their group, but I knew that would be one of my wimpiest moves ever. I had too much pride to admit that at that moment I was intimidated by this climb, so I gamely continued on my solo trek upward toward the ominous clouds. One consolation was that I was no longer bedeviled by the bridleway's horse droppings; the path offered better footing.

An hour from the car I arrived at a jewel of a lake called Styhead Tarn. A solitary orange tent sat in vibrant green grass next to the dark water. I would have taken a picture, but it was still raining lightly. In the distance I could see a prominent mountain ridge rising to a gentle pyramid. I thought it might be Scafell Pike, but I wasn't sure. What I did know was that the sky above the summit did not look inviting.

Just past the tarn lay a trail junction called Styhead Pass. I was following an ancient packhorse route that traversed these mountains, but the only sign of civilization was a wooden mountain rescue container marked STRETCHER BOX. I paused to take a drink from my water bottle, then turned left onto a new path. In less than half a mile I came to another junction. If I had continued forward, I would soon have reached the Grains Gill trail and would no doubt have been reunited with the Gang of Eight. Instead, I turned right, onto what I assumed to be the Corridor Route. Previously called the Guides' Route, this was said to be the most scenic way to Scafell Pike, more challenging than Grains Gill—and more satisfying.

I had envisioned that the "corridor" would be a path through a narrow valley, with steep cliffs rising up on both sides, but that was not what I found. There were cliffs above, to my left, but those on my right were below me, and I was traversing a rather steep slope. I was confused, thinking perhaps I wasn't on the Corridor Route at all. If I had paused to study my trail guide more carefully, I would have seen that the cliffs were exactly where they should be, but in the rain I didn't want to stop for map reading.

Then the trail started deteriorating. It had been well surfaced with small stones, but now it became muddy and sloppy, and my footing became tenuous. Rivulets poured down from my left, and I frequently had to jump over them or cross on stepping-stones. I took some comfort from the fact that I was moving generally south-southwest, but it still seemed like the wrong trail. I thought the Corridor Route might be on the other side of the cliffs above me.

My frustrations came to a head when I arrived at a major stream called Piers Gill. It had carved a small ravine, and I had to get to the other side. The track led down to a crossing point just above a fifty-foot waterfall. There were boulders in the stream, and a muddy footprint on one of them showed that someone had come this way, but on the far side loomed a ten-foot cliff. It wasn't sheer, but the wet rock looked treacherous. I stepped carefully over the torrent and began my first move onto the face. That was when I discovered that it bulged out a bit at the bottom. This forced me into a slight lie-back, meaning that my upper body leaned out, away from the vertical plane. To compound the situation, I was holding my two walking poles in my left hand, trying to negotiate the move with only my right hand on slippery stone, while my feet were awkwardly placed. Whoa, I thought, if I peel off, my knapsack will pull my torso down, and—this being England—I'll go ass over teacups into the stream. Then I'll bounce over the water-fall and never be seen again.

I stepped down and took another look. I should have composed myself, collapsed the poles, and strapped them to my pack, thus freeing my left hand. Or I should have returned to the other side of the gill and scrambled uphill, looking for an easier place to cross above the ravine. Instead, I became petulant; I couldn't believe that a simple climbing move was going to stop me. I muttered something rather negative and got back onto the wall, but this time I repositioned my feet. That gave me slightly better balance, and with my left hand—which was still gripping the poles—I found a small nub that I could use to steady myself. Then, with my right hand, I hauled myself up with a loud grunt. It wasn't elegant, but I overcame the bulge, found new footholds, and finished the pitch. Once above the gully, I looked back. When I realized what I had done, I became even more cross—this time with myself. I had taken an unnecessary risk, and I should have known better.

I knew that I would never down-climb that pitch in such wet conditions, so now, regardless of where I was on the map, I was going to continue upward. I wondered how the guided group would ever make it down this way. When I turned around to look at the path ahead, I saw that there was no path at all—only a grassy, rock-strewn slope. The thought returned that I probably wasn't on the Corridor Route and that I was hopelessly lost. One thing was becoming clearer by the hour: whether it was my map reading, route finding, decision making, vacation planning, or any of the other skills I had employed to get me to this place, I was an idiot.

MY INCIDENT AT PIERS GILL was reminiscent of something that happened to no less an eminence than Samuel Taylor Coleridge, in his case while descending one of these peaks. In 1802 the renowned poet accomplished what was the first recorded ascent of Sca Fell, at 3,163 feet the second highest peak in England and a near neighbor of Scafell Pike. Then, somewhat foolishly, he decided to traverse to Scafell Pike along a ridge called Mickledore, an airy climb that even today is considered difficult and dangerous. Before long he found himself forced to work his way down a series of ledges, and here is how he described what happened:

> I came . . . to a smooth perpendicular Rock about seven feet high—this was nothing—I put my hands on the Ledge, and dropped down / in a few yards came just such another / I dropped that too / and yet another . . . but the stretching of the muscle of my hands & arms, & the jolt of the Fall on my Feet, put my whole Limbs in a Tremble.

Eventually, he came to some taller cliffs:

> The first was tremendous / it was twice my own height, & the Ledge at the bottom was exceedingly narrow, that if I dropt down upon it I must of necessity have fallen backwards & of course killed myself. My Limbs were all in a tremble—I lay upon my back to rest myself, and was beginning according to my Custom to laugh at myself for a Madman, when the sight of the Crags above me on each side, & the impetuous Clouds just over them, posting so luridly and rapidly northward, overawed me / I lay in a state of almost prophetic Trance and Delight . . . Oh God, I exclaimed aloud—how calm, how blessed am I now / I know not how to proceed, how to return / but I am calm & fearless & confident.

Coleridge survived, of course. After his reverie he noticed a "rent" in the rock, a chimney that he was able to down-climb. At that point he abandoned his traverse and descended the mountain in one piece. He returned to his writing and his opium addiction, and he died in his bed in London thirty-two years later.

TURNING AWAY FROM SINISTER GULLY, I moved up the slope, now on grass, now scrambling over rocks. After a few minutes the angle leveled out, and there to my surprise lay a well-worn trail. Once on it, I looked back to see where it had come from, but it simply petered out. I didn't understand how this could be a major route up Scafell Pike and have a section that gave no sign that anyone had ever walked there.

In any event I was grateful for the path, and I picked up the pace. I soon came upon three young men who appeared to be in their late teens. They had done a high camp the night before and had summited Scafell Pike an hour earlier. Now they were heading down to where I had just ascended. After looking at my map, they affirmed that I was now and always had been on the Corridor Route. Then they pointed upward to a saddle in the skyline ridge ahead. The path would lead me directly there, and that was Scafell Pike's summit to the left. Above the col there wasn't much of a trail, the boys said, but the way was marked by rock cairns. It would be a waltz. As they left, I warned them of the ravine at Piers Gill, and I suggested they look for a better crossing point higher up.

It had stopped drizzling, so I gratefully took off my pack and sat on a boulder for my first break, two and a half hours under way. I drank some water and ate a handful of ginger cream cookies, which I then and there declared to be England's foremost contribution to the world of cuisine. I quickly cheered up, my mood enhanced by the food, the lack of rain, and the moments of companionship I had just had with other humans. Best of all, it felt good to know where I was.

Ten minutes of vigorous walking brought me to the saddle, Lingmell Col, low point on the ridge between Scafell Pike and a lesser peak called Lingmell. There I met a woman who had come up from Wasdale Head on the back side of the ridge. We looked in that direction, and there lay the prominent Wasdale path, with Wast Water in the distance. In fact, from here to the top of Scafell Pike, I would join the Wasdale Route. The woman was going to wait at the col for her husband, who was climbing Lingmell.

Continuing uphill, I followed a series of cairns on an extended boulder field punctuated by patches of grass. To my surprise, sheep were grazing here and there; I hadn't seen any animals down below. At one point a young man and woman came bounding down in tennis shoes and running togs. I had heard about "fell runners," a hard-core bunch who dress lightly and carry nothing more than a small water bottle. I have never been a runner of any sort, and while jogging up a mountain has no appeal, dashing downhill strikes me as utter madness. The woman at the col had told me that the couple were in the middle segment of a marathon that had begun on Ben Nevis in Scotland and would end on Snowdonia in Wales. The two waved cheerily and continued their quest.

The vegetation disappeared, and I was on the final scramble up a massive pile of rocks that Dorothy Wordsworth described as lying "in heaps all around to a great distance, like skeletons or bones of the earth not wanted at the creation." At ten forty, three hours and twenty minutes after leaving the car, I arrived at the summit of Scafell Pike. This point was 3,209 feet above sea level and 2,759 feet above Seathwaite Farm. I was at the very top of England and absolutely alone.

IT IS SAID THAT FROM the summit of Scafell Pike, on a clear day, you can see five countries—England, obviously, but also distant shores of Scotland to the north and Northern Ireland to the west. The fourth is the self-governing Isle of Man in the Irish Sea between Britain and Ireland. Then, if you crane your neck and gaze upward, you can behold the kingdom of heaven. I decided to have a go at it, but I needed to act quickly. There was a stiff breeze, and I was still clammy from the earlier rain, so as soon as I stopped climbing, I began to get cold.

Looking north, I could make out Styhead Tarn, Derwent Water, and a few indistinct mountains beyond. One of them was probably Skiddaw, which towers above Keswick. Just over a mile to the southwest, Scafell Pike's hulking twin, Sca Fell, was clear enough. Beyond it lay Wast Water and likely a segment of Cumbria's west coast. All in all I could see fifteen miles at best. England was a world of gray, the other terrestrial lands were lost in the gloom, and heaven formed a sinister canopy over everything. Shivering, I took shelter behind a large cairn and began to eat my lunch.

As I started in on a sandwich, I noticed that clouds were rapidly moving in from the east, and they were *below* me. This gave me a jolt. I realized that within a short time I might be socked in, and I didn't want to descend a new route in zero visibility. While finishing just half my lunch, I was on my feet and staring intently toward Broad Crag, a quarter-mile northeast of Scafell Pike. I needed to drop to a saddle, then scramble back up to Broad Crag and follow the path northeast to a third peak, Great End. I tried to memorize the route, fearing I would have to negotiate it by feel.

A scant fifteen minutes after arriving at the summit, I left Scafell Pike in a hurry. Still, I did not try to run down the boulder field. I had Whernside on my mind, and I imagined that every one of the summit rocks had a sharp edge waiting to tear my leg open. I had to be careful, while moving as quickly as possible. One thing in my favor was that it hadn't rained for more than an hour, and the rock surfaces had dried out.

After reaching the first saddle, I started ascending Broad Crag. At first I followed a series of cairns but soon decided that the route zigzagged too much, so I headed straight up. This put me onto sections where actual climbing was involved, and at the first pitch I had the presence of mind to collapse my poles and attach them to my pack. Unlike the ravine at Piers Gill, I enjoyed this bit of rock work. My hands were free, and the rock was sound. I felt like a mountaineer again, and I quickly scrambled to the Broad Crag plateau. From there the path was well-worn and relatively flat, so I started jogging to beat the incoming storm.

After passing very near the summit of Broad Crag, the trail dropped slightly to a second saddle and then up to the flank of Great End. There it made a sharp turn to the east. At that bend I had a clear view to where, half a mile away, the path turned north at Esk Hause, then west toward Grains Gill. Still running, I noticed the sky lightening, and I looked up to see that the approaching clouds were beginning to dissipate. Even more pleasant, the breeze was becoming warmer, and so I paused to remove my jacket. For the first time that day, I began to feel optimistic.

I allowed myself to slow to a brisk walk. An hour after leaving the top of Scafell Pike, I was at Esk Hause, at 2,486 feet the highest pass in the Lake District. A quarter-mile farther, I turned west and began to descend alongside Ruddy Gill. Flanking this cheerful stream was what I soon called the "Endless Staircase," a series of flagstones set as steps by some trail builders who had evidently had lots of time on their hands. Even though the stairs went on and on, they were dry underfoot and easy to negotiate. After nearly half a mile the stream and the path turned north and began to drop gradually into the Grains Gill valley. At that point it occurred to me that I had never encountered the Gang of Eight. If they had gone up the Grains Gill route, as planned, we couldn't have missed each other. I assumed that after an hour or two of rain they had abandoned their trek.

As I moved down the valley, the sun began to peek through, and I realized that the hillsides were luxuriously green. Now thoroughly enjoying myself, I came to Stockley Bridge, where my loop was completed. From there it was another mile to Seathwaite Farm. I arrived at my car at one fifty-five, three hours after leaving the highest point of England, six and a half since I had set out. The vehicles of the guided party were gone.

As on The Cheviot, I had set out for Scafell Pike alone and in questionable weather, and on the ascent I had been beset with unease about what I was doing. And then, despite what seemed like an imminent downpour in both instances, the storm gods had backed off. I had carried on to both summits and was rewarded with increasingly pleasant conditions as I descended. The babbling and splashing of the trailside streams as I headed home had affirmed everything that is wonderful about climbing a mountain. It is worth the effort and a bit of unpleasantness to hear such music.

12

Wet Wool and Flavored Tea

SHORTLY AFTER I RETURNED FROM Scafell Pike, the Italian Woman and I presented ourselves at the NHS Minor Injuries Clinic, where my wife signed in for treatment of her wound. She had been in the procedure room for twenty minutes when the doctor emerged to summon me.

The Italian Woman, on the verge of tears, lay on a white examining table. The doctor led me to the patient's exposed leg, and there was concern in her voice when she pointed out that she had removed only six of the nine sutures. The remaining three were in an area that appeared ready to burst open like an overripe tomato (or more clinically, there was subcutaneous tissue protruding between the edges of the wound). The entire area was red and ugly, obviously infected.

"I'm afraid it isn't as good as we might have hoped," the doctor commented.

"Well," I responded, trying to stay calm, "what do you think is indicated?"

She paused, made a slight *hmmm*, and replied, "Why don't we have a cup of tea."

"You want to go out for tea?"

"Oh no, we'll have it here."

"You want to have tea here in the surgery?"

"Of course, it won't be any trouble at all." Then, to the Italian Woman, she added, "Dear, would you like a cup as well?"

"Well, I guess so," replied the patient. "Can you help me off this table?"

"Oh, you don't need to move. Here, let me raise you to a sitting position."

The doctor stepped out of the room and returned several minutes later with three steaming cups on a metal tray of the sort that would ordinarily hold scalpels and sterile dressings. "Now," she said, as if what we were about to do was the most normal thing in the world, "does anyone take milk? Would either of you fancy a biscuit?"

I began to wonder whether my brain had somehow slipped out of gear. Was this really happening? After all, we were supposed to be on sabbatical in Italy.

Oddly, the tea had the precise effect of calming the patient and her dumbfounded husband. The three of us made small talk about our summer in Britain and the doctor's past trips to America. Such a pity, she said, that we had missed the peak of the daffodils. Eventually, she remarked that she wanted to wait until the next day before removing the final three stitches. When the Italian Woman asked whether antibiotics might be a good idea, the doctor replied that two weeks after the accident was far too early to consider such a drastic step. The appropriate time to discuss medication would be when the lower leg was green and hanging by a couple of tendons.

After leaving the doctor's office, and to assuage the Italian Woman's frustration, we stopped at a Mexican restaurant and threw ourselves into the task of consuming large margaritas. I had been hoping to say, "Blimey, they're limey," but they had no citrus flavor at all. After that we were not terribly surprised when the enchiladas tasted like bangers and mash covered in ketchup. This was, after all, a country where South of the Border means the English Channel. And yet, with all of that, the dinner succeeded as some form of comfort food.

The next day we returned to the clinic, and as I fidgeted in the waiting room, I noticed that two chairs away sat Priscilla Trousers from St. John Church. We reintroduced ourselves, and she said that Gordon was being treated for a tact gland disorder. When the two patients were released—the Italian Woman now free of sutures—the four of us walked together to a nearby restaurant, The Filling Station Cafe. The place catered to the motorcycle crowd, which in Britain is the *motorbike* crowd. Just to make conversation, I mentioned that to an American *motorbikes* are low-powered sissy machines, not the beefy vehicles shown in posters throughout the restaurant. Gordon responded that any debate over American usage versus British should, in the proper scheme of things, be resolved in favor of the inventors of the language and not their colonial offspring. He said this diplomatically, thus demonstrating that his tact hormone replacement therapy was beginning to show results.

We learned that Gordon had worked as a lawyer with an international bank and the Trousers had lived in the United States, New Zealand, and Bermuda. They now ran a small business that included a post office, computer center, news agency, and souvenir stand, all under one roof on Keswick's market square. Gordon had recently served as mayor of Keswick, and he talked about the frustrations of running a local government within a national park, which added an unwelcome layer of bureaucracy. To illustrate, he called over the restaurant's proprietor, a leather-clad man named Keavon, to ask about his recent application to extend the restaurant's business hours. Keavon reported that the Keswick town council had unanimously approved the proposal, but Lake District National Park authorities had rejected it out of hand.

The Trousers were now on the verge of retiring, trying to decide whether to stay in Keswick or move on. Neither was a native Kezzickian, but after their itinerant banking years they had happily put down roots, and by now they knew everyone in town. Looking ahead, they were torn between the desire to live someplace sunnier than North West England and the comfort of spending their golden years in the company of friends. The Italian Woman and I could offer little advice; we were sabbatical wanderers, and settling down was the farthest thing from our minds.

After coffee the Italian Woman and I returned to our apartment for the next installment of "what is this summer all about?" The local doctor had counseled us to remain in the area for three weeks so she could continue to monitor and treat the patient's leg. We would of course follow her advice, but it meant yet another revamping of our agenda. As we talked, we realized that three weeks seemed like a very long time, and it was difficult to make any plans beyond Keswick. We might resume our tour of the national parks, or we might not. I could climb other mountains, or I could drop the whole business. The crystal ball was cloudy, and Keswick's silent *w* seemed to have addled our brains, so we decided not to even try to decide. On the bright side, extra time in the Lake District was hardly punishment.

YOU DON'T HAVE TO DRIVE far to find literary hotspots in the Lake District. The birthplace and boyhood home of William Wordsworth sits just thirteen miles northwest of Keswick, in a village with the why-oh-why-didn't-we-hear-about-this-place-in-middle-school name of Cockermouth. The Wordsworth House and Garden is a National Trust property on the town's main street, which, defying all logic, is called not High Street but Main Street. Nearly torn down for a bus garage in 1937, the home has been fully restored with period pieces, few of which, unfortunately, were actually used by the Wordsworth family. Even then, it gives a wonderful feel for life as young William would have experienced it. A costumed docent in the kitchen demonstrated gingerbread making and talked about what the poet's family would have eaten. A children's room displayed eighteenth-century toys. Even better was the garden, where a gazebo along the River Derwent offered recorded readings of Wordsworth poems. It was a setting that surely inspired the creative boy, and he would have been amazed to hear a voice coming from that metal box on the wall.

Just down the street stands a pub called the Fletcher Christian. The famous sailor was born near here, and at one point he and Wordsworth, who were distantly related, were contemporaries at the Cockermouth Free School. This might have led to a most interesting schoolyard conversation:

"When I grow up, I'm going to sea and visit strange new lands."

"Well, I'm going to explore the beauty of nature right here in the Lake District."

"I'm going to marry a *wahine* and foment a mutiny."

"I'm going to write about daffodils."

As we were returning to our car, we stopped to admire a statue of Wordsworth in a small plaza along the street. Just then a fellow wearing a Liverpool FC football jersey came walking by. When he saw us, he leaped over a park bench, stood next to the statue, and pointed first to his own face and then to Wordsworth's. "Look, it's me!" he said.

Assuming it was best to treat him gingerly, I responded: "Yes, yes, very nice. I see the resemblance."

The man then whipped out his wallet and showed us an identification card that said William Graham Wordsworth. "I'm his great-great-grandson," he exclaimed, and then, just as quickly as he had arrived, he bounded over the bench and disappeared.

CONTINUING OUR SEARCH FOR THE real Wordsworth, several days later we drove to Grasmere, perhaps the most picturesque village anywhere. Subtract a few tourist shops, and I would delete the *perhaps* in that sentence. Grasmere is host to several Wordsworth homes, and we headed for Allan Bank, a hillside manor where the poet and his family lived from 1808 to 1813, with fellow writer Samuel Taylor Coleridge as a long-term guest. The house had been damaged by fire in 2011, but several rooms were open to visitors. Instead of poring over Wordsworth memorabilia, we took the opportunity to sit in one of the upper rooms, drink a cup of tea, and gaze out the window. The view to a small lake and the green hills beyond was so sublime that Wordsworth called Allan Bank "the loveliest spot that man hath ever found." For half an hour the Italian Woman and I discussed cleaning out our savings, buying a cottage in Grasmere, and never leaving the Lake District.

Down in the village we encountered a tour group frantically making the most of their twenty minutes of shopping time. To avoid them, we ducked into St. Oswald's Church, which has stood in one manifestation or another on the same spot since AD 642. The current building dates back to the fourteenth century but is exceptional only for its age and its lovely setting along the cascading River Rothay. Stylistically, its sanctuary is a mishmash, and most visitors pause only briefly before heading to their real goal—the Wordsworth family graves in the churchyard.

The Wordsworth headstones were unremarkable, and I wondered what the fuss was about. I had asked the same thing twenty years earlier at the burial place of Jim Morrison in Père Lachaise Cemetery in Paris. Remarkably, in a city with the Louvre, Sainte-Chapelle, and Notre Dame just for starters, Morrison's resting place is one of the French capital's most popular attractions. When the Italian Woman and I strolled by, there were so many Door Heads crowding around that two policemen were needed to keep things in order. Jim Morrison? Granted, "Light My Fire" is one of the greatest songs ever, but what is so interesting about the grave of someone who flamed out at the age of twenty-seven? Or, come to think of it, the burial place of a president or a potentate. Unless the tomb is ornate or unusual—think Christopher Columbus, whose sarcophagus in the Cathedral of Seville is held aloft by four kings— why do you want to stand around and look at a piece of marble with a name on it?

If I want to think about the person's life, I prefer to read a biography or sit in a place like Allan Bank. To me a grave is nothing more than a place to hold a decaying body. Tell that to the Mexicans, who revel in Dia de los Muertos and decorate their homes with colorfully decked-out skeletons and pictures of departed family members. I appreciate Mexican culture, and I love a good fiesta, but really.

And speaking of cemeteries, Grasmere's true claim to fame just may be the legacy of a gravedigger's wife. In the nineteenth century one Sarah Kemp Nelson supplemented her husband's meager income by baking pastries for a Lady Farquhar (oh, how I love that name), and her gingerbread developed a reputation as best in the Lake District. Sarah's life was rather unhappy— dinner table conversation with her husband always came around to his work—but her recipe endured, supposedly handed down through the years and still followed today at the Grasmere Gingerbread Shop. Whether the current version is authentic or not, it was wonderful, worth the long queue and ridiculous prices. And the fact is, you need to eat it immediately. We saved a piece for the next day, and it was hard as a rock. It's nice, in a way, that the treat has to be experienced right then and there, warm and fresh, near Sarah's own shop and the marble orchard where her husband wielded his shovel.

AFTER OUR SECOND SUNDAY SERVICE at St. John, Gordon Trousers greeted us and asked us to join him that afternoon for a "strawberry tea." Before I could respond that I preferred my tea without any fruit flavoring, the Italian Woman had accepted the invitation. Priscilla joined our discussion and said that she would be going early to help set things up. She said that the event was a St John's fund-raiser for blinded cats, so we would be expected to make a small donation. And no, unlike Bridget Jones, we would not be required to dress as tarts or vicars.

At one forty-five we met Gordon at the Keswick station, where we began our one and only bus ride in England. It was one of those red double-decker affairs, and we sat upstairs. Gordon explained that the tea was taking place in the tiny hamlet of Ruddy and that parking was so limited that people were encouraged to take public transport. As we rode along, I was amazed to have such a commanding view of the countryside. In our car we were always below the level of the hedges and stone walls, but now we could look right over them. Our daughter and son-in-law had ridden many UK buses the previous summer; they had done so because they couldn't afford a rental car. For the first time I realized that their drives through the countryside had been far more scenic than ours.

Another advantage of the bus was that I didn't need to have my eyes focused on the road at all times, and the Italian Woman—who was convinced that I was an accident just waiting to happen—could relax as well. We discovered that the landscape was filled with rhododendrons, slightly past full bloom but still vibrant. As a transplant to Seattle nearly forty years earlier, I had fallen in love with the elegant bushes, their year-round greenery, and their spectacular spring flowers. They are especially suited to the showery Pacific Northwest, and they actually grow wild in lowland forests near Puget Sound. Seeing so many rhodies in the Lake District, we realized how much we had missed them during our years in Omaha, and we felt homesick for our beloved rain country.

It turned out that a strawberry tea was simply an afternoon tea in which the featured dish was fresh strawberries topped with heavy cream. The event took place at the home of an imposing man named Reginald Timberlodge, who ten years earlier had been named a member of the Most Excellent Order of the British Empire simply for being "so damned English." In any event the rain falls on an MBE as well as on the rest of us, and what was going to be a garden party turned into a let's-see-how-many-people-can-fit-into-the-conservatory event. As the Italian Woman and I wiggled our way onto a single chair, we inhaled the fragrance of wet wool and greeted our new friends. Immediately, someone said, "Do I detect an accent?" I responded that I had no accent, and everyone burst into laughter. It was all good-natured, I think.

As the afternoon wore on, I chatted with several people who lived in Ruddy. For some reason a common theme in our conversations was that in a rural village like this, there are no class distinctions. Who your ancestors were, where you come from, and where you went to school don't matter here. Everyone is a valued and equal member of the community. The people I spoke with may have felt it important to make the point because everyone at the event seemed so obviously cut from the same cloth. I saw only businesspeople and professionals, many of them retired. The car mechanics and farmers would no doubt have been there extending their pinky fingers and saying "Ah, yes" to everything—that is, if they hadn't been tied up rebuilding someone's carburetor or tending to the landlord's sheep. And racial prejudice? None whatsoever in this multicultural melting pot. Several of the rosy-cheeked folks earnestly noted that there was a South Asian doctor, a decent chap, living just down the road. The whole event seemed strangely familiar, and I finally realized that this was one of the lost episodes of *To the Manor Born*. Come to think of it, that woman making the egg salad sandwiches looked a lot like Audrey fforbes-Hamilton.

Americans have been curious about tea ever since we dumped a load of the dried leaves into Boston Harbor in 1773 to protest taxes imposed by the British Parliament. My first exposure to English tea-drinking practice was at a banking seminar in London in 1980. After the first morning session we were released to an adjacent room for our stimulant. There we were directed to a table to pick up a cup and saucer, then proceeded to a second table, where a woman poured the tea, and finally shuffled to a third table to receive a biscuit. As I approached the first table, I noticed that there was a half-inch of milk in each of the cups. I had never had milk in my tea, so I turned to the pouring woman and asked if it was possible to have a cup without milk. She did a double take but then quickly composed herself and said—and this is absolutely verbatim—"Well, Love, I suppose we could do one up special for you." I took this as a polite way of saying, "Get thee behind me, Satan," and slunk back for a cup that was pre-milked. Surprisingly, I discovered that ordinary black tea is far more palatable with milk than without, and I have gone English ever since.

I have not, however, taken sides in the debate on whether milk should be poured into the cup before the tea or afterward. The London seminar ladies were clear as to where they stood, but no less a personage than George Orwell was of the opposite mind. In a 1946 essay called "A Nice Cup of Tea," he offers eleven (yes, eleven) detailed rules for making "one of the main stays of civilization." Here are his thoughts on the milk:

> Tenthly, one should pour tea into the cup first. This is one of the most controversial points of all; indeed in every family in Britain there are probably two schools of thought on the subject. The milk-first school can bring forward some fairly strong arguments, but I maintain that my own argument is unanswerable. This is that, by putting the tea in first and stirring as one pours, one can exactly regulate the amount of milk whereas one is liable to put in too much milk if one does it the other way round.

The tea-and-milk dispute seems indicative of an island nation whose people are, perhaps, too insular. I once heard a segment of a three-hour BBC Radio program devoted entirely to the origins and uses of brown sauce.

13

A Sweet Mess

JUST SOUTH OF KESWICK, NEAR the south end of Derwent Water, sits the Lodore Falls Hotel, and directly behind the building you will find the Lodore Falls, a cascade on a stream called Watendlath Beck. These falls were a favorite destination of Victorian tourists and are still an item on many a book lover's bucket list, all because of a poem.

Robert Southey was one of the principal Lakeland poets, along with his close friends Wordsworth and Coleridge. Coleridge was in fact Southey's brother-in-law, and the two once famously experimented with nitrous oxide—laughing gas—as a means of getting high. Southey is noted for writing biographies and travel books, being the first English author to publish the folktale "The Three Bears," coining the word *autobiography*, and advising Charlotte Brontë that women should not be writers. Yet his most recognized accomplishment is an 1820 poem titled "The Cataract of Lodore."

In the eleventh grade literature course that changed my life, at one point each student was required to find a Romantic movement poem and read it to the class. In the school's stuffy little library I stumbled upon Southey's masterpiece, and reading that the waterfall came down "from its fountains / in the mountains," the aspiring mountaineer in me was immediately drawn to it. I also loved its use of onomatopoeia, a technique we had just learned how to spell, and I was delighted to learn that if you display the poem with each of its lines centered on the page, it is actually shaped like a waterfall whose spray widens at the bottom. So, I told Mr. Vanden Bosch that I would read "Cataract" as my presentation. He rolled his eyes, thinking: "Great, every five years someone picks that piece of crap. Once again, I will have to endure it." What he said to me was, "Fine, just practice because it has tricky pronunciations."

I regretted the choice soon afterward. At 121 lines the poem was far too long, and I didn't think I could ever articulate it with the necessary vivacity. Also, I felt silly reading all of those perky little words ending with -*ing*, as in "eddying and whisking, spouting and frisking." They seemed rather unmasculine, and I was sensitive about liking poetry when my basketball teammates could only talk sports.

When the day came, my recitation started well because the poem told a story:

"How does the water
Come down at Lodore?"
My little boy asked me
Thus, once on a time;
And moreover he tasked me
To tell him in rhyme.

But soon I was mired in an endless section in which each line contained two rhyming words:

And pouring and roaring,
And waving and raving,
And tossing and crossing,
And flowing and going,
And running and stunning,
And foaming and roaming,

My classmates began to look out the windows, and Mr. Vanden Bosch squirmed in discomfort. I just wanted to crawl under a rock, thinking, "Now I am dying, and soon I'll be crying." Eventually, and not a moment too soon for me, Mr. V said between gritted teeth: "Thanks, Steve. We appreciate the alliteration, but it's rather long. So, thanks, we need to get on to someone else."

That was that, except for the fact that I have never been able to get "Cataract" out of my head. While still in high school, in 1966, I actually won the school's poetry contest with the following little verse:

> The crabgrass creeps,
> The locust leaps,
> The willow weeps,
> The gardener sleeps.

Even today I cannot look at a running stream without hearing Southey's words "here it comes sparkling, and there it lies darkling." *Darkling*? Is that even a word? It sounds like a soot-covered hobbit, doesn't it? Not long ago, while cutting the grass, I found myself looking at a bare patch and thinking, "There it needs sowing, but here it is growing, and now I am mowing." Oddly, my ophthalmologist recently told me that in a few years I will have to submit to cataract surgery. No doubt she will sedate me with nitrous oxide.

When the Italian Woman and I drove to the Lodore Hotel to see the falls for ourselves, we discovered that the adjacent parking lot was for guests only. A public pay and display lot across the street was completely full, and elsewhere the roadway was peppered with NO PARKING signs. We simply turned around and drove back to Keswick. Until I return to the Lake District, my only impression of the Lodore Falls will be that maddening poem.

ON THREE SUCCESSIVE WEDNESDAY EVENINGS we joined the Trousers for Pub Quiz at a Keswick watering hole called the Packhorse. Their son Ben was quizmaster, and in our honor he included a smattering of questions on American life. Nevertheless, despite our cultural mix and 264 years among us, our team did poorly, primarily because none of us knew anything about music after the sixties. We were certain that if there were a version of the game called Trivia for Old Farts, we would win every time. Once, during a lull in the proceedings, Gordon leaned across the table and said: "Well, quiz night is one thing, but there is also a British tradition of going to the pub after Sunday church services. Do you know what it is called?" We had no idea. "A thirst after righteousness."

A week after arriving in Keswick, on our third trip to the Minor Injuries Clinic, the doctor finally acknowledged that antibiotics were in order. She was not struck by lightning, and neither was the pharmacist who handed the tablets to us. Within three days the Italian Woman experienced noticeable improvement, and at the end of her seven-day course the redness had disappeared and the swelling had gone down. She began walking more comfortably, and she declared that she would soon be able to travel. She wanted to reinstate our earlier plans and go to Scotland, and it would be fine with her if I tackled a few mountains up north.

Since I had been granted dispensation to climb again, I suggested that to stay in shape I should do another peak in the Lake District. The Italian Woman concurred, and on a sunny day I set out for Skiddaw. At 3,054 feet it is the national park's fourth highest mountain, and its three-mile ascent promised a good workout. Skiddaw dominates the skyline north of Keswick, although whoever nicknamed the low-angle green hill "Keswick's Matterhorn" must have been smoking tea leaves. It has absolutely no alpine features.

I found the trailhead easily, and with clear weather, well-trodden paths, and more than fifty people sharing the experience, the climb was a pleasant ramble. It took just over an hour and a half to reach the top of Skiddaw. At the summit there was a stiff breeze, but the sky was clear, and to the north I could see distant mountains. They were likely in Scotland, and I began to think about climbing in the Highlands. The far-off peaks looked mysterious and forbidding.

To escape the chilling wind, I sat behind a low rock wall and ate lunch with four taciturn people from Manchester and two affable Canadians. Then I rose and visited with a man who had set up a fifteen-foot radio antenna held in place by several guy wires. He told me he belonged to a society whose members walk up different peaks on the same day, set up their radio gear, and talk to each other at an appointed hour. The fellow was checking frequencies in a notebook for the call-in that was about to start. Curious about the whole business, I showed him my cell phone and asked whether it might not be easier just to carry one of these. He responded: "Mate, you've got no coverage up here. I do." I checked, and he was correct, but as I walked away I was wondering what the Gathering of Radio Nerds would actually discuss once they established contact. What could they possibly come up with after "loud and clear"?

That evening the Italian Woman and I were invited to dinner at the home of the Trousers. The final dish (the "pudding") was something Priscilla called "Eton mess." I had heard the term but had thought it referred to the confusion caused in the students of a boys-only boarding school for whom sexual experimentation in the dormitory is followed by public lives as government ministers, captains of industry, and the like, always parading about with wives or girlfriends. There must be an undertone of awkwardness in these postgraduate relationships: "My great-grandmother was your great-great-grandfather's mistress, so let's first establish that you're on my side of the street, and then how about it?"

As for the dessert, it consisted of fresh berries and pieces of dried meringue folded into whipped cream. There was nothing fancy about it, but the Italian Woman became an instant addict. As we traveled beyond Keswick, she regularly asked for it, and we discovered that while the recipe was generally the same, the name depended on where you were. We found "Scottish mess," "Caernarfon mess," and even a "second-pub-south-of-the-double-roundabout mess." In the village of Ruddy they prefer to call it "that meringue dish."

DURING OUR FINAL WEEK IN Keswick I started planning for the mountains I might climb in Scotland, while the Italian Woman researched other things to see and do in the land of haggis. Then one morning, out of the blue, she said, "Let's go to Ireland."

"Why?"

"I've always wanted to go there."

"And what will we do in Ireland?"

"We're going to take a bus tour."

"You're joking, right? We have never taken an organized tour of any sort, much less one on a bus. Whenever we see a tour group, we thank our lucky stars that we're not wearing name tags and being herded around by someone holding up a little pennant."

"No, I'm perfectly serious, and if you have an ounce of good sense, you will now say 'Hey, what a great idea, and hats off to my long-suffering wife who has sacrificed life and limb to be with me on my mountain adventure.'"

In short order we had booked a rather expensive, twelve-day grand tour of Ireland and Northern Ireland. Prior to the bus journey we would spend six days in Dublin at—I could hardly imagine it—a Riverdance festival. As the Italian Woman completed the reservations, I was required to take a solemn oath that I would be sweet and compliant, never sarcastic, for eighteen entire days. What I chose to write after the tour would be my business. Our trip would begin after a two-week swing through Scotland.

I knew, of course, that Ireland would kill our on-again, off-again national parks itinerary. There simply wouldn't be time to complete the list after we returned in early August. I also knew that I owed it to the Italian Woman to just let it go. The fact that she was on her feet again and eager to travel should be enough for both of us. Then again . . . well, I would hold my mountain thoughts and ponder them in my heart.

OUR THIRD SUNDAY AT ST. John was notable for the baptism of a baby whose parents had obviously never been to church since their own christenings. The mother looked mortified to be standing in front of an audience, and the father looked as if this was the first time he had worn a necktie—he kept tugging at it as if it were alive and slowly tightening its grip. The pair had no clue what to say at any point in the ritual, and meanwhile, their four-year-old daughter was running laps up and down the center aisle. No one seemed to flinch at this, but I wondered why the little brat couldn't just sit in the kids' area and start banging blocks.

We were reminded of a baptism we had witnessed twenty years earlier at a Catholic church in Bend, Oregon. The parents and godparents were clearly uncomfortable in their roles, but the star of the event was the middle-aged aunt, who was handed a camera—one of those inexpensive pre-digital Kodaks with a built-in flash—and entrusted with capturing the precious moment. The woman stood in the aisle, looked through the viewfinder, and then started moving, first away from the baptismal party and then closer to them. She seemed to be having difficulty getting the perspective right. Eventually, she realized that the sacrament was proceeding apace, so she decided to try her luck. She paused, took a breath, and pressed the shutter. The flash went right into her eyes, thus signaling to everyone in the pews that she had held the camera backward.

Now, blinded by the flash, Auntie staggered about, trying to stay on her feet. At last she recovered, moved toward the font, turned the camera over a few times, and again raised it to her eye. This time, somewhat more confidently, she touched the shutter, but again the flash exploded directly into her face. By now, chuckles were rolling in little waves throughout the congregation. Tears ran down my face, and I had to lower my head to keep from howling. I am sorry to report that neither I nor anyone else in the audience had the presence of mind or the basic human decency to stand up and approach the hapless woman, who was again lurching around like a drunken sailor.

Meanwhile, the sacrament had concluded, and the priest and baptismal party had lined up behind the font for a final photo. Now completely sure of herself, the woman strode directly to the group, raised the camera, then took several steps back, raised the camera again, and for the third time shot herself in the eyes. Neither the cleric nor any of the family seemed to realize what had happened, but from the congregation there arose a great rejoicing. The photographer seemed to believe that everyone was commending her performance, and so, with a self-satisfied look on her face, she felt her way back to her pew and sat down, clutching the camera. One can only imagine the scene at the drugstore later that week when the proud father picked up the developed pictures, only to discover that each one was a dramatic close-up of Auntie's teeth.

WE CONCLUDED OUR DAYS IN the Lake District rather quietly. There was another failure at Pub Quiz and a final trip to the clinic, where the Italian Woman was pronounced ready to move on. I spent a pleasant afternoon fantasizing at several outdoor shops. We attended a National Garden Society fundraising tea at the bishop's house, met a man selling zebra steaks at a fair, and stopped briefly at Keswick's Midsummer Festival, where a solo singer-guitarist was performing an off-key rendition of "House of the Rising Sun." He apparently thought the song related to the solstice, and he unforgivably flubbed the legendary opening riff. On my sixty-fifth birthday, July 1, we invited the Trousers to dinner to thank them for their hospitality. The Italian Woman made a Herdwick lamb shepherd's pie, and Priscilla brought a birthday mess. We agreed to keep in touch.

During our final evening in Keswick we ate at a restaurant called Sienna, which advertised a fully stocked bar. Both of us were long overdue for a proper Italian Woman Formula One Martini, but outside the United States one has to be very careful about these things. Several years earlier, on a trip to Greece, my wife had ordered a martini and had received a tumbler full of Martini & Rossi dry vermouth. When she tasted it, the look on her face was comparable to the time she had tried raw herring in Amsterdam. We have traveled enough to expect the unexpected in our food, but like the law of the Medes and Persians, which altereth not, my mate's martini has to be just so. It's Bombay Sapphire and dry vermouth in a ratio of ten to one, shaken not stirred, straight up, three olives—nothing more, nothing less. When in doubt, send your husband to the bar to respectfully talk the bartender through every step, then compliment the man for his excellent work and leave him a generous tip.

On our way out of town we delivered a box of chocolates and a note of thanks to the staff at the Minor Injuries Clinic. They had put the Italian Woman back together again and had not charged us a penny. In the renowned Lake District, with all of its literary history and natural beauty and with the highest mountain in England, the thing that most impressed us was the National Health Service.

14

Embracing the Velar Fricative

WE HAVE DONE A BIT of sea cruising, especially during a brief period when I was giving onboard lectures for Holland America Line. During those trips we often made six-hour forays into port cities that we had not visited independently. In one sense any chance to see someplace new is rewarding, but the toe-in-the-water approach has serious limitations. You leave your hermetically sealed floating hotel to find a bus or taxi waiting for you at the dock. You are then deposited into the heart of a city ("Where are we today?") to wander around with a small map, locate the cathedral, grab lunch in the tourist area, and then find your way back to the pickup point to retreat to the ship and a clean stateroom with fresh towels. The Italian Woman likens cruising to riding an elevator. You just stand there, and every time the door opens you catch a glimpse of a different floor. Then the door closes.

If you want to make cruising even easier, you can sign up for guided tours on which every move is choreographed and you never once have to think for yourself—essentially, a walking travelogue. The problem with a shore excursion is that you don't really belong on the land. The ship owns you, much as a penitentiary controls a prisoner who goes out on work release. Also, the city you visit lacks any context. You have no sense of the countryside or how the urban area relates to its surroundings. You don't appreciate how local people make their way into the center to work, and you don't know where they shop for groceries. By never spending a night in the place and never even being there after dark, you have little feel for the rhythm of life. If someone asks whether we have been to Le Havre, we are likely to answer, "Not really, just a few hours once from a ship."

I say these things because in 2008 we had spent a day in Edinburgh while on a cruise. Nevertheless, until our UK summer we had never really been to Scotland.

NO PLACE IS REALLY LIKE its popular image. Most Frenchmen don't wear berets, just as most Americans don't carry guns, and most Canadians don't end their sentences with . . . well, actually they do, eh. When we think of Scotland from afar, we envision misty, barren moors. We see men named MacTavish in plaid kilts, drinking single malt whiskey and tossing telephone poles for sport. Afterward they play bagpipes, eat sheep organs, and drink more whiskey, although they hate paying for it because they are so tightfisted. Their children are called "lads" and "lassies," and they all have red hair.

Our first impression of Scotland was when the M6 motorway north of Carlisle became the A74/M74 at the border, and our first hour in the country was spent dodging the same cars and trucks that had threatened us in England. It then took quite some time to bypass Glasgow, Scotland's largest city and home to the Glaswegians. Permit me to add for my Seattle friends that a Glaswegian is not a Ouija board designed by Dale Chihuly.

At the west edge of Glasgow we skirted Paisley, where everyone stops to purchase a necktie before proceeding north into Argyll to find a pair of socks. A few miles farther we crossed the River Clyde on the elegant Erskine Bridge, which has the distinction of having been hastily redesigned during construction because of the collapse of a similar structure in Melbourne, Australia. We held our breath.

Once safely across, we were purportedly in the Scottish Highlands, although by some definitions the boundary was farther north. Wherever the line is, the Highlands are more than Scotland's mountain areas; they are the entire northwest half of the country. They include the central mountain ranges but also the Atlantic west coast and the Hebrides, Orkney, and Shetland island groups. The Lowlands are everything else, including most of the east coast on the North Sea, the population centers of Glasgow, Edinburgh, and Aberdeen, and the entire south. Historically, the division between Highlands and Lowlands was based on cultural and linguistic variations. In modern times these differences have faded, although the regional names have hung on.

Our final taste of the cities was just north of the Firth of Clyde, where we passed through Dumbarton and Alexandria, and just like that we were on the shores of Loch Lomond. The national park called Loch Lomond and The Trossachs is, as its name implies, a bit of this and a bit of that—not unlike an Eton mess. Anchoring the south end of the park is its crown jewel, Britain's largest fresh water lake. West of there is the Argyll Forest, whose hills bear the aspirational name of the Arrochar Alps. The eastern section is The Trossachs, an area of hills and lakes, famed as the setting for Sir Walter Scott's *Lady of the Lake*. Less known and somewhat out of the way on the north end of the park is an area called Breadalbane, home to the highest peaks in southern Scotland. Loftiest of that bunch is Ben More, whose name means "great mountain"—actually, since *ben* is the generic Scottish word for "mountain," it is literally "mountain great." Weather permitting and the Italian Woman willing, I would try to climb Ben More.

As anyone who has studied a foreign language can attest, *loch* is one of the most useful words in English because its throat-clearing *ch* sound—a voiceless velar fricative, if you must—is rare in our language but common in so many others. When you learn the Spanish *gi* or the Dutch *ge* or the Russian *x*, the phrase book always says "sounds like the *ch* in *loch*." I realize that most Americans pronounce *Loch Ness* as *Lok Ness*, but softening those vocal cords and releasing a hearty fricative is not only linguistically proper—it can also clear out some unwanted phlegm, so why not give it a go?

The road map of Great Britain shows the A 82 as the primary north-south highway in western Scotland. Do not be deceived. Its southern portion is a two-lane road that winds in tight curves along Loch Lomond's western shore, and it reminded us of US 101 along Lake Crescent on Washington's Olympic Peninsula. You should not be in a hurry on either of these highly scenic byways. At one point on the A 82 we were forced to wait at a sharp bend while a bus worked its way forward and back to avoid leaving its outside mirror in a tree. At times we were so close to the water that it felt like being in a boat.

Loch Lomond is shaped like an upside-down kite, and in its center lies a group of islands. One of them, like Indonesia's Bali, is famous for hosting wild Australians, but the Aussies on tiny Inchconnachan pose little threat to the local beer supply. They are wallabies. The colony was planted in the 1940s by a Lady Colquhoun, who evidently thought the adorable animals would look good in kilts. Unfortunately, they would not sit still long enough for a fitting, and the critters have been breeding and jumping about ever since.

As we proceeded northward along the narrow tail of the kite, the hills along the loch's eastern shore became more and more impressive. One of them, Ben Lomond, rises majestically to 3,196 feet and is the highest peak in the Loch Lomond section of the national park. Interestingly, even though the lake is far better known than the mountain, the mountain's appellation had to have come first. The word *lomond* (*laomainn* in Scottish Gaelic) means "beacon," a term that hardly applies to a body of water. Logically, the loch must have been named for the "beacon mountain" that towers above it.

Moving as we were, along the lakeshore road while looking across to the mountains, there was no chance we could escape the song:

Oh, ye'll tak' the high road, and I'll tak' the low road,
And I'll get to Scotland afore ye;

But me and my true love will never meet again
On the bonnie, bonnie banks o' Loch Lomond.

Those first two lines are emblazoned in the mind of everyone who grows up speaking English. The words just pop up automatically anytime any two people set out to do the same thing in two different ways. Sadly, the grammatical travesty at the start of the third line has become normal usage among American youth. I cannot believe that on a regular basis I need to remind my law students that *me* is not a subjective pronoun. Then I have to explain what a subjective pronoun is.

I was surprised to learn that the song's high road and low road do not refer to a choice between a mountain track and a lakeside highway. It is generally thought that the singer is a Scot about to be executed in England, and he is foretelling that his soul will be speedily transported back home by the fairies on a subterranean path. The person hearing the song will avoid death and return to Scotland by a slower, more conventional route aboveground. In that sense the A82 is the high road.

EIGHT MILES BEYOND THE NORTHERN tip of Loch Lomand, the A82 meets the east-west A85 at a place called Crianlarich. I use the word *place* because Crianlarich didn't feel like a town or even a village. It boasts a railway station on the West Highland Line from Glasgow northward, but that doesn't seem to have attracted much settlement. The ninety-six-mile West Highland Way—a spectacular walking path from near Glasgow north to Fort William—also passes nearby, but with little resulting civilization. I had hoped for another Leyburn or Keswick, where we could enjoy ourselves for several days, so I was sorely disappointed to find essentially nothing. No bank, no gas station, just a tiny grocery and a pub that was closed.

The one thing Crianlarich had plenty of was traffic. You can't get from Glasgow to Inverness, Scotland's northernmost city, without passing through here, and there was a never-ending

stream of tour buses and trucks negotiating the highway intersection. It seemed as if someone was missing a golden opportunity to open a truck stop. Travelers should be happy to pause
for fuel and a burger and then browse for naughty magazines,
NASCAR jackets, and Bruce Lee DVDs. Before returning to their
vehicles, they could grab a half-gallon soda and a platter of
nachos made with artificial cheese sauce.

While searching online in Keswick, I had found exactly two
B&BS in Crianlarich. One was full, so I had booked us at the
Breadalbane Lodge, which described itself as having "cosy timber cottages" plus a restaurant and bar. As we arrived, we felt
as if we had passed through a time warp and emerged somewhere in central Wyoming. The guest rooms were indeed separate log cabins—not the sort of thing you associate with the
UK. At the main building I met my first Scot in Scotland. She
was the manager, and a dour young woman she was. You can
pronounce dour to rhyme with *moor*, which suggests a gloomy
place, or with *glower*, which suggests a frown. Either way, that
was the manager. She was not hostile, but she lacked any warmth
whatsoever.

If the cabin looked like Wyoming on the outside, its interior reminded me of the cheap bungalows my family stayed in
during a trip to Colorado when I was ten. The furniture consisted solely of a double bed, not a queen or king but an ordinary double whose bedspread was faded and frayed. The single
ceiling light had one bulb that functioned and one that didn't. A
twelve-inch television was perched on a shelf in the corner. The
room was so tiny that there were perhaps ten inches of space
on either side of the bed and at its foot barely enough room to
turn around. We had to stash our suitcases just inside the door.
The bathroom was cramped and cold.

It is fair to say that the Italian Woman and I bring different perspectives to situations like these. I have spent enough
nights in a tent to consider any bed an improvement over sleeping on the ground. My wife is a city woman whose baseline is

a business-class hotel. I thought the Breadalbane Lodge was doable. For her it was dreadful—she simply does not do rustic.

After unloading our things, we walked to the main lodge for lunch. The fish chowder and vegetable plate were actually quite good, but as we ate, my companion looked more and more unhappy. Even the Guinness didn't erase her scowl. Finally, I said: "You don't want to stay here, do you? Shall we look for something else?"

"Whatever you want," she responded, which translates into "Do you even need to ask?"

We drove back into Crianlarich, and at the highway junction we saw a large white building called the Crianlarich Hotel. We hadn't noticed it earlier as we had sat at the intersection trying to decide which way to turn. The woman on duty said she had rooms available for fifty pounds, and she seemed a little surprised when we asked if we could look before we committed. The room was small (although twice the size of our cabin), but it was well appointed and relatively modern. It would do, but back downstairs we asked if there was possibly anything larger. Yes, indeed, a deluxe king, and its price was sixty-five pounds. We were thrilled. I returned to the Breadalbane Lodge alone, where I loaded our bags into the car, then went to the main building, where I told the sullen manager that we would not be staying. I had booked three nights, and she told me I should pay for one. I didn't want to argue, so I meekly handed over sixty-six pounds for an hour and a half of suitcase storage, and left.

To our considerable delight, the Crianlarich Hotel had a cozy bar and a first-rate restaurant staffed by earnest young men who drove in from other parts of southern Scotland and lived on the premises during their workweek. They responded to our every request with a spirited "Sairtenly!" The dining room was decorated with stuffed animals, and the fox draped over my settee brought back memories of my grandmother, who wore a red fox stole around her neck in church during the winter. I was fascinated by its beady eyes and tiny feet, and I would stare at it, certain that if I looked long enough, it would reward me with a knowing wink.

Back in our room it was time to negotiate the next day's activities, and what better occasion than when we had just enjoyed an excellent meal and a bottle of wine.

"So," I began cautiously, "should I try climbing Ben More tomorrow?"

My wife looked at me as if I had just asked her what her name was. "Why else would we be here in the middle of nowhere?"

"Well, we want to see Scotland, and we're headed north. We had to stop somewhere."

"And one of your high points is sitting there right outside our window."

"Yes, but I said I would give up the climbs, and I meant it. We're at the edge of the national park, and we could explore it together by car."

"I really have no interest in . . . what is this place called again?"

"Loch Lomond and The Trossachs. Wouldn't you like to see where *Lady of the Lake* takes place? It was in the Authors card game."

"That doesn't interest me even a little. Look, you were very sweet to spend three weeks in the Lake District without complaining, and so I'm okay if you want to run up a few hills in Scotland, as long as we spend most of our time on other things. Just go and do your climb so we can move on."

15

Tilted Bogs and Cold Toast

THAT NIGHT I WAS ANXIOUS about climbing Ben More. During the evening the peak had been shrouded by a dark cloud cap, and the forecast for the next day had ranged from nonstop rain to intermittent showers. Also, an online description of the mountain reported that "there are no obvious easy approaches . . . the ascent is unrelenting . . . there are pathless sections with boggy ground, and some dangerous terrain if the route is lost." I had dismissed these warnings, but at 3:00 a.m. I was second-guessing myself. Could Ben More really be *dangerous*? Intellectually, I knew that it was just another British walk-up, not the north face of the Eiger, but I had never set foot on a Scottish mountain, and the unknown was nagging at me.

At 7:00 a.m. Ben More was still socked in, so I went back to bed. Up again at eight thirty—still no summit. By eleven we had had our breakfast and were about to set out for a driving excursion, when the Italian Woman looked out and said: "I can see the mountain. It's clearing up. You ought to go right away."

I quickly changed clothes, grabbed my knapsack, and picked up a box lunch from the front desk. A mile east of the hotel I parked at the trailhead near Ben More Farm. Three women were standing there, waiting for a man to join their party, and they told me they intended to work their way up the valley on the west side of Ben More to a saddle south of the peak, then climb a path up the south side of the summit pyramid. Theirs was a longer but easier route than the direct line up the northwest slope above us. I told them I was going straight up.

I started on what was at first a zigzagging gravel road, and in short order I met a man coming down. He had summited from the northwest side, but on top he had seen nothing but cloud. He had then traversed the peak down to its south saddle and returned by way of the valley. I told him I was going to climb directly up and return by that route, but he urged me to consider the traverse for its variety, with the caveat that the lower slopes would be soggy no matter which way I chose. As proof of the wet conditions, he pointed to the mud covering his lower legs.

The man was right. Ten minutes later the road turned to the right, but I continued upward onto what soon became a tilted bog. The track was visible enough, and it avoided most of the wet spots, but here and there I was forced into mud nearly to my boot tops. As on The Cheviot, I was surprised that on the angled slope the water didn't just run to the bottom—apparently, the grass and heather were holding it in place.

After an hour of climbing, I was above the wet ground, and I reached a horizontal rocky ridge that had been the skyline for twenty minutes or more. At this point I was sorry I didn't have my altimeter. The peerless mountaineer Reinhold Messner once wrote that on a training walk he likes to ascend a thousand meters in an hour. For me half that pace would be good enough, but without an altimeter I had no idea how I was doing. The total ascent of Ben More is precisely one thousand meters, 3,280 feet, and I hoped I was halfway.

When you do something repetitious like hiking, it is easy to have a tune playing over and over in your head. On Scafell Pike I had been hearing Howard Goodall's lovely musical version of the Twenty-Third Psalm that introduced *The Vicar of Dibley*, and the experience had been appropriately English and rather comforting. Unfortunately, during the previous evening's dinner at the Crianlarich Hotel, melodies from the fifties had been playing softly, and now, on Ben More, the Connie Francis standard "Lipstick on Your Collar" was stuck in my brain. It had been popular when I was a boy working in my father's grocery store in Sioux Center, Iowa, and even then I had thought it was annoying. As I climbed, I tried to exorcise it by concentrating on the most grating tune I could think of—it was "In-A-Gadda-Da-Vida"—but like a stubborn case of the hiccups, the lipstick kept coming back. Now, simply writing this paragraph has got me hearing the cursed song.

Above the small ridge I found the lower end of a crumbling rock wall that ran straight uphill. At one time it must have separated two pastures, but it had been abandoned. Other than the path and wall, there was no trace of civilization.

As I gained altitude, a breeze came in from the south on my right side. At first it was pleasant, and it dissipated any clouds remaining around the peak, but the wind became stronger and stronger until it was so powerful that I was forced to lean into it for balance. I retrieved a hiking pole from my pack to steady myself, but when I lifted it, it would blow against my leg with a snap.

The path angled to the left over a rib of rock, and beyond it I found myself on the north side of the summit block in the lee of the mountain. I was able to move more efficiently, and in twenty minutes I arrived at the top of Ben More. It had taken exactly two hours to get there.

THE SKY WAS CLEAR OVER the summit, where a cement pylon marked 3,852 feet above sea level. Despite the sunshine, the wind was daunting, so I sought shelter behind a man-made mound of rocks, where I was welcomed by a couple who were drinking tea from a thermos. The woman said they were Leez and Veronica from Glasgow. It took me several tries to understand Leez's name, so I asked Veronica to spell it. It was L-E-s. So, he was Les, but her pronunciation, with its long *ee*, was reminiscent of New Zealanders, who don't use a short *e* at all, as in "I'm tired, and I'm going to beed."

Veronica and Leez had taken the same route that I had, setting out an hour ahead of me. They had seen me coming up behind them, and they thought I was moving very fast. The couple had climbed this mountain once before, and today they were going to descend to the south saddle and return through the western valley. When I asked if they minded some company, they said they would be happy if I joined them. As we talked, I quickly ate an orange and half a sandwich.

Before we started down, I stepped a discreet distance away to relieve myself. I carefully took a stance with the breeze at my back, and this worked for a few seconds, but then the wind suddenly shifted and began spiraling like a tornado. My output began to swirl around me like dollar bills in one of those Grab for Cash machines, and I became immersed in a vortex of golden droplets. They hit my clothes, my sunglasses, my cheeks, and my lips. *Hmmm*, salty. Mortified, I desperately contorted myself to correct the situation. I was completely unsuccessful. The shower continued, and at one point I saw a small rainbow, like the ones created by a lawn sprinkler. When I was finally finished, my entire body was speckled with moisture. I waited until it dried before returning to Veronica and Leez.

Once, back in 1967, after sampling a few beers in South Dakota, some friends and I lined up on a bridge west of Rock Valley, Iowa. We were leaning over the railing and delivering a message of good cheer into the Big Sioux River, when a fellow named E.J. said something to me. I turned to him, and he has never forgiven me for pivoting my whole body and soaking his shoe. I would like him to know that after all these years I have made an appropriate penance for that wrong—I have pissed on my own face.

The path down Ben More's south side was well worn and dry. Leez led the way, followed by Veronica and then me. She used the occasion to talk a blue streak about past walks, previous travels, whatever came to mind. The pair had only a few ascents left to complete all 282 of Scotland's "Munros"—mountains over three thousand feet in elevation. Still, she insisted that she and Leez were not mountaineers; on the most technical Munros on the Isle of Skye, they had hired a guide. Outside Britain the two had hiked in the Alps and Pyrenees, trekked to Everest base camp, and climbed Kilimanjaro. For non-mountaineers, they certainly had covered a lot of high country.

As Veronica maintained the flow of chatter, I grunted my approval from time to time. I had the feeling Leez was glad that his wife had someone new to prattle on with so he could descend in silence. Actually, Veronica was delightful. One slight challenge for me was that her Scottish accent was so thick—she had grown up in Glenlivet—and the wind so loud, I missed half of whatever she said, but no matter. What her pronunciation lacked in clarity, her thoughts made up in enthusiasm. Interestingly, I could understand everything coming from Leez, but there was very little of it. It was not surprising to learn that he was an engineer, while Veronica worked in retail sales.

In half an hour we reached Bealach Eadar dha Bheinn (try saying that after two Guinnesses), the saddle between Ben More and its slightly lower twin, Stob Binnein. The two peaks are often climbed in the same day, as Leez and Veronica had once done, but none of us was interested in a second summit in that roaring wind. At the col we met the three women from the trailhead. They seemed surprised to see me coming down, and one of them said sheepishly, "Oh dear, we *are* slow, aren't we." The three were resting while their male friend scrambled alone up Stob Binnein. The four would then climb Ben More together.

For more than an hour below the saddle the three of us worked our way down a long, gently angled slope that was a continuous bog. Overall it wasn't bad, because by hopping around we could find the firmest ground and avoid sinking in more than a few inches. Also, as we descended, we dropped below the summit winds into the quiet of the valley.

At last we reached the rough road across Ben More's lower slopes. We were able to walk three abreast, and it was finally my turn to talk. Veronica and Leez asked about my travels and my work, and I was happy to oblige them. At the cars we parted in friendship, they for Glasgow and I for the hotel, having shared the pleasure of a mountain afternoon.

BY THE TIME I RETURNED to the Crianlarich Hotel, the cloud cap had returned to the summit of Ben More, and by evening the peak was totally obscured. My five hours on the mountain had been the only period of clear weather for several days.

The Italian Woman had spent a relaxing day reading and doing Sudoku in the hotel library. When I saw the pleasant room, I realized how dreary it would have been for her at the Breadalbane Lodge. I reported that I had reached the top of Ben More, and it didn't take my companion more than a moment to decide that we would leave Crianlarich the next morning and move further north. I again floated the idea of taking a day to channel some Walter Scott, but my suggestion was summarily dismissed. So, I called our next B&B, in Fort William, where the owner was happy enough to accommodate us a day early. My wife and I spent another pleasant evening over a fine dinner and the day's reports from Wimbledon.

CONVERSATION WITH THE WAITER AT breakfast the next morning:

"Excuse me, but why do you bring out the toast in a wire rack that separates the slices?"

"To allow each piece to cool properly."

"Why don't you want the toast to be warm?"

"Well, ye wouldn't want the butter to melt, now would ye?"

I had never really given much thought to the matter of butter on toast, but I had always assumed that toast should be warm to the touch and that you buttered it immediately after extracting it from the toaster, so the butter would melt. In fact, you kept the butter next to the toaster, knife at the ready, prepared to immediately do the spreading. If you were quick enough, you could take satisfaction in seeing the butter saturate the toast. The height of luxury, I believed as a boy, was to have breakfast in a café and have someone back in the kitchen do the buttering so the stack of toast arrived already glistening and still warm. In my world the role of butter was to enhance the toast.

Now my assumption had been turned on its head. I needed to appreciate that for some people—the entire British nation, apparently—it is butter that is king of the breakfast table. The ideal is for the butter to retain its yellowness and creamy texture at all times, and toast is merely a vehicle to deliver the marvelous mucilage in its proper state to your longing lips. Cold toast preserves the essential character of the butter. To use warm toast would be to abet the unholy transmogrification of the sacred golden spread into an unrecognizable, disappearing goo. Thus, should the toast be greater than room temperature when it is set before you, the proper thing is to sit patiently and take a sip of your coffee or a bite of your black pudding until the moment is right. When the correct approach is taken, cold toast will deliver a sensuous experience and a jolly good start to your day.

Text from British tourist to friend in the UK: "Doing gr8 in US, but toast is warm LOL."

16

Sensory Overload

I HAD WANTED TO CLIMB Ben Nevis since I first read about it as a boy. At 4,409 feet it is the highest mountain in Britain, and like England's Scafell Pike, it has played host to generations of British climbers cutting their teeth for the Alps and Himalayas. From my small town in Iowa the Highlands of Scotland seemed impossibly romantic, and I vowed I would get there one day, ascend Ben Nevis in a kilt, and then roll around in the heather with a redheaded lassie named Fiona.

Well into my adult years in Seattle, I was once planning a business trip to London, and I nearly took the Ben Nevis plunge. I found that there was an overnight train, the Caledonian Sleeper, from Euston Station to Fort William, at the foot of the great mountain. I could have my meeting in London, sleep on the train that night, climb the next day, and then overnight back to London and fly home. The problem with the plan—beyond the fact that it was desperately loopy—was that it was November and conditions on Ben Nevis were described as grim. I needed to go there in summer and allow enough time to get a day of good weather. I decided to forgo the mad dash to Scotland. Fiona wrote to say that she was heartbroken.

Now it was summer indeed, and we were in the Highlands. We had eleven days before heading to Ireland for our bus tour, so this was a perfect opportunity to tackle Ben Nevis. The fact that it was not in a national park but in a "national scenic area" didn't matter to me; it was the top of Britain, after all. Furthermore, the possibility of actually getting to the high points of all fifteen national parks still seemed far-fetched, so it made sense to have a back-up plan. If nothing else, I could climb the tallest mountains in England, Scotland, and Wales and rest on my laurels. England was already in the bag. We would stop in Wales on our return from Ireland. For now Ben Nevis was at hand.

A MOUNTAIN RANGE AND AN open road are a magical combination. When I think of my favorite high country drives in the United States, I always start with the North Cascades Highway in Washington, Trail Ridge Road in Colorado, and the Going-to-the-Sun Road in Montana. All three traverse national parks and are justifiably renowned for their engineering wizardry and sweeping vistas. Less famous but just as rewarding are Colorado State Highway 9 and central Oregon's US 97; I have traveled those elegant routes many times and will never tire of them. In England I had enjoyed driving through Yorkshire and Cumbria—more accurately, I had appreciated the landscape during those precious moments when it didn't seem as if a head-on crash was imminent—but the green hills of the Dales and Lakes had never felt like true mountain country. What a pleasant surprise, then, to find that north of Crianlarich there lies a wonderland of towering peaks.

The A82 is classified as a "trunk road"—British-speak for a major highway. Interestingly, when such a road is supplanted by a new motorway, the older highway loses its primary status and is said to be "de-trunked," a rather disturbing term that smacks of ivory poaching. I expect that one day, somewhere in the UK, I will come across a road sign that says, CATS EYES REMOVED—DE-TRUNKING IN PROGRESS—ANIMALS RUN FOR YOUR LIVES.

It was a sunny morning in the Highlands as we left Crianlarich, heading northwest. For the first five miles the A82 and the east-west A85 ran together, before separating at the village of Tyndrum. The shared section gradually ascends Strath Fillan, a lovely valley flanked by heather slopes and occasional stands of dark-green trees in neat rows that have obviously been planted by humans. Scots use the word *strath* to describe a broad, gently sloped valley, while a *glen* is usually narrower and more precipitous. Usage, however, is not always precise. I found one reference to "the glen of Strath Fillan."

A notable feature of Strath Fillan is the railroad tracks on either side of the road. The West Highland Line splits in Crianlarich, with the track on the right side of the highway continuing northward to Fort William. The track on the left turns west at Tyndrum to follow the A85 to Oban on Scotland's Atlantic coast. Curiously, when the two branches reach Tyndrum, each line has its own stop, less than half a mile apart. In fact, the village bears the distinction of being the smallest community in Britain with two railway stations. It also seemed to have a spark of life that Crianlarich had lacked, including a busy truck stop called a "transport café."

We continued north on the A82, and now on our right the Fort William rail line and the West Highland Way footpath ran in parallel. On that beautiful morning the trail was dotted with long-distance hikers, as both the railway and path traversed along the side of a prominent mountain called Ben Dorain. I told the Italian Woman that one day I simply had to return to walk the entire West Highland Way and savor this landscape at a much slower speed. My wife wished me Godspeed and invited me to send her a text now and then.

Beyond a tiny hamlet called Bridge of Orchy, we entered onto the Rannoch Moor, an endless bog that under gray skies would perfectly illustrate the concept of dreary. The ancestral home of Clan McDuck, the moor was no doubt responsible for the sour disposition of the most notable McDuck, Donald's Uncle Scrooge. For us, however, the tarn-filled countryside sparkled cheerfully in the sunshine of early July, the wetlands shimmering like silver coins in Scrooge's Money Bin.

The highest spot on the A82 sits at 1,142 feet above sea level, some fifteen miles north of Tyndrum. It isn't a pass but simply a point where the gently climbing highway takes a bend and begins dropping gradually to the west. Over the space of the next few miles, the mountains on either side began to close in, with the Black Mount range on the left counterbalancing a trio of unpronounceables on the right. A sign announced the Glencoe Ski Centre, and just beyond it stood the King's House Hotel, a seventeenth-century inn that is one of Scotland's oldest. Its setting was so magnificent that I regretted not booking a night there.

The hotel marked the entrance to Glen Coe, a valley that outdoor writer Simon Warren claims "is often voted the most beautiful and spectacular location in the whole of Britain." The accolade is well deserved. Precipitous green slopes and rocky buttresses rise up on both sides, as the highway and the River Coe twist and snake along the valley floor. At one turnout after the next we pulled over to step out of the car and gape at the peaks and ridges above us. We quickly experienced sensory overload, as if entering a Thai restaurant when famished and being assaulted by the fragrances of lemon grass, cumin, and coriander. The highest of the Glen Coe mountains reaches a modest 3,766 feet in elevation, but the peaks tower so dramatically over the valley that I will rank this piece of Scotland among the most impressive high country vistas I have ever seen. I want to go back and hike and climb and take a thousand photographs. I would be happy to return just to drive the highway again. If I lived within striking distance, I would sally forth whenever possible, in all kinds of weather, just to experience the A82 through Glen Coe.

WEST OF GLEN COE, WHERE the River Coe empties into the sea, lies the hamlet of Glencoe. The village serves as a bustling center for mountain and water sports, and its cottages look as if they have been lifted from the Norwegian countryside. The idyllic feel of the place, however, belies a bloody past. This was where the 1692 Massacre of Glencoe occurred, in which members of the local Clan MacDonald were rudely dispatched by

Clan Campbell during a dispute over stolen livestock, fealty to this king or that, whether to wear briefs or boxers under your kilt—the usual things people fought about back then. If this sort of history tickles your fancy, you are welcome to it. Take a room at the Clachaig Inn, where a brass sign says, NO HAWKERS OR CAMPBELLS. Dress up in your Scottish finest (go commando if you dare), inflate the bagpipes, and lay into "The Campbells are coming, Ho-Ro, Ho-Ro." Afterward, heat some soup from a red-and-white can and serve it up with a Big Mac.

If Glencoe reminded us of Norway, so did the road beyond. For fifteen miles from Glencoe to Fort William, the A82 hugs the shores of two narrow bodies of water, Loch Leven and Loch Linnhe. Despite sounding like lakes, they are saltwater "sea lochs" that most of us would call "fjords." The views along the way were stunning, and I was transported back thirty years to a weekend excursion with clients in western Norway. We drove inland from Ålesund along the splendid Romsdalsfjord to the village of Andalsnes, where we spent two days drinking beer, eating *gravlaks*, and telling tales that became increasingly unbelievable. It was my first trip to Norway, and I was impressed with the scenery but also with the warmth of my hosts. After dozens of subsequent visits to the country, I remain convinced that its people, despite their reputation as spiritual cousins to the gloomy Scots, are cheerful, welcoming, and full of life.

Our destination was Fort William, terminus of the West Highland Way walking path and slightly more than halfway from Glasgow to Inverness. The town is indelibly associated with Ben Nevis and its neighboring peaks, but it is also very much a seaside community. In that sense it is a miniature Seattle, whose own fjord—Puget Sound—is ringed by mountains. Seattleites (yes, that's what we are called) often boast that we can ski in the morning and sail in the afternoon. Williamites can do the same. The town calls itself "the outdoor capital of the UK"—not to be confused with Keswick's claim to be "the outdoor retailer of the UK, if not Europe!"

We needed to find the Benloch Bed & Breakfast, which was located along the A82 on the approach to Fort William's town center. The owner, Michael Hill, had told me on the phone that the house was a stone Victorian half a mile before the first roundabout. When I asked how I would know when I was half a mile from something still ahead of me, he paused, as if that question had never occurred to him. Perhaps he had never had a lawyer or engineer as a guest. In the end his best suggestion was to drive to the roundabout, then go round about it, and head back out for—you guessed it—half a mile.

Our room at the Benloch was the single nicest accommodation of our entire summer. In earlier days it must have been the second-floor drawing room. It was large and elegantly furnished in Victorian period pieces, but its outstanding feature was a bay window with an unobstructed view of Loch Linnhe just across the road. Along the water ran a grassy lawn with daffodils and flowering bushes, a paved walk, benches, and picnic tables. People strolled by at all hours, walking to and from the town center, pausing now and then to sit and savor the scenery. We paid rather dearly for this piece of Highland Heaven, but as we settled in we were certain that it was worth every penny. Unfortunately—and nothing is ever perfect in this world tainted by original sin—Michael proved to be the worst breakfast chef of the summer. Everything he served was gray. Never before had I seen real eggs and bacon that looked like a black-and-white photograph.

Fort William's town center was, I am sorry to say, a disappointment. Its High Street was for pedestrians only, and that gave it a relaxed feel, but there were too many empty storefronts. Where Keswick had been lively, Fort William was forlorn. On the plus side, it did have an excellent tourist information office, where I was able to obtain brochures and maps of Ben Nevis. The posted weather forecast for the next five days was for clear skies, little wind, and temperatures in the upper sixties—perfect conditions for a climb.

To my great surprise, Ben Nevis was nowhere to be seen. Descriptions of Fort William tell how the mountain dominates the town, but nobody ever mentions that what you really see from High Street is a ridge of intervening hills. We later learned that if you drive west a few miles along Loch Eil, you can look back and see Britain's highest peak in all its glory, hovering over the foothills, with the town tucked below. Many people visit Seattle and go away frustrated that they have not seen the iconic Mount Rainier, but that is a function of western Washington's frequent cloud cover. The glaciated volcano is actually out there, and when the sky is clear, it is an eye-popping sight. You could visit downtown Fort William every day of the year and never see Ben Nevis.

We needed lunch, and in a High Street pub we found ourselves cheek by jowl with a raucous crowd watching the men's final at Wimbledon. The excitement was over the fact that Scotland's own Andy Murray had the chance to become the first British man in seventy-seven years to take the championship. He did win, and the United Kingdom went wild. That evening the Glen Nevis Restaurant offered strawberries and cream, Wimbledon's traditional dish, to honor the occasion.

Our waitress at the Glen Nevis was a university student named Kim, a native of Fort William, and she was thrilled about the Wimbledon result. Yet, voicing a complaint heard often in the Highlands, she noted that all the news reports from London that day had referred to Murray as British. "Whenever he wins, he's a Brit," she said. "When he loses, he's a Scot." Kim had gone up Ben Nevis several times, and she was glad that the English had to travel to Scotland to climb the UK's greatest mountain.

17

One Brief, Shining Moment

THE GLEN NEVIS VISITOR CENTRE is an unassuming structure that plays host to the 100,000 people who ascend Ben Nevis
every year and many times that number who drive into the valley just to picnic and stroll along the River Nevis. Every July a
few extraordinary folk participate in the Glen Nevis River Race,
negotiating a two-mile stretch of the frigid water on air mat-
tresses. If that isn't daunting enough, the racers begin by leap-
ing from a small cliff, and then they encounter obstacles named
Gurgling Gorge, Dead Dog Pool, Leg Breaker, and Lower Falls
Leap. They do wear helmets and wetsuits, but the event reinforces
my belief that mountaineering is a measured and thoughtful
activity when compared with many other so-called adventure
sports that are designed for idiots. Incidentally, to distract themselves from the dangers of the River Race, a few competitors
have eschewed the traditional air mattress in favor of a blow-up
woman that likely proves useful on non-race days as well. It
does get lonely on those long winter nights out on the moors.

At the visitor center I inquired about signing in for the ascent,
and the host informed me that they don't keep a register because
they close at 6:00 p.m. Many climbers return later than that,
and all of them would be classified as missing in action if they
could not sign out. If a few people do not return, their bodies
will be located in due course.

MY TREK BEGAN BY CROSSING the Nevis River on a suspen-
sion bridge. On the far side, 200 feet above the river, the path

began traversing upward along the slope of a 2,333-foot mountain called Meall an t'Suidhe, the "hill of rest." It did look like a whale in repose, but the trail was far from restful. It became surprisingly rough as I worked my way around the snout of the beast.

An hour under way I felt a chill, which was odd because it was windless and hot. I realized that this was the beginning of heat exhaustion, so I stopped to drink half a bottle of water and eat a few ginger cream cookies. I also used the time to roll up my pant legs and apply sunscreen. After fifteen minutes—an unusually long break when I am hiking alone—I felt better and resumed the climb.

The path entered a high valley between Meall an t'Suidhe and Ben Nevis. Ninety minutes after leaving the visitor center, I arrived at a trail junction called Halfway Lochan. The point is somewhat short of the midpoint of the five-mile ascent, but the Halfway name offers cheer to the weary. The word *lochan* is a diminutive of *loch*, and several hundred feet below, in the broad saddle between the two peaks, lay a lovely tarn whose proper name is Lochan Meall an t'Suidhe. Its deep blue offered a sharp contrast against Meall's green slopes.

Oddly, my Lonely Planet guide described the trail to that point as a "good path" while referring to what lay beyond as "much rougher." I experienced just the opposite. The segment around Meall an t'Suidhe had been uneven and jumbled. Above Halfway Lochan I found the path—now on the flanks of Ben Nevis itself—to be smoother. The first stretch ran two-thirds of a mile and was bisected by Red Burn, a lively stream that wasn't the least bit red. Its gully was picturesque, and the breeze from the rushing water was cool and refreshing. Less enticing was the sagging metal bridge across the cascade. As I approached, other hikers were standing there daring themselves to set foot on the rickety span. I cheerfully volunteered to lead the way, and after I scampered across with no loss of life, they decided they could follow suit.

Beyond Red Burn I came to the first of many switchbacks, as the path aggressively ascended Ben Nevis's prominent western ridge. The slope was steeper, but I was delighted with the conditions. A slight breeze offered relief from the heat, and I settled into what I thought was a productive rhythm, but then two young runners in gym trunks and athletic shoes breezed by me. They weren't carrying so much as a water bottle.

An unexpected pleasure just below the rocky summit dome was a sloping patch of snow a hundred feet across, with the path running up its center. As with the bridge below, I found several people who had paused to discuss whether they could safely make it through. The snow was consolidated and granulated, perfect for climbing, and with a whoop of joy and many pleasant memories of mountains in the Pacific Northwest, I floated upward. A snowfield is clean and friendly, unlike a rocky path, which is constantly trying to throw you off balance. This was the only snow I touched the entire summer, and it was delightful.

The final section of the route wound its way past several precipitous gullies on the mountain's sheer north side. My hiking brochures had warned that in poor visibility people have veered over the edge and into a free fall. The last of the defiles was Gardyloo Gully, a curious name for a mountain feature. "Gardy loo" (from the French *regardez l'eau*, "watch out for the water") is what people in earlier times in Paris—and in Edinburgh as well—called out as they emptied their chamber pots onto the street from upper-floor windows, and it was intended to alert pedestrians below that a downpour most foul was about to descend. Now it could be that Scottish men have traditionally stood atop the Ben Nevis fissure to relieve themselves, generously calling out to any rock climbers unlucky enough to be ascending the vertical cliffs below, but I doubt it. Most gullies high on mountains are subject to updrafts, and word would soon have spread throughout the Highlands that if you heed the call of nature at the top of Gardyloo, you will find yourself in a shower of your own making. No intelligent climber would allow that to happen.

THE ACTUAL SUMMIT OF BEN Nevis, at 4,409 feet, was unsightly. The scattering of boulders was a natural phenomenon, but the remnants of old buildings were jarring. I had climbed 4,379 feet and nearly five miles to be confronted by another set of British ruins. Even worse was the garbage that lay everywhere. I had seen no litter on Scafell Pike or any of my other climbs, so this was a shock. The highest point in the UK deserves better, and in a modest gesture of civic spirit, I picked up several plastic bottles and stuffed them into my trash bag.

The second thing I wasn't expecting was that most of the thirty-odd people spread around the summit area were speaking German. I was reminded of my American friend Peter Jacoby, who underwent emergency surgery while on a visit to his family in Frankfurt. When he awoke, his daughter was at his bedside, and his first words were "Why are the nurses speaking German?" I asked one of the Germans on Ben Nevis what was going on, and he said that he was as surprised as I was, and frankly, he hadn't come to Scotland to mingle with his fellow countrymen. These people were intruding on his British holiday.

The third surprise was myself. They say that as you age you lose your inhibitions, and that might explain what I did next. Or perhaps it was because I had written a book called *The Naked Mountaineer*, and even before its release people were starting to ask, "Did you really . . . you know . . . climb like that?" Maybe I wanted to be able to answer in the affirmative. Maybe I just had fond memories of a woman I once saw relaxing au naturel on the summit of Norway's highest peak. Regardless of why, I decided for the first time in my rather prudish adulthood to soak up the summer sun without the interference of my clothing.

When you share a mountaintop with thirty others, you don't just drop trouser and start singing "Take Me Out to the Ball Game." People do that sort of thing on street corners in Seattle, and we have nice places where the state takes care of them. But on a populated mountain you need to use a bit of discretion. Even in your boldness, you must keep your wits.

I wandered about the plateau, and fifty yards away from the relaxing summiteers I spotted a low, circular stone wall. It sat off by itself, a small shelter that had no doubt protected climbers during a storm or provided a bivouac site for overnight campers. Casually, I sauntered over, glancing back from time to time to see if anyone was looking. When I was certain that nobody had spotted me, I scrambled over the wall and into the circle.

I located a flat rock facing south, toward the sun, set my pack next to it, and began shedding my garments. The shirt was easy enough, but to go further, I had to first take off my boots. My feet were immediately attacked by sharp stones. I endured, but as I loosened my belt I felt a flush of shame and heard a small voice saying, "Mr. Steve, what doest thou?" I ignored it, and a moment later I was sitting on that flat rock in the altogether. The solar rays felt good on parts of me that had not experienced any direct sunlight since my cousins and I had gone skinny-dipping in the Big Sioux River some fifty years earlier.

I closed my eyes and tried to be at ease, but I just couldn't. Sharp rocks protruded into my back and feet, and I couldn't find a comfortable posture. At the same time, I felt certain that the Germans were headed toward me with Leica cameras at the ready. Under the circumstances I concluded that, like Camelot, my shining moment would have to be brief.

Opening my eyes, I looked down, and next to my left hand I saw a bit of matted white paper. More litter, I thought. Do people have no manners? Then I looked more closely at my surroundings. There were more clumped-up bits of tissue on the rocks, a fact that I had missed in my anxiety as I made ready for sunbathing. Then I noticed that there were dry lumps of organic matter strewn about, and the truth hit me like a freight train: I was sitting in the summit latrine.

I was dressed and on my feet faster than a visiting mailman who hears the words "Honey, I'm home!" Like a steeplechase racer, I hurdled the wall and sprinted away from the enclosure. I kept checking my arms and legs to see if I was bearing any marks of shame. I wanted to get off that mountain, back to Fort William, and into the shower in our nice, sanitary bathroom at the Benloch.

I may have been chastened in my attempt to act Scandinavian, but at least there were no cosmic consequences. Contrast that with the fate of four climbers—two Canadians, one Dutch, and one British—who were thrown into a Malaysian jail in June 2015 for baring all atop Borneo's Mount Kinabalu. They were part of a larger group of visitors engaged in a contest to see who could longest endure the cold at the 13,453-foot summit, and they had chosen to ignore the fact that the peak is sacred to the local Kadazan people. As fate would have it, a magnitude 5.9 earthquake occurred several days later, killing eighteen climbers on the same mountain and stranding more than a hundred others. A local official declared that the catastrophe was divine retribution for the strippers' act of desecration.

I quickly realized that, stain or no stain, I had to eat my lunch, and then it would be a long slog to the car. I had to descend safely, and obsessing about human detritus would be a waste of energy. I humbly rejoined the summit crowd and, trying to avoid eye contact, sat on a boulder to eat an apple and some crackers. It was only when I paused to take in the view that I realized how fortunate I was to be there on that beautiful day. Southwest, at the mouth of Loch Linnhe, I could see the Isle of Mull. North and west, those bumps on the horizon may have been the rugged Cuillin range on the Isle of Skye. The wonderland that is western Scotland was laid out before me. All of Great Britain, land of my mother tongue, where they eat black and white pudding for breakfast, was at my feet.

PERHAPS IT WAS THE LUNCH or the relaxation, or perhaps the extra dose of sunshine, but as I started to leave the summit I felt amazingly refreshed and energetic. I discovered that I could move rapidly and with catlike agility, or at least the sixty-five-year-old version of it. I kept my feet apart for balance and my knees flexed, like a football player dancing through a set of tires laid out in two lines. I held my hiking poles up, like a skier, not using them except occasionally to catch myself. In that manner

I started prancing down the path. In short order I was hearing the song "Dancing Queen," and I had a vision of Pierce Brosnan in his bell-bottoms and platform boots in the final scene of the movie version of *Mamma Mia!* I leave it to you to psychoanalyze the preceding sentence, but as I have said before, once a tune gets into your head, there is nothing you can do about it.

Heading down, whenever I met people ascending the upper part of the mountain, I said something like: "You're doing great. Almost there. Congratulations." Most responded gratefully, but some seemed to resent my geniality, preferring to wallow in whatever discomfort they were experiencing.

At the lowest switchback on the western ridge, I came upon a small drama. There were two women and a man, and one of the women was bent over, gasping and whimpering in a most pathetic manner. She was in a panic. In response to my questions, the other woman said that her friend Darla had not injured herself, was not asthmatic, and wasn't having chest pains. Trying not to sound pushy, I suggested that this might be heat exhaustion or just fatigue. Why not stop here and take a rest? When Darla was breathing normally, she might want to eat some food and take a drink of water. When she felt better, they could decide whether to continue up or turn back. But there was no hurry. It was one forty-five, daylight would last until eleven, and the weather was perfect. Just rest a while, and everything should be fine. As we talked, Darla had already calmed somewhat. I offered to stay awhile, but the three said it wasn't necessary. They thanked me, and I resumed my descent.

When I reached the trail junction at Halfway Lochan, I stopped to visit with an older English couple who were on their way up. They asked about the path from that point, and I assured them that it was much smoother than the first half of the climb. They were delighted to hear this. As we talked, a thin, white-haired man joined us. He had been descending just behind me, and as he came near, I turned to him and said, "Lovely day, isn't it?"

He said, "Yes indeed," and then launched directly into a speech that must have been forming in his mind as he approached: "Think of it. There are 365 days in a year. On three hundred of them Ben Nevis will be cloudy with no visibility at all. Of the remaining sixty-five, thirty-five will be overcast but with a clear summit. That means that only thirty days in the whole year will be as nice as this."

I mentioned that this was my first time in the area, but the man continued as if I hadn't spoken: "Everybody wants to come here in July and August. What they don't realize is that it rains more in summer than in spring. The best months here are April, May, and June. A perfect day like this, in July, is most unusual. We are all lucky today."

It was clear that the fellow was eager for company, so I suggested that he and I walk down together, and he readily agreed. He said his name was Brian, he was seventy-eight, and if he was too slow for me, I could pass him by. I responded that companionship can be better than speed. The fact was, I had trotted all the way from the summit to Halfway Lochan, and I was ready to slow down.

Brian and I spent more than an hour together on the lower half of Ben Nevis. He talked of his career in insurance, his long-distance walks in England and Scotland, and his thoughts on hiking etiquette. He hated it when he said hello to someone on the trail and they didn't respond. Just plain rude, he called it. The world is so much better if people greet each other with a smile. Brian had married and divorced long ago, but then, seventeen years earlier, he had met the love of his life. He called her his "Dear Ellen." They had had a wonderful year as best of friends, traveling, gardening, reading books, and listening to music. Two peas in a pod, they were. The two were planning to marry and spend the rest of their lives together, but then one day, without warning, she dropped dead. His mother died three months later. For sixteen years now he had been alone, with no family or friends. He still had his books and those other things, but he would never be able to replace his Dear Ellen. He just couldn't make sense of it.

The trail around Meall an t'Suidhe was awkward, with tilted steps, ankle-twisting holes, and loose stones. Brian was painfully slow, and several times he fell back onto his rump, struggled to his feet, and immediately said to me, "Now, watch what you're doing there." I never fell, but once my feet slipped on some gravel, and he turned back and said, "Steve, you need to be more careful." Then he fell down again and warned me to pay more attention to the path. At several points I nearly told him I would just play through, but after his sad story about losing his love, I felt it would be unkind to abandon him.

At the visitor center they were selling "I Climbed Ben Nevis" certificates to anyone who said they had done so and was willing to part with three pounds. I bought a cold soda instead. I was thrilled to have made the ascent so long after first reading about this mountain, I was grateful for the exceptional weather, and above all, I was thankful that the Dear Italian Woman was alive and with me in Britain. I didn't think that a certificate, with my name written in ballpoint pen by a store clerk, would add anything to the experience.

THE ITALIAN WOMAN AND I celebrated at Crannog, a fish restaurant on the town pier in Fort William. The baked cod fillets on leek mash, asparagus with hollandaise sauce, and apple-rhubarb cobbler, accompanied by locally brewed beer, added up to one of the best meals of our summer. As dinner came to an end, I asked my wife whether she would prefer to spend another day in Fort William or move on. There might be some car touring or easy walks in the area.

All she said was, "Let's blow this pop stand."

18

Close Encounters

AS A BOY, I WAS a fan of those Saturday night television shows known as "creature features," the programs whose on-air host was a slightly inebriated local merchant promoting his aluminum siding business. The movies were *Dracula* or *Frankenstein*, anything whose title begins with "House of" or "Curse of," or Japanese films like *Mothra* or *Godzilla*. Every one of these stories begins with a peaceful, sunlit scene—a quaint fishing village, a mountain hamlet with fresh-faced wenches, or perhaps a little town in the American Southwest where everyone is named Johnny. Of course, we, the viewers, know from the first minute what the rubes do not—namely, that night will descend or fog will roll in and something too horrible to imagine will awaken from a millennium of slumber. Fortunately, after the planet is all but reduced to a smoldering cinder, the evil one is defeated by a battered yet indefatigable hero, but then, maddeningly, the movie concludes with the words *The End?*

There is a reason for these reflections at this point in our narrative, and it is that legends of fantastical creatures are not just a Hollywood concoction. Monster mythology is universal, and no matter where you travel, the bogeyman or chupacabra may be lurking just out of sight. As the Italian Woman and I approached Scotland's Cairngorm National Park, we should have realized that when you least expect it, mischief may be afoot.

We followed the A 82 northeast out of Fort William. Had we carried on toward Invergarry and Fort Augustus, we soon would have arrived at Loch Ness, second largest and most famous of all the Scottish lakes. That morning a certain plesiosaur was no doubt swimming laps and waiting for the Italian Woman to capture the footage that would finally and conclusively establish Nessie's existence. Our story would be dramatized in a made-for-television movie called *They Came from Omaha*. Enticing as this prospect was, we turned east at Spean Bridge, onto the A86. Our plan was to spend a few days in Aviemore, where I hoped to attempt a third Scottish mountain. We would then travel to Inverness and approach Loch Ness from the north. Our monster experience could wait a few more days . . . or so we thought.

Aviemore is the northern gateway to the Cairngorm mountain range. Within a short distance to the south of the town you can go skiing, mountain biking, pony trekking, and something called snow holing (without knowing more, I respectfully decline). Aviemore calls itself the Adventure Capital of the United Kingdom, but its surfeit of activities is counterbalanced by a dearth of charm. The town presents itself as little more than a collection of shops strung along the B9152. It has no market square and, despite being within the national park, evidently no standards on architectural style. The Macdonald Aviemore Resort, with its "Decade Explosion 2" song-and-dance extravaganza, seems to be the town's main attraction.

When we arrived at our B&B, the manager seemed perplexed. Her name was Justine, and she said she wasn't expecting us until the following day. Unfortunately, her six rooms were completely booked that night. I told her I had talked to her husband, Dennis, the previous afternoon and he had agreed to advance our arrival by twenty-four hours. In a fluster she went next door and came back with the news that the neighboring lodge had a room and would honor the seventy-five-pound rate we had been quoted. We moved the car, and as I was unloading our bags, a red-faced Dennis arrived. He told me that I was wrong, and now he and Justine would have to absorb the cost differential between the two rooms. He was so upset that he could barely get the words out, and it looked as if he would stomp his foot into the ground, like Rumpelstiltskin.

Not taking the hint that I should offer him some money, I responded: "What did you suppose was the purpose of my call yesterday? What did you think I meant when I ended our conversation with 'Okay, I'll see you tomorrow'? And if you had told me you were full, why would we have shown up today? We could have stayed in Fort William."

Seething, Dennis turned his back and left. As I was carrying the last bag into our new accommodation, he reappeared, now purple, spitting and sputtering madly without using actual words. His arms flailed around, and it looked as if he would beat his chest and emit a loud roar before lunging at my throat. Fearing that I would be attacked if I turned away, I maintained eye contact and slowly backed into the house. I later learned that the going rate for our new room was 150 pounds.

Having survived the Attack of the Bellicose Proprietor, we drove to Leault Farm, where a "true native highland shepherd" named Neil Ross offered a herding demonstration. This was stand-and-gape tourism at its finest, and twenty-five of us paying customers slouched indolently in the heat—yes, it was sunny and hot—as a dozen border collies chased a group of terrified sheep this way and that for half an hour. The dogs responded instantly to whistles and strange sounds emitted by their master. Remarkably, one of the females was totally blind and yet was an efficient herder. Even more intriguing to us was Ross's comment that the dogs—all of them—sleep in his bedroom. We surmised that taking a girlfriend home for the night could be a delicate business. "Listen, dearie, afore we go in, there's a wee somethin' I'm needin' t' tell ye."

BEN MACDUI RISES IN THE heart of the Cairngorms to 4,295 feet, the loftiest mountain in any of Britain's national parks. It is the second highest peak in Scotland and in the UK overall, yielding only to Ben Nevis's 4,409 feet. Although MacDui is only slightly lower than Nevis, from a climber's point of view it is a far less strenuous outing. The Nevis trailhead sits a scant 30 feet above sea level, leaving an ascent of 4,379 feet. The Mac-Dui walk begins at 2,116 feet at a ski area, requiring an absolute gain of only 2,179 feet to the top. Granted, the MacDui route does undulate somewhat, and if you do a loop and climb the mountain Cairn Gorm as well, the total gain comes to just over 3,000 feet, but that is still significantly less than Ben Nevis. Both walks are roughly ten miles round trip, but by any account Ben MacDui is gentler and easier.

After a restful night in our expensive room, the Italian Woman turned me loose, and I drove from Aviemore into the mountains, through a broad valley of farms and woods, past a Hilton resort, and then into the Glenmore Forest Park. Glenmore is a park within the national park, a doubly protected stand of ancient Caledonian pinewood, and yet it is not a wilderness. At its center lies Loch Morlich, with an enormous swimming beach, windsurfing concession, bike rental, and campground. Also on hand is the Cairngorm Reindeer Centre, which offers close encounters with Donder and Blitzen—well, now, really. Fortunately, beyond these distractions the countryside began to feel wilder. The road climbed out of the trees onto open slopes, and after several large switchbacks I pulled into the ski area, forty five minutes after leaving the B&B.

Ski resorts are always a harsh intrusion in alpine country, and there's no way to hide or beautify them. As a skier and snowboarder, I see them as a necessary evil. As a climber, I hate them. In any event, my ascent started at the massive parking lot. A hundred cars sat there, and a funicular was already ferrying sightseers up a steep slope to a viewing platform above the barren ski runs.

I have known many well-toned mountaineers, but the man who signed me in at the ranger base was the most robust-looking person I have ever met. Shaved head, legs of steel, biceps beyond all telling. If our species were headed for extinction and if Darwin was right about survival of the fittest, that ranger would be the last man standing. I felt sheepish to be in his presence, and I nearly blurted out: "Excuse me, where can I buy a ticket for the funicular?" Then I realized that I should be happy to have McBuff on the scene. If I hurt myself on Ben MacDui, this fellow could carry me out with one hand.

Horizontal visibility was unlimited at the level of the parking lot, but a thousand feet above hung a heavy blanket of gray cloud. Yet it didn't appear to be raining up there, so at ten o'clock I set out. Immediately, "The Happy Wanderer" started playing in my head. This happens now and then on my walks, and it makes me feel ten years old. That's a good feeling, but it's a silly song. I'm afraid I will start singing out loud and meet another hiker just as I'm bellowing "Val de rah ha ha ha ha ha."

As the crow flies, the summit of Ben MacDui lies four and a third miles directly south of the ski base. The path deviates slightly from this straight line, running in a shallow westward arc to bypass an intervening mountain called Cairn Lochan. What an excellent path it was, and in the cool air I was able to walk at a good clip.

For the first half-hour the track ascended gradually, but after crossing a stream, it started more steeply up a ridge on the northwestern flank of Cairn Lochan. The buttress rose 950 feet in just under a mile—a perfect angle for energetic hiking. I noted that higher up the path disappeared into the clouds, but I still saw no signs of rain. My outing in the Cairngorms was off to an excellent start.

JUST BELOW THE CREST OF the ridge, I entered the cloud zone. I was carrying one of my extendable walking poles in my right hand, but not using it. I held it in the middle of the shaft, horizontally, with the point forward and the handle toward the rear. All of a sudden I felt something tugging on the handle behind me. Startled, I stopped and looked back, but nothing was there. When it happened again, I paused to analyze the situation and thought that I might have bumped the handle against the bottom of my knapsack. Satisfied, more or less, with that explanation, I continued.

A few minutes later a gray figure emerged from the mist just ahead of me. I had seen passing references to the legend of a Yeti-like creature known as the "Big Grey Man of Ben MacDui," and the apparition caused the hairs to rise on the back of my neck. I froze and stood there until I realized it was only a solitary hiker descending. He told me he had summited Ben Mac-Dui but had seen nothing, due to the cloud cap.

Beyond the ridge I was moving through dense fog across a plateau, near a place marked on my map as being at 1,083 meters (3,553 feet). The path was mostly sand and gravel, and it crunched loudly underfoot. I gradually became aware that my footsteps were reverberating behind me. At first I thought this was like the noise created by the tails of my skis biting into firmly packed snow when I am carving turns. Under some conditions it sounds exactly as if someone is skiing closely behind me, and more than once I have stopped to let them pass, only to discover that I was alone. Well, on that mountain path I speculated that the gravel was settling as I lifted the heel of each boot, or else my footsteps were simply echoing in the dense atmosphere.

Then again, as I proceeded, I started listening more closely, and I gradually realized that the steps behind me were occurring at a different pace than my own. For every three or four of my own footfalls, I heard one or two echoes. I stopped, and the other sounds ceased as well. I turned around and saw . . . nothing but mist. I continued, and the sounds behind me resumed, again at their own rhythm.

Now a chill ran down my spine. Had I offended the mountain gods by stripping down on Ben Nevis, and had they sent the Punisher to dispense retribution? I would not succumb without a fight. I stopped, raised my walking stick like a spear, and spun around. The sounds abruptly stopped, and I stood there, ready for battle. After a long pause in the silence of the mist, I started walking again.

After I had shown that I would defend myself, the echoing unexpectedly ceased, even though the path remained gravelly and the fog persisted. Ten or fifteen minutes later the secondary footfalls started again, this time ahead of me and at a much faster pace than I was keeping. I stepped off the path, spear at the ready. Moments later a figure appeared. It had arms and legs and a human head—a runner, a thin man in his forties. I quickly lowered my stick, and as the man passed, he grunted, "Lovely day," and was gone. After that I never heard another footstep other than my own.

I have two questions: Was there someone or something walking behind me before the runner jogged by? If not, then what were those earlier sounds?

Six months after the incident, while preparing to write this account, I surfed the internet looking for more information on the Big Grey Man of Ben MacDui. Much of it is predictably batty, coming from sources like "ghostclub.co.uk" and *Wormwood Chronicles*, but I also learned about J. Norman Collie, who was prominent in British mountaineering circles during the late nineteenth and early twentieth centuries. He led the first expedition to Nanga Parbat in the Himalayas, pioneered dozens of ascents in the Canadian Rockies, and served as president of the venerable Alpine Club. He was also a renowned organic chemist, professor at University College London, and Fellow of the Royal Society. He was definitely a cut above the ghost hunter crowd.

In Collie's 1943 write-up in the obituary notices of the Royal Society, the reporter mentions "a strain of mysticism in Collie" and quotes Collie's own report of an experience in the Cairngorms in 1891:

One day at Eastertime I was climbing Ben Macdhui. It was very misty and I was only able to see a few yards from me. When not very far from the summit, I suddenly heard footsteps in the snow behind me. Confident that some man was following me, I waited for him to join me, but the moment I stopped the footsteps also stopped. When I started on my way again, once more I heard the footsteps clearly. More than ever convinced that some man was on my track, I turned and ran back for some distance, but found no one. Once again I started on my way to the summit and once again I heard the footsteps which stopped whenever I stopped. When at last I reached the summit the footsteps did not stop but came nearer and nearer until they came right up to me. At that instant I was seized with an intolerable fright and I ran my hardest down the mountain side. No power on earth will ever take me up Ben Macdhui again.

In other accounts Collie is reported to have described the steps pursuing him as "three or four times the length of my own." He also spoke of an "eerie crunch, crunch" in the snow behind him, and he concluded that "there is something very queer about the top of Ben Macdhui." Other climbers have told of being driven into panic by some unseen force on the mountain. A few claim to have come face to face with Grey Man himself.

I had been rattled by the phantom footsteps on Ben MacDui, but nothing came of them, and I carried on. If I had known of the other accounts beforehand, the mysterious noises would probably have caused me to follow Collie in a mad dash down the mountain, and I wouldn't have stopped running until I reached the parking lot and loving embrace of Ranger McBuff.

AS IF TO COMPENSATE FOR my close encounters on the approach, the clouds parted just as I arrived at the summit of Ben MacDui, and I was bathed in sunlight. My only companions on the broad boulder field were a party of six Germans, and five of them were being bored to death by an older fellow who was blathering on—in German, of course—about how his camera had failed on Mount Kenya and how he now carries a spare. To prove his point, he dug into his pack and grandly produced two identical cameras. I was happy that I could barely understand him. His companions looked as if they were hoping for Grey Man to show up and drag him off.

One of the younger Germans and I looked at my map and discussed the route back. They had planned to walk the loop to the east of Cairn Lochan and then up and over the summit of Cairn Gorm, directly above the ski area. That route involved dropping down from Ben MacDui the way we had come, then skirting Cairn Lochan, and finally slogging eight hundred feet up the steep western slope of Cairn Gorm. The Germans hoped to descend the north side of Cairn Gorm to the top of the funicular and ride back down to the ski base. This plan sounded far more interesting than retracing my steps, and I felt ready for more climbing. I said I would do the loop as well, and what a great decision that was.

The Germans and I left the summit at the same time, but I didn't have to coordinate my pace with any companions, and I soon pulled ahead of the others. At a jewel of a tarn called Lochan Buidhe my earlier trail continued straight ahead, but I bore right. The next mile was a level traverse across a pristine grassy meadow at 3,700 feet. Along the way I stopped several times to look back at gently rounded Ben McDui. On an intervening ridge lay a large patch of snow, and I recalled reading that on a nearby peak called Braeriach there is a similar snowfield. Legend has it that if the Braeriach snow ever melts completely, the chief of Clan Grant will die within six months. If I were that man or woman, I would commit all of my resources to fight global warming.

A quarter-mile east of Cairn Lochan's high point, the path stopped abruptly at the top of a precipitous cliff. Below lay a deep concave valley, Coire an t-Sneachda. In Scottish English an amphitheater of this sort is called a "corrie," while American climbers generally use the French word *cirque*. In any language this was a spectacular feature, with a vertical drop of seven hundred feet to a cluster of small lakes on the valley floor. From this vantage point an on-again, off-again path wound its way to the right along the ridge, staying very near the corrie's rim. I don't mind exposure when I am engaged in technical climbing, but at times this track was too close to the edge for my comfort. Nevertheless, the ensuing mile to the base of Cairn Gorm was one of the most scenic mountain paths I have ever walked.

The top of Cairn Gorm is the sixth highest point in the United Kingdom. It had been shrouded all day, but just as on Ben Mac-Dui, the cloud lifted as I arrived. A collection of radio antennae showed that civilization was near. I paused to visit with a young German couple (they're everywhere!) and then descended a staircase to the Ptarmigan Station at the top of the funicular.

My final challenge of the day was getting into the station. A viewing deck one floor above ground level was filled with chattering people, but I was alone on the rocky soil below, and there was no obvious way to get in. As a concession to environmental groups, the builders of the funicular had agreed that summertime visitors would not be allowed to leave the viewing area. They were sealed in, just as I was sealed out. I was lucky that Grey Man was not in hot pursuit.

I circled the building twice before I found a nondescript door with what appeared to be a bell. I rang several times, and eventually the door opened a crack. A young man in a fleece jacket peered out, and when I asked if I could please be admitted to the inner sanctuary, he cautiously acquiesced. In a small, dimly lit room, I had to sign a register, attesting that I had gotten to that spot under my own power. If I wanted to leave the building later, the staff would verify my identity before I could be released into the wild. After being advised of my rights, I wound my way up a cement staircase, and when I finally entered the restaurant area, the smell of food and coffee was almost more than I could take in.

After a quick descent in the funicular, I returned to the ranger station to sign out. A different man was on duty, because McBuff had gone to the gym for a session of power lifting. The afternoon attendant told me that he had hiked all over the UK, and he firmly believed that the Ben MacDui–to–Cairn Gorm loop is the most beautiful walk in the entire country. With my limited experience to that point, I couldn't disagree.

19

Passing through the Kingdom

I HAD SCAMPERED UP THREE Scottish mountains in five days during an unusual spell of dry weather. I was on a roll of sorts, but I had to accept the fact that it was time to set my knapsack aside and accommodate the Italian Woman's desires for activities that involved no elevation gain. We would explore Scotland for the coming week as ordinary tourists and then make our way to Ireland for eighteen days featuring—I still couldn't believe it—the Riverdance festival and a twelve-day bus tour. The next four weeks would obviously take a big bite out of the summer, but I would keep calm and carry on.

We were planning to spend a few days in Inverness, thirty miles northwest of Aviemore. From there we would explore Loch Ness and then follow the North Sea coast eastward before turning south to Aberdeen and Dundee. While I was climbing Ben MacDui, the Italian Woman had been surfing for our next lodgings. What she found was that in city after city and in towns along the way, there was nothing available except rooms in a few ridiculously expensive deluxe hotels. Eventually, she looked at Edinburgh, but she couldn't find anything with all of our must-have requirements: parking, washer-dryer, and internet. She broadened her search and finally located a self-catering cottage not far from Edinburgh in a place called Fife.

When my wife described her search and informed me we were heading not north but south to a place we had never heard of, we sat back and laughed. Back in Omaha I work with a fellow who plans a month-long trip every July, normally in the

American West. One October he asked my advice about Washington's Olympic Peninsula. He was already making arrangements for the following summer, and he appeared to have laid out each day's activities and reserved a hotel room for every single night. Apparently, the only spontaneity in his trip would be where to stop for gas, although I suspected he had marked his map to show every Chevron station along his route.

I suppose there is merit to meticulous planning. If you really want to stay in a particular town, you can avoid disappointment by booking early. But for us, during our entire summer in Britain, I believe that the only thing we arranged more than a day or two in advance was the tour of Ireland. As a consequence, we would not see Inverness or Loch Ness, but we would visit a place called Fife.

LEAVING AVIEMORE, WE DROVE NORTHEAST along the River Spey. This was the beginning of the famed and commercially trademarked "Malt Whisky Trail." The previous evening a bartender named Ben had given me several samples of single malt, including his favorite, Knockando, which he pronounced *no can do*. Frankly, it all tasted like an ashtray, but I was willing to explore the subject a bit further, and I thought a distillery tour would be interesting. The Italian Woman—well past her Scotch phase—nixed the idea, and I was reminded that at this point in our travels, I was not calling the shots.

The map showed hamlets with intriguing names like Boat of Garten, which did not appear to be on any water, and Skye of Curr, where all dogs are of questionable parentage. My personal favorite was Maggieknockater, which suggests some sort of whiskey-fueled adventure with a girlfriend named Margaret. We bypassed these treasures and turned southeast at Speybridge, headed for more mundane places like Bridge of Brown and Bridge of Avon. Farther on, however, we came close to Roughpark, Sinnarhard, and Kildrummy—towns that are not for the faint of heart.

Along the way we were treated to impressive views westward, over fields and pastures, toward the Cairngorms Mountains. I was certain it was Ben MacDui that stood out as highest of the bunch, and it was satisfying to see the mountain from this perspective only a day after standing on its summit. Equally impressive was the Scotch broom along the roadside. *Cytisus scoparius* is a spectacular shrub with dazzling yellow flowers. To people from Seattle, however, it is the plant they love to hate.

In 1849 Captain Walter Colquhoun Grant, a British Army officer and a Scot, brought a touch of the Highlands to decorate his new settlement on Vancouver Island, and his Scotch broom quickly spread from Victoria to Nanaimo and Campbell River. It then caught the Tsawwassen ferry and established itself on the British Columbia mainland. In due course it became fed up with Canada's high taxes and migrated south into Washington. Many years later a brilliant Department of Transportation official decided that the hardy immigrant would be ideal for erosion control along Washington's roads, so government workers planted it in ditches and alongside freeway exit ramps.

Today, if you drive through Washington during May and June, you will be overwhelmed by a sea of yellow. It is an impressive sight, but the flowers stink to high heaven. Most Seattle people also blame Scotch broom for their springtime allergies, although studies have shown that its pollen is too heavy to be much of an irritant. The biggest problem is that the broom is intractable. It wantonly pushes aside native plants and destroys animal habitat; it has deep roots, massive numbers of seeds, and no natural enemies; it is impossible to eradicate. The shrub is now designated as a Class B noxious weed. Throughout the Pacific Northwest it is firmly believed that after a nuclear conflagration, the only surviving forms of life will be cockroaches and Scotch broom.

WHEN I WAS GROWING UP, Balmoral was a pipe tobacco, just as Pall Mall was a brand of cigarette. As I entered adulthood, I became aware of Balmoral as an estate in Scotland where

Queen Elizabeth sought refuge whenever her children set out to embarrass the royal family with their chaotic marriages and affairs. Perhaps because all of this news came from London, Balmoral Castle was always described as a gray and forbidding place where the atmosphere was bleak and the inhabitants perpetually brooding. As the Italian Woman and I plotted our trip from Aviemore to Fife, we noticed that the most direct route would take us directly past Balmoral, and my companion insisted that we stop for a look.

Like most Americans, I am puzzled by the concept of royalty. I find it hard to understand how self-respecting democratic nations like the Great Britain, the Netherlands, and Norway—countries with highly educated and sophisticated citizens—would perpetuate their monarchies. Under what sense of propriety should people be pampered from cradle to grave, bowed to and fawned over, and have their profiles put on postage stamps, just because they were born into a particular family? My Aunt Betty was once Queen for a Day on the 1950s television program, and to me it seems reasonable that everyone should have a chance to sit on a pedestal for a short time, perhaps by lottery. But royal by birth? It doesn't make sense.

On the other hand—and I would not be on this subject if there were not an "other" hand—I, along with many of my fellow ex-colonial republicans, am fascinated by all those dithering kings and queens and those misbehaving princes and princesses, particularly the ones in Britain. I am not into movie stars or sports celebrities, but I do love the goings-on at Buckingham, Kensington, and Windsor.

I am particularly intrigued by the Prince of Wales. I am several months older than he, and my middle name is Charles, so I grew up believing that he was named after me. My mother was aware of this, and on occasion she would feed my ego by calling me "Prince." As I have lived my life, trying to accomplish what I could, I have often wondered what I might have done if I had actually been a prince. Would I have finished college and gone to law school? Would I have worked as hard as I have? Or would I have adopted an air of insouciance and simply allowed my retainers to dress me, squeeze paste onto my toothbrush, and keep their lips planted firmly on my powdered buttocks? I will never know, but from afar I have enjoyed following Charles and his most peculiar life.

As if to blow the "gloomy Balmoral" stereotype right out of the water, it was another dazzlingly sunny day in Scotland when we paid our call. At a well-guarded entrance we boarded an open wagon and were towed onto the estate. There we learned that we would be allowed to see only one room inside the castle—the ballroom—but we would be free to roam the grounds with a map and audio set. As a result, we spent most of our time looking at flower gardens and cottages.

Most fascinating were the museum displays set up in horse barns. We were treated to photo montages, dioramas, and short films showing the Royals cavorting in their kilts. There was Charles himself walking through a field of heather, shotgun in hand, ready to shoot a grouse that some gamekeeper would no doubt release from a nearby ditch. Okay, that wasn't nice. The fact is, for most of my life I have been envious of Charles. As a boy, I longed to be him, and I vowed to marry his sister. Later I lusted after Diana, and I wanted to drive an Aston Martin. From today's perspective, however, looking from afar at the aging heir to the throne—seventy years in the wings, no real job, and no longer bonny—I'm grateful for my own career and my modest life . . . although I really would like to take a spin in that car.

IN A LAND OF MANY peninsulas, Fife is a modest one, and yet it has the temerity to proclaim itself the Kingdom of Fife. It is actually a county, but in ancient times it was a Pictish Celtic kingdom called Fib, so the modern day people of Fife—known as Fibbers—have some basis for their boast. This is the opposite of the situation in Colorado, where people outside the university town of Boulder sarcastically call it the "Kingdom of Boulder" to highlight the fact that its liberal politics put the community into a realm of its own.

Bounded on the north by the narrow Firth of Tay and on the south by the broader Firth of Forth, Fife is a distinct geographical area, but it is hardly isolated. It is bisected by the A92 and the M90, it is crisscrossed by National Rail, and it anchors major bridges across both of the fjords. The county serves as a bedroom community for countless workers who commute south to Edinburgh or north to Dundee—respectively, the second and fourth largest cities in Scotland. Even so, Fife is surprisingly pastoral, and our lodging—only a few miles off the A92—was in the boondocks.

Finding our cottage was one of those episodes that at the time you are sure will never come to a successful conclusion. The emailed driving directions were at best confusing, in reality pure Fibberish. Our quest involved poorly marked intersections, road closures, and a one-lane track on which we met a farm tractor pulling a wagon. We were further confounded by several phone calls to the cottage's owner, whose verbal suggestions were wildly dissimilar to his email, and our road atlas was of no help, because Coaltown of Burnturk and its seven buildings had been overlooked by the mapmaker. Luckily, July days are long in Scotland, and there was still plenty of light when we buzzed into Burnturk and nearly ran over the proprietor, who was standing in the roadway listening for the sound of my shifting gears. And just remember, I did all of this while driving on the left side of the road.

What a lovely little house it was—every bit as nice as our self-catering place in Northumberland, but this one was not propped against a busy highway. It had a garden, comfortable furnishings, and a well-equipped kitchen. After leaving Keswick, we had just spent seven days on the move, and we happily unpacked our bags and settled into what would be our home for a full week. It sat on a hillside and was called Granny's Cottage. I should say that I was perplexed by a placard in the bathroom that warned me not to deposit anything but my "personal production" into the toilet. Was this a reference to my academic publications? There was no mention of "peer review."

The nearest supermarket lay six miles away, in the town of Cupar, and so, bravely setting out with no assurance we would ever find our way back, we went shopping. Wishing to avoid unnecessary trips off our hill, we bought a week's worth of everything. Then, hoping the ice cream wouldn't melt during our second search for Coaltown of Burnturk, we headed home. We had tired of eating out during the past six days, and we were looking forward to some of the Italian Woman's home cooking. I had also grown weary of the big B&B breakfast, and I was happy that for the next week I could have my cold cereal every morning without feeling I should be getting my money's worth by eating the eggs and picnic beans. And now, having raised the subject of breakfast cereal, I feel I must address the matter of Weetabix.

I grew up in the 1950s, when the primary sponsors of kids' television programs were Kellogg's, Post, and General Mills. The Cheerios Kid was always able to rescue Cheerios Sue, because "he's feelin' his Cheerios." Tony Tiger pitched for Kellogg's Sugar Frosted Flakes ("They're Grrrrreeeeat!"). There was even one called Sugar Corn Pops ("Sugar Pops are tops!"). There seemed to be an unwritten rule that other than the amount of sugar coating, the prime virtue for any cereal was crunchiness—more than looks, flavor, or if it was mentioned at all, nutrition. The proof of a proper crunch ("Snap, Crackle, Pop") was that no milk ever extracted from any cow could penetrate your flakes, nuggets, or amorphous bits. The ideal cereal was one that floated on top of the milk, like a cork. If it floats, it crunches. If it crunches, it's good.

In Britain they apparently took the opposite approach. The picture on the Weetabix package screams: "Whole grain! Fiber! Healthy!" I wanted all of that, so in Cupar I bought a box, and the next morning I eagerly put a biscuit into my bowl and poured on the milk. In an instant—really, a split second—it was a puddle of goop. I thought something was wrong, so I poured that bowlful into the sink and tried again. This time I put a dry biscuit into the bowl and just looked at it sternly. There, right before my eyes, it disintegrated. Well, I thought, maybe it is supposed to be this way. I dutifully added milk and tried a spoonful of the mush. On my lips it felt wet and cold, like a dog's nose. Was this a dog's breakfast? No, it looked more like a dog's personal production. It was too much to bear. I reached for a slice of bread and popped it into the toaster. The whole episode leaves me wondering whether the British reputation for drollness is somehow connected to their taste in breakfast cereal.

OUR WEEK IN FIFE WAS a pleasant mixture of relaxing at Granny's Cottage and setting out on day trips. We drove one morning to St. Andrews, past several golf courses that looked a lot like every one I have ever seen—green spots, little flags, patches of sand. I wondered what would possess golfers from Japan, Korea, and every other country in the world to make the pilgrimage. Yes, it is supposedly the birthplace of the sport, but it seems a long way to travel to chase a little white ball across a lawn. On the other hand, I was smitten by the old city center, and I fancied myself someday giving a lecture in a red robe at the renowned University of St. Andrews, which was celebrating its six hundredth anniversary. To be fair, the Japanese golfers would no doubt wonder what would be the fun in that.

Unexpectedly, at a nondescript St. Andrews café called Jannetta's, we found a sensational plate of food. The smoked salmon was Scottish enough, but it was served with a jalapeño-laced tzatziki, cilantro couscous, and crostini with spinach and melted goat cheese. I'm reeling after just writing that sentence, but the diverse dishes complemented each other like a golfer and a grass stain. Even more surprising was the piece of "butter tablet" that was served with our coffee. It's a Scottish spin on fudge, with an intense caramel flavor. Neither of us is much of a candy lover, but this sweet was instantly addictive. I never thought I would be writing this, but here you are: you must visit Scotland for its food.

The same afternoon we drove to Anstruther, a coastal village, to find its famous Fish Bar. I hardly qualify as an expert on the subject, but I now understand those who believe the restaurant's fish and chips to be the finest in the world. Locally caught haddock in a light and crispy batter—that's the whole story. The place was so confident of its food that as you stand in a snaking queue (oh, yes, you must queue up), you are greeted by a sign that invites you to nip off to one of the restaurant's competitors for a little something to eat while you are waiting your turn for the premium stuff. That's a bit snotty, but the Anstruther Fish Bar delivers the goods. We ate ours on a park bench at the marina.

None of our travel information recommended Dundee, but we wanted to see the city because Dundee was the name of our neighborhood in Omaha. The waterfront area, along the Firth of Tay, was torn up by a massive renovation project, but still we felt there was something appealing about the city. Perhaps it was the shrimp cocktail at a firthside restaurant. Perhaps it was seeing the *Discovery*, the ship used by Robert Falcon Scott on his one-way trip to the South Pole. Or the modern shopping center wrapped around an old church. For whatever reason this city provided us a pleasant Sunday afternoon.

We did a rather bad job of visiting Edinburgh. I am quite certain it is one of the nicest capitals in Europe, and we had wanted to spend a week there, but the best we managed was a day trip by train from Cupar. That took us to Waverley, a station in the center of the old city. Probably due to lack of imagination, we found ourselves back in the same places we had visited during the shore excursion on our 2008 cruise. We walked up and down the Royal Mile, chose not to pay the outrageous entrance fee to Edinburgh Castle, and drank a Guinness at the same pub. We again browsed the tartan shops and bought nothing. We tried for tea at Clarinda's but found that five o'clock was too late, so we jumped on a train and left. Frankly, we disappointed ourselves, and we vowed to return and give Edinburgh its due.

WHEREVER WE WENT IN SCOTLAND, we saw signs and posters announcing the local Highland games. There are more than eighty of these events each summer, and we wanted to see what all the fuss was about. Nearest to Burnturk were the games at Burntisland, across from Edinburgh on the Firth of Forth, and they are touted as Scotland's second oldest, having started in 1652. Now if you look at the word *Burntisland*, doesn't it make sense to pronounce it as *Burntiss Land*? That's how we said it, and when we asked our proprietor for directions, he was perplexed.

"Burntiss Land?"

"Yes, we want to go see the Highland games there."

"Highland games . . . Do you mean Burnt Island?"

Once there, we had to negotiate the largest amusement park midway I have ever seen. We felt violated just walking through it, but beyond the cotton candy and thrill rides we found the grassy pitch, a fenced-in oval where the contests were held. Interestingly, in contrast to thirty thousand carnival goers, the number of spectators at the competition seemed to be no more than a few hundred, and they all seemed to be related to the participants. We found a seat at the far side of the field.

The games themselves were a three-ring circus, albeit a modest one with a homemade flavor. On one side, children in Scottish costumes danced on a raised platform. Around the perimeter there were running races for different age groups. All winners were rewarded with a ribbon and a kiss from Mum. A local charity sold hot dogs and sodas at a kiosk. For the most part it felt like a Lutheran church picnic or a small town Fourth of July in the American heartland, with a large contingent of paunchy bagpipers.

It was the third venue that attracted us. There, eight beefy lads in kilts provided what for us was the day's primary entertainment—the heavy events. The contestants had to prove their mettle by tossing a large rock (the "stone put"), hurling a weight attached to a rod (the "Scottish hammer throw"), and flinging an iron ball attached to a chain (the "flinging an iron ball attached to a chain"). Most fascinating was the "weight over the bar," in which the competitor stood with his back to a raised bar and then, with one hand, flung a fifty-six-pound cube of metal back and over the bar. With his non-throwing hand he held his kilt in place to avoid titillating the gray-haired ladies who sat with binoculars pointed toward his private parts. I later learned that dark underwear was mandatory, to keep the competition focused on how strong the man was.

The caber toss was the final event and most iconic for all Highland games. The idea is to vertically hoist a telephone pole and flip it away from yourself so that it falls end over end. Only half of the competitors were successful, but it was an impressive display. The crowd favorite among the eight strongmen was a fellow from Iceland, of all places. He sported a shaved head, bushy red beard, and perpetual smile. The winner, however, was a local man, a blond giant aptly named Bruce Robb.

On our last day in Granny's Cottage, I visited with our host, Raymond, who had been sitting in the garden playing gentle melodies on an acoustic guitar. He told me that he had built the bungalow for his mother when his father died, and Raymond and his wife had moved into the family home next door. When his mother passed away, they decided to rent out the smaller place. He said that one day he and his wife will move into the cottage and their son will take over the main house. "We only live a short while," he reflected. "I see that. My time will run out, but this house will remain, and others will live in it." There was a hint of melancholy in Raymond's words, and yet he seemed content. He recognized that in this ancient land—the Kingdom of Fife—each day could bring pleasure, but in the end he was just passing through.

20

Dancing in the Streets

AFTER A WEEK OF EXCURSIONS from Granny's Cottage, I still managed to get us lost as we left Coaltown of Burnturk for the last time. Even now, looking at a detailed map of Fife, I can't fathom where we were or how it happened. After trying this way and that, leftward and rightward, downhill and back up, we finally lurched onto a road that connected us to the A92 at Glenrothes. From there it took five and a half hours to leave Scotland, bypass the Lake District, and make our way into Wales.

Our ferry to Ireland was from Holyhead, a port town on the Isle of Anglesey in the northwestern corner of Wales. As we entered the island, we paused to top off the car's fuel tank in the town of Llanfairpwllgwyngyllgogerychwyrndrobwllllantysiliogogoch, the bane of all typesetters. The community originally bore what locals considered to be the simple name of Llanfair Pwllgwyngyll, but it adopted the longer version in the 1860s, hoping a new image would attract tourists. (Hot Springs, New Mexico, did something similar in 1950, when it renamed itself Truth or Consequences for the privilege of hosting once each year a popular radio program of that name.) On Anglesey the official translation of the town's name is "Saint Mary's Church in the hollow of the white hazel near a rapid whirlpool and the Church of St. Tysilio of the red cave," but this is offered with a wink, and inside sources confirm that the actual meaning is "If you try saying this and can't otherwise speak the Welsh language, you are a fool."

Fully aware that they are being taken for a ride, the English simply refer to the town as "L" (visiting Spaniards call it "el L," while Israelis say "El Al"). The Monty Python ensemble most likely had Wales in the back of their minds when they wrote a sketch about a German baroque composer by the name of Johann Gambolputty de von Ausfern-schpleden-schlitter-crasscrenbon-fried-digger-dingle-dangle-dongle-dungle-burstein-von-knacker-thrasher-apple-banger-horowitz-ticolensic-grander-knotty-spelltinkle-grandlich-grumblemeyer-spelterwasser-kurstlich-himble-eisen-bahnwagen-gutenabend-bitte-ein-n-ürnburger-bratwürstle-gerspurten-mitz-weimache-luber-hundsfut-gumberaber-shönendanker-kalbsfleisch-mittler-aucher von Hautkopft of Ulm.

At the L gas station I handed the cashier a twenty-pound note from the Bank of Scotland—while traveling up north we had learned that both the Bank of England and Bank of Scotland issue British currency, and both are valid throughout the UK. The young woman did a double take and then turned to her much older boss and showed him the money. They had an animated conversation in Welsh, and after he had expounded on the implications of the small country's membership in a united kingdom, she turned to me with an awkward smile and said, "It's okay." I responded, "I'm glad, because otherwise I don't know how we would get the petrol back out of the tank."

Just beyond L lay the village of Gaerwen, where we were to return our rental car. We had rented from a major company that for present purposes I will call "Shady Lane." Its Gaerwen office was a portable trailer in a quiet industrial park, where two young men greeted us and started inspecting the vehicle. One of them, Robert, quickly pointed out some damage to the front end grill, and I said, "That was there when I picked up the car in Worcester, and they said it would be no problem." He asked me to accompany him into the trailer while he called Worcester. The Italian Woman remained in the car. After a brief wait for information, Robert said thanks, hung up, and cheerfully reported: "They confirmed the damage. So everything is fine." I was highly relieved.

Robert and I returned to the car, where the other man, Gareth, stood shaking his head. "Mr. Sieberson, I want you to see this." Near the rear of the vehicle, just ahead of the left taillight, was a deep scratch around three inches long. I asked Gareth to measure it, and it was a quarter-inch longer than the maximum allowed; thus, it was my responsibility. I responded that I had inspected the car that morning and the mark hadn't been there. That was true; I had given the car a careful going-over, and since then it had never left our sight, and nobody had come near it. What was most suspicious was that the scratch was in a concave, sculpted part of the rear side panel, and nothing could have rubbed against the vehicle at that spot without causing other marks. The damage appeared to be deliberately inflicted, as you might with a screwdriver or the tip of a knife.

I protested, but Gareth was unmoved. Rules are rules, and a contract is a contract. He filled out a damage report and explained that my credit card would be charged one thousand dollars. Then, after the repair had been made by an independent body shop in Llandudno, I would be refunded anything above their invoice. This was outrageous, but unfortunately, there was no time for a protracted discussion because we had to catch our boat to Ireland.

By prearrangement Robert drove us to Holyhead to the Irish Ferries terminal. He was friendly and wanted to chat about this and that, but I was seething. I asked him if Shady Lane received a kickback on the cost of the repair. Oh, no, not at all. I asked him whether employees were trained to "key" a car and then charge the customer for the damage. Certainly not. I told him the scratch should not receive a Rolls-Royce treatment—our car was a Vauxhall. He agreed. I told him I would need full paperwork on the repair. He promised to provide it. I told him I had been a Shady Lane customer for many years and I didn't deserve to be jerked around. He assured me I would be treated fairly. When it finally soaked in that I was really upset, Robert became apologetic and said he would do whatever he could to help us. He seemed sincere, and he struck me as an enterprising young man, but I doubted anything would come of it. When we parted in Holyhead, he told me not to worry. That was of little consolation because I was convinced that we had been shafted.

While waiting to board our ship, we sat near an Irish mother with five young children. The older two—a girl and a boy, probably five and six—couldn't sit still. Instead, they ran in circles, jumped on the furniture, threw things, and generally acted as if they were on amphetamines. Rather than get up off her bench to calm them down, the mother—who was nursing a baby—just screamed repeatedly. The children were obviously used to this because they ignored her. At last the woman set the infant down, covered her breast, and with arms raised, she lunged at the little malefactors. All of us spectators drew in a breath. The woman swung a fist directly at the boy's head but stopped it an inch short of contact. Then she turned to the girl and did the same. Meekly, the children returned to sit with her—for about five minutes. Then it all started again. First the rental car and now mayhem in the waiting room—our trip to Ireland was off to a dubious start. If we hadn't prepaid for everything, I would have suggested heading back to Scotland or the Lake District.

THE *ULYSSES* BRIGHTENED MY MOOD. It was a clean, modern ship, loaded with amenities. We ate well in the restaurant and then chose a movie in the two-screen cinema. Later we enjoyed cappuccinos and pastries. We have traveled on many day ferries in the United States and Europe, and in comparison to the *Ulysses*, all the others resemble transit buses. We sailed to Dublin in style.

Through the Irish Ferries the Italian Woman had booked three nights in a hotel, the Regency. On arrival we discovered that it was nowhere near the city center, as we had expected, but out on the road to Dublin's airport. It was a building well past its prime, obviously catering to low-budget tourists on package deals—come to think of it, that's exactly who we were. As we were checking in, an American family from Colorado was departing, having taken one look at their room and concluding that it was not acceptable. Ours was tolerable, not quite bad enough to cause us to leave. Our primary problem was that the room faced west. It was a hot afternoon, and there was no air conditioning. Later, after dark, I found that if I left the door and window open, a slight breeze would pass through. We kept the lights off to avoid attracting insects, and I sat next to the window, working on my laptop. The unintended result was that folks passing in the hallway would stop and stare at the apparently naked man whose face and shirtless torso were bathed in the blue light of a computer screen. Actually, I was wearing gym shorts, but there was no way for our neighbors to know that, so I had given them something to write home about.

My only previous experience in Dublin had been a two-day business trip from Amsterdam in 1980. At that time my overwhelming impression was that the Irish capital was dingy and depressed—nothing like London, Paris, or Amsterdam. Ireland had joined the Common Market seven years earlier, but it didn't feel like modern Europe. What a surprise, then, to see Dublin in the twenty-first century. It was such a different city, with public art, an attractive riverside promenade, and well-dressed people scurrying about. Glass and steel office buildings are not always appealing, but they do reflect commerce and affluence, and Dublin had its share. Ireland experienced its "Celtic Tiger" boom years in the 1990s, when the English-speaking nation with low taxes became the European location of choice for many American firms, especially in the technology field. The 2008 recession and a bursting property bubble hit the country especially hard, but by the following decade the economy was percolating once again. Wherever we walked in the city center, it felt alive. Spit and polish may not eliminate the undercurrent of melancholy in the Irish soul, but today's Dublin is vibrant. It is also expensive, so much so that you will think twice before ordering that pint of Guinness in its hometown.

IRIS STEP DANCING HAS ANCIENT roots, but its modern popularity began in 1994, when a seven-minute number called "Riverdance" was performed at the Eurovision Song Contest, whose venue that year was Dublin. The piece enjoyed an enthusiastic reception, which spurred its creators to expand the work into a full-length show. It has been a phenomenal success ever since, with three different touring companies now performing around the world. At the same time, Irish dance studios have sprung up in virtually every country on earth, attracting countless fleet-footed young girls—and the odd boy—who dream of a career under the lights.

Before visiting Dublin, when I thought of Irish dancing, my mind's eye saw a line of men and women standing stiffly at attention, moving only their feet and looking as if they were trying not to break wind. If they weren't holding something inside, wouldn't they relax and let loose? My attitude was no doubt influenced by a Seattle television comedy show, *Almost Live*. Poking fun at a rural area southeast of the city and at the *Riverdance* show itself, which was heavily promoting its performances in Seattle, the *Almost Live* troupe did a sketch called "Green River Dance." The players wore plaid lumberjack shirts, jeans, and work boots, and their number was a Pacific Northwest raspberry to what many people viewed as an overhyped and overpriced stage production.

Despite the naysayers, *Riverdance* continued to draw an audience, and after two decades of success, the show's producers felt it appropriate to celebrate by returning to Dublin and staging a weekend festival called Riverdance—The Gathering. Through our Irish Ferries package, we had tickets to every event. Starting as the uninitiated (and on my part, the skeptical), we would undergo a total immersion.

The first affair took place on Saturday afternoon in a street outside Merrion Square Park. The brochure promised, "*Riverdance* will teach the audience how to dance . . . and then everyone will be invited to show off their Irish dancing skills, whether experts or beginners." An enthusiastic man with a microphone ran up and down the street, forming lines and organizing the routine. With some trepidation the Italian Woman and I stepped forward. The MC described the first sequence as "very basic, no more than lift, toe, heel, kick, cross, kick, stomp, now other foot lift, toe, heel, kick, cross, kick, stomp. Okay, everybody got it? Now music, and here we go!" Actually, we never made it to *toe*. We stood there like mannequins, which is exactly what Irish dancers are when they stop moving their feet. A blonde girl named Kelly O'Cork took pity on us and slowly demonstrated the pattern, inviting us to follow. We simply couldn't manage, and she graciously left it for us to say, "Thanks, we'll just watch." We retreated to the ice cream stand, laughing at ourselves, but in retrospect let it be said that for a fleeting moment—a single leg lift in a Dublin street—we were part of *Riverdance*.

That evening we sat on chairs in the same street for an outdoor concert of *Riverdance* music accompanied by film clips from the past two decades of performances. Dancing stars, musicians, and producers stepped onto the stage to reminisce about their experiences. Not having seen the show, we quickly grew tired of the anecdotes, but we came to appreciate how *Riverdance* had put Ireland on the map. Then, on Sunday morning, we gathered at the river to watch 1,629 dancers from eighty-five countries perform the longest Irish line dance ever. In so doing, they crushed the record of 652 previously set in Nashville, Tennessee. Officials from Guinness World Records were on hand to observe and bestow their imprimatur. It was quite a spectacle. If we had had more success on Saturday afternoon, we might have been in that line, but I suspect someone from Guinness would have spotted us and disqualified the entire event.

We finally saw the real show on Sunday evening at the Gaiety Theatre. The idea of any big stage production, such as a Broadway musical, does not appeal to me in the abstract. But then, it always happens that when the lights dim and the curtain rises, I'm a dolt who is easily entertained by all the flash and dazzle. So it was with *Riverdance*. I have to say that I was puzzled by the flamenco and Russian numbers, but the show's creators must have realized that at some point the audience would want to see an arm lifted. The foreign segments were reminiscent of Tchaikovsky, who didn't hesitate to spice up his ballets with everything but a dancing samovar.

My only complaint about the show was that I sat behind a man with the World's Largest Head, and I had to bob from side to side to see around it. It was not as miserable as the time I sat next to OCD Woman at a performance of *Tosca* in Perugia. In thirty-second cycles she would cross her legs, open her cell phone, snap it shut, fiddle with her necklace, recross her legs, and say something in a loud whisper to the man on her other side. By golly she was wired—so much so that during the first intermission a dozen people in the vicinity simply packed up and left. The *Riverdance* Head was less annoying, but really, I should have called the Guinness people to come to the Gaiety with a measuring tape.

BETWEEN THE DANCE FESTIVAL AND the start of our bus tour, we had three days to explore Dublin on our own. We extended our stay at the Regency because the Italian Woman couldn't bear the thought of packing and moving if she didn't have to. She knew that our eleven nights on the tour would be spent in eight different cities, and she wanted as little disruption as possible beforehand. At the Regency she wouldn't even transfer to a room on the shady side of the building.

Our first destination was Christ Church, a Church of Ireland (Anglican/Episcopal) cathedral whose choir had taken part in the world premiere of Handel's *Messiah* in 1742. A wall of the church's nave is noticeably out of perpendicular and proudly called "the leaning wall of Dublin." More impressive was the crypt, which runs the entire length of the large building and is the largest burial chamber in the British Isles. It is also the oldest structure in Dublin, dating back to the eleventh century. I tend to be a bit claustrophobic, but this cellar was so large that I felt comfortable wandering around. Remarkably, there is a coffee shop down there, and we decided to sit down for a sandwich. As we ate, I commented to the Italian Woman that I had never spent so much time in a crypt. Without a moment's hesitation she responded, "At your age you'd better get used to it."

Sticking to our hard-and-fast "one monument per day" rule, we waited until the following afternoon to visit St. Patrick's Cathedral. I was excited to see it. In this, one of the most Catholic of all nations, to visit the cathedral of Ireland's patron saint would be special. The building didn't prove to be as magnificent as Notre Dame or Chartres, but the thirteenth-century Gothic structure was grand enough. As we moved about St. Patrick's interior, various signs explained that this church had welcomed Methodists and Huguenots at times of persecution. Imagine, a Catholic congregation with such a generous and ecumenical spirit. I began to have a new appreciation for Irish priests and bishops, whom I had always thought to be conservative and inflexible. It was only near the end of our visit that the truth came out: St. Patrick's was not Roman Catholic at all but Church of Ireland. That explained why much was made of Jonathan Swift, author of *Gulliver's Travels* and onetime dean of the cathedral, and his complex relationship with a woman named Esther Johnson. I wondered how many Irish American Catholics on pilgrimage to Dublin had swooned over this cathedral without realizing that it is Protestant. Shaking our heads, we left the church and made for a pub.

We had put in many hours on the streets of Dublin, so on our third day we left the city center on a local train to the seaside village of Howth. Located on a rugged peninsula, the town is both a bedroom suburb of the capital city and a perfect day trip for tourists and Dubliners alike. Walking along the harbor past a fleet of commercial fishing boats, we felt as if we were at Salmon Bay in Seattle, and we developed a craving for seafood. At several points along the pier there were restaurants, but we were aghast that the price for a simple plate of haddock and chips was well over twenty dollars. We weren't *that* hungry. I wanted to stop and ask what was so special about their food, and if it was that great, why not charge a hundred? Instead, we just walked by, satisfied that we were two tourists who were not going to be ripped off. Back in the village we found a "chippy," a little stand with perfectly serviceable fish and chips for six dollars. We ate them on a park bench, never once wishing for a white tablecloth.

We spent that evening in our room organizing ourselves for the bus tour, which began the next day. I have always wanted to end a chapter in the fashion of Stephen King or John Saul, and I think this is the appropriate place: Steve realized that regardless of what had got him to that dark moment, they were going to get on a bus, and it was too late to turn back. Then the screaming began.

21

Don't Talk about the Troubles

THE MUCH-ANTICIPATED TOUR STARTED on Thursday afternoon at the Conrad Dublin, an establishment so self-important
that it doesn't use the word *hotel* in its name. It was elegant, but
we were not happy when a rain shower forced us to eat in the
hotel's lobby bar, where an order of fish and chips was priced
like those on the pier in Howth. Still, the waiter assured us,
"These are no ordinary fish and chips." True enough. The pieces
of cod were tiny, and the chips turned out to be long, curving
potato sticks jutting from a cup of mayonnaise, like a bouquet
of unopened calla lilies. The food was presented on a faux-Asian
square plate. Add a couple of twelve-dollar beers, and the meal
was indeed far from ordinary.

Our tour group—nine men and eighteen women—assembled
in a conference room, where we met our guide, Declan, and our
driver, Roy. Declan, who also answered to "Dec," began with a
lecture: If we didn't wear our seatbelts on the bus, we would be
thrown into Maze Prison with a few remaining IRA terrorists.
Don't drink the water anywhere in Ireland; it's safe, but it tastes
bad. Don't use the bus toilet except in a dire emergency; if you
do, Roy will pull over to the side of the road and the other pas-
sengers will sing a song until you are finished, and then they
will applaud you as you return to your seat. Don't be late, ever;
the difference between a tourist and a local is ten minutes—if
you are more than ten minutes late, you will be left behind.
The Irish electrical current can kill you; that's why there are no
outlets in the bathrooms, and that's why you should never use

a handheld dryer when your hair is wet. Seating assignments on the bus will be posted every morning, to give everyone an equal chance to sit up front and close to Dec, now in his thirty-eighth year as Ireland's greatest guide.

After the briefing the group made an excursion to Dublin Castle, a rather unremarkable building. The only thing of note was an offhand remark by a castle guide. She said that the white makeup worn in Georgian times was made with beeswax, and if you stood too close to a fireplace, the cosmetic would run and you would "lose face." If you kept your distance or used a small screen to ward off the heat, you could "save face." It occurred to me that learning this sort of thing might be the benefit of a guided tour. If I had wandered Dublin Castle by myself, I would have spent the rest of my life without this piece of trivia. Then again, now that I've written it here, I'll never be able to use it again.

THE NEXT MORNING WE WERE up at six o'clock. I need to repeat that: the next morning we were up at six o'clock. For many people that is normal, but the Italian Woman and I had gotten ourselves thoroughly onto Madrid time—that meant breakfast at eleven, lunch at three or four, and dinner at nine or ten. At six in the morning we were just getting into REM sleep. In Ireland the set routine would be that our suitcases had to be in the hall by seven. Then we would eat breakfast, and the bus would leave at eight. Fortunately, in three cities we would stay two nights, so on a few mornings we would not have to deposit our bags into the hallway, but even then, we would set out at eight. This tour would test our mettle.

Standing bleary-eyed in the Conrad's lobby at seven, wondering where the breakfast room was, we were barely functioning. Trying to pep things up, I looked at the Italian Woman, and in my best bright and cheery voice I chortled, "Good morning, Sweet Cheeks." A nearby porter turned his head and responded, "Good morning!"

After Dublin we would spend two nights in Belfast, one in Londonderry, two in Westport, one in Bunratty, two in Killarney, and one in Waterford. The final night would be back in Dublin. This itinerary worked a counterclockwise swirl around the coast of the island, with many stops along the way. Given how slothful my wife and I are when it comes to sightseeing—a day's tour is often no more than strolling and sitting at sidewalk cafés—we would see far more attractions in a week and a half of touring Ireland than we had seen during five months in Spain.

As we drove north out of Dublin, Declan reminded us that we would spend the next several days in Northern Ireland, where the wounds of sectarian strife have not yet fully healed. As a result, he said: "Don't be an idiot. Don't talk about religion or politics up there." He then commenced a rambling lecture about religion and politics in the North, and he never really let up until we returned to the Republic of Ireland three days later. Nearly everything we saw reminded our guide of some nasty business between Protestants and Catholics. His favorite topic was the Troubles, the period of strife that began in 1969 with protests in Belfast and Londonderry, and officially ended with the 1998 Good Friday Agreement. Dec claimed to have personally witnessed or taken part in many significant events, and he assumed we would be fascinated to hear of his exploits. Serious as the Troubles were, his stories and the gentle swaying of the bus put most of us to sleep.

Once over the all-but-invisible border and into Northern Ireland, we stopped in the village of Downpatrick, where Saint Patrick is supposedly buried in the churchyard of Down Cathedral. The church sits on a hill surrounded by trees and water, a setting the Druids would have considered sacred, and that is why Patrick is said to have chosen the place to preach the Gospel. But the man was even more culturally sensitive or, if you prefer, wily. He took the pagan sun symbol and imposed it on the Christian cross, thus creating what we now call the Celtic cross. The saint was also something of an engineer, because the sun circle served as a structural element to support the cross's horizontal arms.

Inside Down Cathedral an animated tour guide named Joy talked about Saint Patrick, and she proceeded to debunk all of our favorite myths. Patrick's color is not green but blue. He didn't drive the snakes out of Ireland because there weren't any to start with. He didn't use the shamrock as a symbol. On the saint's day, March 17, locals do not dye their hair and drink green beer; instead, they come to the cathedral for an ecumenical service. Wait just a minute—an ecumenical service? How is that possible? It turns out that just like St. Patrick's Cathedral in Dublin, the saint's own Down Cathedral is not Roman Catholic but Church of Ireland. It does make sense, actually. Patrick was born in England, and he preached in Protestant Northern Ireland (I know what you're thinking, but give me this and stay with me). In earlier chapters this book has exposed the scandalous truth about black pudding and Weetabix. Now the biggest shocker of them all: beloved Patrick, patron saint and cultural icon of Catholic Ireland, was Anglican.

AS WE SETTLED INTO THE Belfast Hilton for the first of two nights, the Italian Woman and I discussed the possibility of my leaving the group the next day and climbing a mountain. I had floated this idea several days earlier, and she had not rejected it out of hand. Now, since she knew she could tour the Titanic Museum with our group, it didn't matter much to her if I headed off on my own, but I shouldn't expect her to justify my actions to Declan or anyone else. She also reminded me that we needed to do some laundry, and since the hotel service was ridiculously expensive, we would have to find a self-serve place. I suggested that we take care of it when I returned from my climb or later in Westport or Killarney.

Online research had turned up the fact that along the southern coast of Ulster, between Dublin and Belfast, stands a group of peaks called the Mountains of Mourne. Belfast native C. S.

Lewis visited them as a boy, and he wrote that "under a particular light [they] made me feel that at any moment a giant might raise his head over the next ridge" and that "one almost expects to see a march of dwarfs dashing past." That mysterious landscape inspired the realm of Narnia, and I could travel there without passing through a wardrobe.

The Mournes lie in County Down, thirty miles south of Belfast and not far from Downpatrick. They are the highest mountains in Northern Ireland, positioned just above the coastal town of Newcastle, and tallest of the group is Slieve Donard. *Slieve* is the Gaelic word for "mountain"; Donard was a local Christian saint. The peak's natural elevation (the os map refers to it as "living rock") is 2,785 feet, although its trig point sits at 2,799 feet on a stone tower. If I could climb Slieve Donard and then Snowdon on our return to Wales, I would have ascended the highest mountains in the four countries of the United Kingdom— enough, perhaps, to satisfy my peculiar need for a definable set of accomplishments.

I would have only one day available to attempt Slieve Donard, and the Mountains of Mourne are one of the wettest places in Ireland, so the weather would have to cooperate. Still, I would have a shot.

Our Saturday in Belfast dawned sunny and warm, and I began my excursion with a mile and a half walk through the city center to the Botanic Station. As I approached the train and bus terminal, I came across the prominent entrance to Sandy Row, a neighborhood that has been a hotbed for the ultra-loyalist Ulster Defence Association and was the scene of politically motivated violence during the Troubles. Despite somewhat inflammatory murals celebrating the Protestant freedom fighters and their hero William, Prince of Orange, the neighborhood appeared tidy and tame on that pleasant summer morning.

After purchasing my ticket to Newcastle, I bought food and water. The double-decker Ulsterbus left at ten. I took a seat on the upper level just behind the stairwell, where I had an excellent view to the front. As the trip began, I reflected on Sandy Row and the Troubles. From my perspective Northern Ireland was artificially carved out of the Irish island as a result of what today appear to have been petty differences. Then again, aren't most national boundaries arbitrary? Why is there both a Canada and a United States? Shouldn't at least Anglophone Canada and the United States be a single nation? Why shouldn't Mexico and the Spanish-speaking countries of Central America be combined? Australia makes sense—no artificial boundaries there. The Irish people have their own island, too, and recent steps toward reunification seem long overdue.

I turned my attention to the people around me. All appeared to be locals heading for a day at the seaside. A man, looking the part of a divorced father with custody for the weekend, sat across from me feeding potato chips and Coke to three freckle-faced boys. Behind them slouched a couple with facial piercings and headphones. A group of four young women chatted merrily in the rear. The older folks had stayed below, to avoid the awkward stairway.

A family of sorts sat in the front row, directly behind the upper windshield. I could see heads and shoulders from behind, but the glass also served as a mirror to their front sides. On the right-hand aisle seat was a very attractive woman, midtwenties, hair colored dark red. She was slightly plump and joyously buxom. Her four-year-old son sat on her right; that is, he sat when he was not bouncing across the aisle to be with his grandmother. The older woman was forty-five or fifty, slightly heavier and less comely than her daughter, but even more chesty. She wore a low-scooped spandex top that revealed tattoos on her upper back and a substantial amount of cleavage in front. The odd man in the group was the fourth member, a stringy-haired, skinny chap in his thirties who sat to the left of the grandmother. Most of the time he was slumped in his seat, his shoes planted on the windshield. He was inebriated. He kept tugging the older woman onto his lap, and he would slide his hands up and down her body. Now and then she would sit up and rearrange herself, only to be drawn back down. The little boy wanted to get up close to the action, but his mother kept retrieving him, trying to distract him with pieces of chocolate.

Now the man lowered his feet, raised his head, and broke into an improvised song: "We're goin' to Newcastle, feckin' Newcastle, feckin' Newcastle. We're goin' to feckin' Newcastle; Newcastle, here we come." He laughed out loud at his cleverness, and the older woman laughed too. He sang it again. As he began for the third time, the woman placed an index finger across his lips and said, "Shush." He responded by resuming his slouch, pulling her down, and sliding his hand under her spandex.

We passed tide flats, a cement plant, and several trailer parks, and then we arrived in the singing fellow's Newcastle. I quickly left the bus. I did not want to see *The Further Adventures of the Thin Man*.

THE ULSTERBUS TERMINAL SAT AT the north end of Newcastle's Main Street, while the mountain trailhead lay more than a mile away at the south end. This forced me to negotiate the entire town center, which was awash in visitors. The street was festooned with little flags and lined with souvenir shops and cafés. The scene reminded me of Main Street in Breckenridge, Colorado, which—depending on your frame of mind—can strike you as festive or tacky. I felt so fortunate to be heading for a mountain that I didn't mind the tourist trap feel of the place.

Just to the left of the commercial strip lay the sea and miles of beach; just ahead, and towering over everything, stood the prominent green pyramid of Slieve Donard. To get to its summit, I would need to gain every one of its 2,785 feet of elevation. Beyond the commercial strip I found a grassy parking field and on its far side a gate that ushered me into the Donard Forest. It was nearly noon when I stepped onto the Glen River Path. The trail was rocky and hard to follow at first, with false leads running in all directions. Eventually, it became more obvious, and the river on my left showed the way uphill.

Half an hour under way, I emerged from the forest into an open valley with slopes of grass and heather. The stream continued to rush and gurgle as it danced over large boulders. It was a peaceful scene, but something peculiar was in the air. When I met a group of walkers coming down from Slieve Donard, I said, "Hello," and they responded with "Hiya." I recalled shopkeepers in Cumbria and Scotland saying *hiya*, and I assumed it was just a variation on *hi*. On the Glen River Path I decided I should fit in, so when I met the next person, I said, "Hiya." She responded, "Hello." When I said *hello* to a couple, they came back with *hiya*, and I began to wonder . . . is there a protocol here? Are *hello* and *hiya* the two halves of a standard dialogue, like "Thanks" and "You're welcome"? I was never able to figure it out, and whatever greeting I tried, I seemed to get it wrong. One time I threw in a *howdy* and got only a puzzled look in return.

The path ascended gently until reaching the head of the valley, where it rose in steep switchbacks to a saddle between Slieve Donard on the left and Slieve Commedagh on the right. Directly between the two mountains runs the Mourne Wall, a stone structure five feet high and nearly three feet thick. It was constructed in the early twentieth century to keep cattle and sheep out of a water catchment area that supplied the city of Belfast. The wall is twenty-two miles long and crosses the summits of fourteen peaks. From the saddle above the Glen River valley, the path to the summit of Slieve Donard runs directly along the north side of the wall.

At the saddle I paused ten minutes for water and a few ginger cream cookies. Then I set out for the summit, and I quickly decided that the Mourne Wall was a nuisance. It was a warm day, and the barrier blocked a cool breeze coming from the south.

I arrived at the top of Slieve Donard at one thirty, nearly three miles from Newcastle and just over an hour and a half after starting on the path. It was windy there, and a few clouds were swirling around. At the square summit tower, the Mourne Wall took a ninety-degree bend to the south. Nearby sat a large conical pile of rocks. I counted twenty adults at the summit, along with two children and three dogs who scampered about. I leaned against the wall and ate an apple.

Fifteen minutes after reaching the summit, I started down. I wanted to get back to Belfast as quickly as possible, to avoid spending the entire day away from the Italian Woman. My mountain excursion had been the result of her largesse, and I needed to be as efficient as possible.

The descent was uneventful, and I arrived at the edge of Newcastle at three fifteen. There was a bus leaving for Belfast at three thirty and another at four thirty. I could either spend a relaxing hour at a Newcastle pub, or I could do something rather insane and sprint the length of Main Street—more than a mile—in my hiking boots, carrying my backpack and two trekking poles. When I remembered that we had discussed doing laundry in Belfast, I decided to run. I can't tell you how many people I nearly knocked over—babies in strollers, old people with aluminum walkers, and children holding ice cream cones. I also startled a number of drivers whenever I sidestepped into the street to get around a slow-moving pack on the sidewalk. I bounded along, bobbing and weaving, and it must have looked as if somewhere in the Mountains of Mourne, I had encountered the Big Grey Man of Ben MacDui.

Chest heaving and drenched in sweat, I arrived at the bus just as the driver was starting its engine. He had already closed the door, but he reopened it for me. I lurched to the rear bench of the lower level, where I hoped I could catch a breeze from the open windows. A woman in a summer dress looked a little startled when I sat opposite her, and as I started to take off clothing, she clutched her handbag and retreated into a Zen space somewhere within her mind. First my shoes and socks, then my shirt, then the lower zip-off sections of my pant legs. When I was down to a T-shirt and my hiking shorts, I stopped, of course. The woman stared ahead, thankful that her worst fears had not been realized.

It was five o'clock when I entered our hotel room in Belfast. The Italian Woman was sitting on the bed, and her first words were: "Don't say anything. Just don't talk to me." I opened my mouth, then thought better of it and stayed silent. She just glared, and her eyes spewed fire like a nighttime eruption of Mount Aetna. I slowly took off my backpack, bent over, and unlaced my boots. I had removed some of my sweaty clothes when I paused and asked, "Have you had lunch?" She hadn't. Would she like to drop down to the hotel bar and order something? Yes, but I shouldn't expect her to engage in conversation. I re-dressed in my damp things, and we went downstairs.

A pint of Guinness and half a club sandwich later, the Italian Woman felt talkative enough to inform me that she had walked for miles that afternoon, wandering the sweltering streets of Belfast like a hobo, toting a heavy sack of dirty underwear and looking for a Laundromat, while I was selfishly cavorting in the mountains and doing nothing whatsoever for her. I felt it prudent not to remind her that I had offered to participate in doing the laundry, that Belfast had taxis, and that we could have waited for a more convenient time and place to wash the clothes. I didn't mention that I had made a fool of myself dashing madly through main street Newcastle and then doing a striptease on the bus—just to get back to her. No, I just told her how sorry I was that she had had such a miserable afternoon, how grateful I would be for the clean clothing, and how, from the perspective of that moment, Slieve Donard had hardly been worth the trouble.

22

Twelve Days on a Bus

IF YOU ARE LUCKY, TRAVEL will bring you face to face with people who will never fade from memory. More than a decade after a Mediterranean cruise, the Italian Woman and I vividly recall our dinner table companions Danny ("I'm in sales; I made two hundred grand last year; we fly first-class") and Pammy ("Today in the spa, just for something different, I had an aroma therapy hot-stone butt massage"), from New Jersey. At the start of every meal they each ordered a green-colored milkshake made with Midori melon liqueur. And then there were Lynnette ("So, you're a lawyer; I could have been one, too, but I decided not to because it would interfere with my medications") and Jerry ("Now don't get the idea that welding is easy; let me tell you how complicated it gets"), from Bakersfield. On formal night Jerry wore a black T-shirt painted to look like a tuxedo. There were times when we thought we couldn't bear another min- ute with any of them, but now, so many years later, we wish we had kept in touch.

After three days on the bus, we realized that nobody on our tour of Ireland was strange enough or sufficiently irritating to earn an entry in our Pantheon of Characters. There was a red- headed woman from the French island of Réunion, but her home address was the only thing about her that was exotic. An Austrian woman seemed ready to assume the role of Constant Grumbler, but it turned out that her complaints were rather muted – and fully justified. We liked the White Plains cou- ple, Kevin and Billie—he a lawyer turned househusband, she a banker and the breadwinner. They had lost all of their possessions to Hurricane Irene in 2011 and then the next year to Hurricane Sandy, and yet they maintained a positive outlook on life. In fact, they were the mellowest New Yorkers we have ever met. We also enjoyed Vivek and Manisha, originally from India but now living in New Jersey. He was an IT manager and she a helicopter mom for their daughter. They were typically American and nice as pie.

We pitied the man who leaped out of the bus at every stop and desperately lit a cigarette. Later he would be last on board as he took one final drag, then joined us with a look of panic on his face, holding in that last lungful of smoke and searching his pockets for a Nicorette. And we couldn't help but notice the woman from Phoenix, recently dumped by her doctor husband. She had had "work" done in various places, and although I am hardly an expert on the subject, the efforts of her surgeon appeared to have achieved the desired effect. She modeled an endless array of sequined blouses and tight-fitting slacks—again, rather successfully. She also expected to be the center of attention at all times. One evening, when our dinner table conversation moved to a subject other than her, she got up and left. In the end, however, neither Mr. Smokes nor Ms. Sequins nor any other member of our group could hold a candle to Danny and Pammy or Lynnette and Jerry.

But we still had Declan. With his ruddy face and close-cropped beard, he looked like a Lego leprechaun, but his initial charms quickly wore thin, and his store of anecdotes soon sorted themselves into a handful of tedious themes: (1) the Troubles and Dec's personal role in them; (2) Irish music, Dec's renown as a singer, and his loathing for "Danny Boy"; (3) hurling, an Irish sport that is similar but vastly superior to lacrosse and field hockey, and of course, Dec's own championship-caliber play as a young man; (4) growing up in Waterford with every Irish artist, athlete, and politician of any significance in the second half of the twentieth century; and last but not least (5) the European Union—to hear Dec tell it, the EU was a Stalinist regime imposed by the British, and every problem in Irish life, including high taxes, a dysfunctional health care system, potholes, and bad cuisine, is the fault of meddlesome Eurocrats. Why, Brussels even requires ear tagging of cows and sheep—a slap in the face of every Irish farmer who knows his livestock by name and has slept with most of them. How much better the Republic of Ireland would be if the country could go it alone. (I note that this was several years before the UK voted to leave the EU, with Ireland retaining its membership, and I would love to know what Dec thinks about it all.)

Another thing about Declan was that by divine right he was intended to be the focal point of our journey at all times. Generally, this was easy for him because on the bus he held the microphone, and each of us sat under an overhead speaker. But it went further than that. He was so enamored of whatever was pouring out of his mouth (see topics enumerated earlier) that he did not brook any interruption, even by a question from the audience. He might grudgingly grant a response, but his facial expression and tone of voice let the questioner know that he or she was a noodlehead.

In stark contrast to Declan, our driver, Roy, was modest and self-effacing, and the more we saw of him the more we liked. It was as if the pair had been issued a standard amount of ego for two people, but Dec had usurped it all. This was not bad, actually, because if Dec got out of control, he would simply bore us into a coma but not kill us. Roy's calmness in maneuvering a gigantic bus on those narrow Irish roads was reassuring. When I asked him one morning how to greet someone in Irish Gaelic, he said he didn't have a clue. It turned out he was a Scot.

AT THE NORTHEASTERN CORNER OF Northern Ireland lies a coastal feature called the Giant's Causeway. It consists of roughly forty thousand vertical columns of hexagonal basalt, some set into cliffs and others appearing like a cobblestone pavement extending out into the sea—a true geological curiosity. For many years I have possessed a nineteenth-century engraving of it, so of course, I wanted to see it someday, but it had never occurred to me how popular it was. Our bus was one of an endless stream, arriving like 737s at Heathrow.

From the visitor center at the top of the bluff, you can stroll half a mile downhill to the Causeway while listening to narration on a headset. Or you can ride a shuttle bus. The Italian Woman agreed to walk down, but after we had taken the obligatory photos of ourselves on the rock formation, she decided that her tender leg had had enough, and we caught the shuttle back. Lucky that we did, because just as we stepped into the visitor center for a sandwich, the heavens let loose with the hardest downpour I have ever seen. The deluge lasted thirty minutes, during which hundreds of drenched souls staggered into the building. They immediately bought up all the "I ♥ Columnar Basalt" T-shirts in the gift shop and stood there in plain sight, stripping to the waist—yes, even the ladies—to put them on. What they took off, they wrung out, and soon the cement floor was a wading pool. In the restrooms people shed their trousers and underthings, wrung them out, and put them on again. Fights broke out for access to the wall-mounted hand dryers. Fortunately, not a single person on our bus had been caught in the squall, so when we left the Causeway, we did not have to endure the fragrance of wet hair.

Our first night out of Belfast was spent in Ulster's second-largest city, officially known as Londonderry, although local Catholics call it Derry to shed any association with the imperial capital in England. A proposal to rename the community Derrière has not gained much traction. Whatever its label, it would be the most uninteresting city on the planet were it not for the fact that it was ground zero during the Troubles. Sectarian strife, however, does not make for much of a vacation destination, and we assumed that our stop there was an act of charity.

The River Foyle divides Derry, with the city's Catholic majority living on the west bank and its Protestant minority on the east. Since 2011 a Peace Bridge for pedestrians has physically and symbolically connected the two sides, but even then the east bank neighborhood, known as Waterside, remains an astounding anomaly. It is a Protestant enclave in a city that is a Catholic enclave in a country that is a Protestant enclave on an island that until a hundred years ago was a Catholic enclave in a Protestant empire. As a Calvinist turned Catholic turned Episcopalian, I can say with some confidence that if I were from Waterside, Londonderry, Northern Ireland, I would chuck it all and become a Buddhist.

During our overnight stay the city center of Derry was crawling with police in riot gear. They were responding to a caller of unspecified denominational affiliation who had threatened to blow the Peace Bridge off its foundations and into the river.

A STANDARD SUSPICION AMONG GUIDED travelers is that their host company or individual guide will receive a kickback from "approved" shops on the tour itinerary. I have no idea whether that was the case in Ireland, but if not, I can't intelligently explain why we were deposited into a woolen mill in Andara, plied with Irish coffee, and then assaulted by fast-talking salespeople. Just to kill time, I asked to see a few items, but when the man realized I was not a real customer, he dropped me like a hot potato famine. The hustle was a little less overt at a marble factory in Connemara and at the crystal showroom in Waterford, but our travel companions grumbled rather loudly about being subjected to these face-to-face infomercials. Collectively, we exacted our revenge in the best manner possible—we bought nothing. Let's see, 15 percent of zero equals . . .

At the Hotel Westport, Declan did convince us to purchase expensive tickets to a show called "The Legend of Gráinne Mhaol," the story of a woman also known as Grace O'Malley. Touted as a "magical production," it is the tale of an Irish pirate queen who enjoyed Celtic songs and dance numbers interspersed with tango and salsa. She also had a thing for a bad boy pirate who wore heavy makeup, a curly black wig, and a tricornered hat. The climax of the story came when the pair declared their undying love for one another in an overamplified and vibrato-filled version of "You Raise Me Up" by Josh Groban. At that point, from the back of the room, I heard a muffled guffaw. I turned and saw New York Kevin trying to contain himself. At least, I thought, there is a Jacuzzi in our room, and the bubbles will raise me up. When the water came out yellow, the hotel receptionist regretted to inform me that plumbing repairs were in progress and the tub was out of order.

Moving down Ireland's west coast, we stopped at Galway Cathedral. A small chapel displayed a mosaic of John F. Kennedy in a profile copied from the half-dollar coin, with the addition of praying hands and a beatific, heavenward gaze. I turned and looked upward to see if Marilyn Monroe had been painted on the ceiling. Now if JFK wasn't bizarre enough, in the cathedral shop the Italian Woman found a small book on how to bypass purgatory and enter the pearly gates immediately after expelling your final breath. The way to accomplish this is to avoid birth control, the use of which violates every last one of the Ten Commandments. One vignette vividly described a sexually active single woman who used a copper IUD, which attracted lightning, which fried her insides. She survived, sans uterus, to warn other women that unless they take a job with the national railway system, they should not become conductors.

That evening over dinner we shared stories with Kevin and Billie and with Vivek and Manisha. When I described our idea of visiting all of Britain's national parks, our companions commented that it sounded like an interesting tour. On the other hand, they couldn't fathom the idea of climbing to the high points of the parks—it was as if I had just tried to explain an obscure section of the Internal Revenue Code. The Italian Woman made eye contact with me and tilted her head as if to say: "Now do you get it? Nobody, not even your friends, cares about your checklist."

South of Galway the rugged coastline is reminiscent of Cornwall. We visited the Cliffs of Moher, where sheer rock plunges hundreds of feet from green pastures directly into the crashing surf. This is one of Ireland's top tourist attractions, a short drive from both Galway and Limerick. It is also the place where Dusty Springfield's ashes were scattered, even though she was English. For the safety of those visitors not engaged in the act of scattering, a four-foot stone wall runs along the cliff top next to a paved walking path. It was raining lightly, and most of our group went directly into the visitor center. I decided to climb some steps above the center, where a section of the cliff jutted out and a terrace offered impressive views.

I was leaning against the retaining wall, looking toward the sea, when I heard shouts. Twenty feet to my left a Japanese man and woman were arguing. You rarely see Japanese people display emotion in public, so this was startling. At first the tussle was simply verbal, but then the pair started slapping at each other, and the man tried to snatch a large camera from the woman. The strap around her neck held fast, so he let go, pointed at the camera, and screamed.

Meanwhile, a second Japanese couple tried to separate them, the second man grabbing the first by the shoulders, while his wife was doing the same to the fighting woman. Frustrated, the fighting man broke away from his friend, placed his hands on top of the retaining wall, and hoisted himself up (climbers call this a "mantling" move). The other three tried desperately to pull him back, but he kicked at them, bellowing something like "I can't take any more of this! I must be united with my beloved Dusty!" He then jumped from the wall onto the narrow strip of grass on the outer side, just inches from the cliff's edge.

The man's wife and friends wailed in panic, arms outstretched, pleading for him to come to his senses. I stood there frozen, expecting to witness a suicide. Instead, in a theatrical gesture, the fellow bent over and picked something up from the grass. Clutching it in his hand, he clambered back over the wall and onto the terrace. He hurled the object at his wife. It bounced off her chest and fell to the pavement. It was a lens cap.

Just then a green tour bus pulled into the parking lot. In large letters it bore the name PADDYWAGON. Good timing, I thought. Here are two characters who need to be trussed up and hauled away.

AS THE TOUR WORE ON, the Italian Woman became increasingly grumpy about our early departures and the degree of regimentation to which we were subjected. There were several times when I was tempted to say, "I rest my case," but I maintained a discreet silence. The fact was, our tour mates were also complaining about the schedule—and even more about Declan. In Westport, Kevin had left the tour for a few hours to visit a doctor. He later reported that in the taxi he told the driver that he was a bit nervous about the appointment because our tour guide had been so negative about Irish health care. "Oh," said the driver, "that would be Declan." Over lunch in Dingle, where we refused to sample the berries, Kevin said that Dec's mind seemed to be on the scramble feature of a digital music player. Billie couldn't bear to hear another word about the Troubles, and she admitted to a fantasy of covering our guide's mouth with duct tape and proclaiming in Yiddish, "*Genug shoyn!*— Enough already!"

I began to think that a song about Declan would be cathartic, and one night I lay awake composing a few verses. The next day I described the ditty to several of our friends, and they told me that if I would print it out, they would sing it. That evening, with Dec and Roy in attendance, our entire group sang a cappella, with me conducting rather awkwardly. The piece was set to "Londonderry Air," the tune of our guide's despised "Danny Boy," and it went like this:

Oh Dec and Roy, the bus, the bus is calling,
By the hotel, it stands there in the gloom.

It's five a.m., our bags are in the hallway,
'Tis you, 'tis you, must drag us from our rooms.
We just can't wait to hear about the Troubles,
The Irish taxes, and also the EU,
And you'll be there to show us more of Ireland,
Oh Dec and Roy, oh Dec and Roy, we love you so.

Oh Dec and Roy, the road, the road is calling.
Please load us up and strap us in our chairs,
And tell us tales of growing up in Waterford,
Of north and south, and Londonderry airs.
With orange and green our flags are all unfurling,
We will be Irish sooner than you know.
A few more days, and we will all be hurling,
Oh Dec and Roy, oh Dec and Roy, we love you so.

As we sang, Roy doubled over with laughter, while Declan
gritted his teeth. When the number ended, most of the choir
applauded loudly, but Ms. Sequins approached me and muttered, "Well, aren't you the belle of the ball." As for the rest of
us, we felt as if a burden had been lifted from our shoulders. We
had expressed our solidarity, and for the remainder of the tour,
whenever our guide became too full of himself, we thought of
hurling and smiled.

NO IRISH TOUR COMPANY WORTH its salt would fail to schedule a visit to Blarney Castle. As we arrived, Declan told us that
he had never kissed the Stone of Eloquence and had no intention of doing so, because he was already loquacious enough.
Nevertheless, he urged us to participate, and he advised us to
ignore the rumor that local boys sneak into the castle at night
to urinate on Ireland's national treasure. He assured us that the
stone was wiped clean every morning. That sounded good to
me—that is, if I could be first in line, like the squeamish people who rush to the front during Communion, hoping for wine
that does not yet contain any backwash. I generally don't worry

much in church, trusting that God Almighty will kill the germs. I wasn't so sure about placing my lips on a secular chunk of rock.

If you haven't heard, the Blarney Stone is built into a wall at the top of a crumbling tower, the highest point in the castle. That means winding your way in a long queue through musty rubble and dark chambers, up tortuous spiral stairways, and ultimately along a crenellated parapet. I didn't mind the stairs, but when I emerged at the top of the tower and saw the folks ahead of me getting down on their backs one by one and putting their heads awkwardly into a hole in the wall, I started having second thoughts. More particularly, I started scrutinizing the people in line, wondering if any of them had a disease that couldn't be defeated by a good, stiff antibiotic. I discussed this with the man immediately in front of me, and he chuckled, but I had planted a seed of doubt, and there was fear in his chuckle. Still, we reassured each other that the folks ahead of us looked fairly healthy, so we shuffled on.

I intended to perform a dry little British peck at the stone. Instead, in the awkwardness of the posture, with my head thrust back and down, I found myself in a full open-mouth French kiss—with a bit of tongue, I'm sorry to say—on a surface that was cold and very wet. I was horrified, knowing that I had just taken a bacterial plunge of some significance. I felt like Lucy in *Peanuts*, when she inadvertently kisses Snoopy and wails: "My lips touched dog lips! Baugh! Agh!" As I struggled to my feet, the man ahead of me was waiting, and he asked what I had thought of it. I was speechless.

The next morning I woke up with a sore throat.

RETURNING TO DUBLIN THE NEXT day, we stopped along the way at the Irish National Stud, a farm where they breed racing horses and sell T-shirts for men that say, "I'm a Gelding." Actually, they say, "Irish Stud," and they are a great conversation starter back at the office. After considerable buildup, our one-hour walking tour netted a total of seven horse sightings.

Our final evening included a gala show at a place called Taylor's. After the obligatory line dancing and fiddling, the program offered a comedian who rattled off a string of Borscht Belt jokes with an Irish twist ("Take my wife Siobhán—please!"). Kevin leaned across the table and whispered, "Who is this, Shecky O'Toole?" The climax of the show was a supposedly famous chanteuse who belted out an emotional rendition of "Danny Boy." At our table everyone was trying hard to avoid eye contact with Declan. Kevin's eyes were filling with tears.

Toward the end of the tour Declan had repeatedly reminded us that it is customary to tip both the guide and driver. And so, on the final morning, he and Roy stood in the lobby as we emerged from breakfast, and it was impossible to avoid passing within inches of them. Meekly, I handed each of them an envelope filled with cash. A bit later, as we again passed through the lobby on our way to a taxi that Dec had arranged, the magnificent one was sitting on a sofa looking at some papers. It turned out that there was a misunderstanding with our driver, and I returned to ask Dec for assistance. He curtly responded, "I'm off duty." Rather than argue, I simply told him that this was the best bus tour I had ever been on and he was the world's greatest travel guide—whereupon he rose triumphantly, stepped outside, and sorted the matter out.

23

Return to the Horseshoe

WE SAILED BACK TO HOLYHEAD in Wales on a ferry that was smaller and less elegant than the *Ulysses*, and in a crowded lounge we sat across from an orthodox Jewish family. The mother and two teenage daughters wore long skirts, the son dark slacks and a sweater, and the father a black suit. The man also wore a black hat with such a wide, stiff brim that once he leaned over to say something to his wife and bonked her on the forehead. They were having lunch. Each of them would take a slice of what appeared to be homemade white bread unadorned by butter or mayonnaise, fold it, insert a few green olives, and then begin eating. They consumed the simple food with gusto, as if a meal of olives on plain bread, washed down with bottled water, was a feast fit for King Solomon.

I appreciated the distraction that the family provided, because I was dreading our reunion with Robert from Shady Lane Car Rental. He was going to meet the ferry and escort us back to Gaerwen to pick up another car, and I was certain he would cheerfully report that the mysterious scratch had been repaired and we were now a thousand dollars poorer. Imagine, then, my shock when the first words out of Robert's mouth were: "Mr. Sieberson, I have good news for you. We decided not to report the scratch on your car. We simply delivered it to another of our offices, and they didn't say anything, so the car is now in the system without any connection between you and the damage."

Despite my relief, when we were introduced to our new Vauxhall, I began to give it the most thorough going-over that I have ever conducted. On the damage sheet I started noting every water spot and speck of bird droppings, every nick in the paint. This quickly tried the patience of Robert's colleague, Gareth, who two weeks earlier had been immune to my protests. It then occurred to me that if I annoyed him too much, he might retract the beneficence that had been granted in regard to the first car, so I backed off. I cheerfully signed the acceptance sheet, and we were on the road again.

IT WAS MONDAY, THE FIFTH of August, when we returned from Ireland, and if we were going to visit Britain's nine remaining national parks, we would have to do so in less than four weeks. Without committing to the entire list, the Italian Woman had agreed that we could visit the three parks in Wales as a reward for my cooperation on the Irish tour. Our first stop would be Snodownia in the north. After that we would drive south to the Brecon Beacons and then west to Pembrokeshire Coast. Because of commitments I had made for the following weekend, we would have to cover the three parks in four days. On the map it appeared manageable.

The mountains of north Wales are the crown of the small country, and the highest of them is 3,560-foot Snowdon. It sits in the northwestern corner of the Snowdonia National Park and is one of fourteen peaks in the vicinity that reach 3,000 feet. Snowdon has ridges emanating in all directions from its central summit, but most climbing activity takes place on the east side.

To visualize the mountain's eastern flanks, think of Snowdon as a euro symbol, €, with the summit located center-left where the two prongs of the "equal sign" join the C. The center of the C is Snowdon's eastern valley, called Cwm Dyli (*cwm* is the Welsh word for a high mountain basin and is pronounced *coom*). The equal sign represents two well-used paths running west to the summit. The upper one is the Pyg Track, which traverses the slopes beneath the upper half of the C. The lower path is the Miners Track, which runs along the valley floor. The two trails merge at the higher, western end of the cwm, and most Snowdon climbers follow one of the two. The curving outline of the C forms a horseshoe, consisting of the mountain's northeast ridge, its summit block, and its southeast ridge. The seven-mile Horseshoe Walk, running counterclockwise along the C, is one of the finest mountain excursions in Britain, crossing three 3,000-foot peaks and traversing several sections of exposed ridge. For those less adventuresome, a narrow-gauge railway runs to the top of Snowdon from the northwest, from the village of Llanberis.

Alone among the summer's mountains, I had previously ascended Snowdon. Thirty years earlier I had taken a vacation from my temporary job in Amsterdam and visited Wales for the express purpose of climbing the peak. I had attempted the Horseshoe Walk but accomplished only the top half of the C. A sudden snowstorm forced me to bail out at Snowdon's summit, and I was fortunate to escape down Cwm Dyli by way of the Miners Track. I had always hoped that someday I would be able to return and complete the southern portion of the Horseshoe.

We had booked three nights at the Beech Bank B&B in Llanberis. The lodging was first rate, and Annie, the manager, treated us as if we were her most important guests ever. We liked her, but my, how she did run on. She couldn't stop talking, and so, when she suggested dinner at a place called the Heights, we thanked her and made a hasty escape.

The restaurant was a rustic establishment with a good beer list and reading material strewn about. As the Italian Woman and I waited for our food, we thumbed through magazines, and that is how I discovered an ancient verse describing the Seven Wonders of Wales:

> Pistyll Rhaeadr and Wrexham steeple,
> Snowdon's mountain without its people,
> Overton yew trees, St Winefride wells,
> Llangollen bridge and Gresford bells.

I am certain that the reference to the absent people of Snowdon was thrown in only because the poet needed to fill out the line and couldn't think of a single other word in the English language that rhymes with *steeple*. I have tried, and—after rejecting a three-base hit in the Mexican baseball league—I have concluded that there is none. Pystyll Rhaeadr, incidentally, is a waterfall and not an electronic device that identifies small weapons. The falls may be worth seeing, and Snowdon surely is, but would you go out of your way to see a copse of yew trees or a stone bridge? Compared to the Great Pyramid of Giza and the Hanging Gardens of Babylon, the Welsh attractions hardly deserve to be called "wonders," and the poem leaves the impression that Wales is a sad little place. Fortunately for me, it offered three national parks and, possibly, three mountains to climb.

While I stood at the bar ordering a second round of Staropramen pilsner, the Italian Woman—who is far better at chatting with strangers than I will ever be—struck up a conversation with a man and woman at the adjacent table. They were Rob Davies and Jindra Kaplicka, he English and she a native of Prague, home of the very beer we were drinking. They lived in Dublin and were in Llanberis to visit a client of Rob's technology consulting business. Rob was also a professional mountain guide, and Jindra was an apprentice climb leader.

Jindra said that she, too, was planning to climb Snowdon the following day, and the two of us quickly agreed that we would hike together. I told her that I wanted to go directly up the well-traveled Pyg Track and then return by way of the southeast ridge. This, I explained, would create symmetry with my previous experience on the mountain. That was fine with Jindra. On the other hand, even though I had previously been up Snowdon and she had not, we agreed that she would "lead." She would then be able to enter the outing in her logbook and credit it toward her guiding certification. We were both happy at the prospect of company, and for me it would be the first time I would set out with a partner since the day the Italian Woman and I had climbed Whernside two months earlier.

I WAS NOT AT MY best the next morning. Ever since kissing the Blarney Stone, my throat had been scratchy, and that morning it was raw. Yet I refused to let it keep me off Snowdon. At nine forty-five Jindra and I caught the Sherpa bus from Llanberis to the Snowdon trailhead at Pen y Pass, a trip of five miles. We could have driven, but we had been warned that parking was limited and expensive. When I had been to Pen y Pass thirty years earlier, there was a youth hostel on one side of the road and nothing more than the trailhead and an untended car park on the other. Today the site has been developed with a national park visitor center and several closely monitored park and pay lots.

We set out at 10:10 a.m. on the Pyg Track in the company of hundreds of other hikers, many of whom seemed poorly conditioned and ill equipped for the excursion. The path was straightforward, even a bit monotonous, but the mountain scenery was impressive—the deep valley of Cwm Dyli with three lakes on its floor, the ragged ridges all around, and Snowdon's summit pyramid towering above.

An hour under way we encountered Gerwyn Lloyd, a local guide and friend of Jindra and Rob, and we spent fifteen minutes visiting with him. He was escorting two clients, a man and woman. I was puzzled that anyone would need professional assistance for such a straightforward hike, and I was even more surprised when I later learned that Gerwyn's fee was nearly $250 for the day. I had once used a guide on the Matterhorn, but that was a technical ascent. I had also hired a trail guide on a walk up Mount Kinabalu in Borneo but only because the local park authorities required it. Snowdon was easy and unrestricted, so guiding made little sense to me, but still I was happy for Gerwyn and his clients. He was earning a fee, and they could have a mountain adventure without worrying about the logistics.

After we resumed our ascent, Jindra asked me several times

if she was going too fast, and indeed, she was racing along, but I told her the pace was fine. I felt feverish, but I relished the challenge of keeping up with a trim, thirty-five-year-old outdoor professional. She also looked rather good from behind, so I had ample incentive to stay close. In this I was following in the footsteps of alpinists worldwide who find relief from the tedium of the trail by focusing on someone just ahead with a good pair of legs and well-toned glutes. In the freedom of the hills, you can choose which gender you prefer to observe, and any climber who denies having taken this sort of enjoyment on an approach hike is a flat-out liar. I distinctly recall a climb in Washington when I was in the lead, and after fifteen minutes on the walk-in, I paused to ask my team if the pace was okay. A woman named Ruth, who was immediately behind me, looked up and said, "Nice definition in those calf muscles, Steve."

Now for those of you who never hike, if you wonder how to relate to the previous paragraph, I have two words for you: *yoga class*. And for those of you who are inflexible of body but lively of mind, I have one word: *escalator*.

When we reached the Snowdon saddle at the upper end of the Pyg Track, I pointed out the large marker stone and told Jindra how I had used it thirty years earlier to find my way off the ridge in a whiteout. Then, as the two of us drank some water, I checked my watch and noted that we were just ten minutes shy of two hours under way. I said to Jindra, "If we go a bit faster, we can make the summit in two hours." She was amused that I cared about the time, but she offered to let me set the pace. I started jogging, and we arrived at the top ten minutes later.

THE ACTUAL SUMMIT OF SNOWDON is a small platform reached by a set of stone steps. In its center stands a three-foot column topped by a brass plaque identifying mountains in all directions. Dozens of people, including twenty schoolchildren, were crowding the monument, jostling for position. Jindra and I snapped a few photos and then retreated to the visitor center.

When I had previously climbed Snowdon, it was October, and the ramshackle summit building was closed for the season, but its leeward side had offered shelter from a howling wind. Today's visitor center, called Hafod Eryri, opened in 2009 and is a modern, stylized glass and concrete affair. Jindra and I managed to worm our way into the cafeteria, but just barely. It was bursting at the seams with patrons, most of whom had arrived by the Snowdon Mountain Railway. There were, however, enough hikers on hand to fill the air with the odor of sweat. In that atmosphere we had to stand in line for half an hour to get a bowl of potato leek soup, but it gave us a chance to get better acquainted.

Jindra had grown up in a skiing and hiking family in the Czech Republic, where she attended university and became a teacher, but she had wanted more. In 2003 her country was on the verge of joining the European Union, but she felt she could have a better life somewhere else. So, in hopes of improving her prospects and her English, at the age of twenty-five she moved to the UK. Eventually, she migrated to Dublin, where she took a succession of menial jobs just to survive. After years of this, discouragement set in, and she wondered whether she should return to her native country. Instead, she turned to her love of mountains. She joined the Irish Mountaineering Club and immersed herself in outdoor activity. One day, on a club outing the year before our encounter in Snowdonia, she met Rob, and she soon knew that he was her perfect partner on and off the slopes. They now lived together and were working to expand Rob's mountain guide service. Their dream was to make it a full-time profession for both of them. Hers was a story right out of the American saga. Like an early pioneer, she had left home and family behind and headed west. Success had never been guaranteed, and she had gone through years of struggle. Now she was thirty-five, and her risk was beginning to pay dividends. The mountains had changed her life and had shown her the path ahead.

OUTSIDE, THE SUMMIT HAD BECOME engulfed in a swirling mist, and I feared that once again I would have to abandon the Horseshoe and return by way of the valley. Luckily, we ran into Gerwyn and his clients, and he said that if we descended the Watkin Path just a few hundred feet, we would likely drop below the cloud. We should then have clear conditions to tackle the mountain's southeastern ridge, the second half of the Horseshoe Walk. He was correct. A few minutes under way, we reached a point of good visibility and could see the entire route. We would descend to a saddle, then cross over a 2,946-foot peak called Lliwedd, and then head down to the lakes at the floor of Cwm Dyli. From there we would join the eastern segment of the Miners Track and return to Pen y Pass.

Thirty minutes below the summit, we reached the col between Snowdon and Lliwedd, at the head of Cwm Llan, a prominent valley south of Snowdon's summit block. We paused, and I told Jindra about King Arthur's final battle.

The story begins with Arthur and his Knights of the Round Table in semi-retirement after repelling the Saxon invaders and bringing peace to Wales and western England. Unfortunately, Arthur's past came back to haunt him in the person of his bastard son, Mordred, whom Arthur had sired with his half-sister Morgause in a moment of sibling naughtiness. The crazed and perpetually disgruntled offspring, being far less patient than the current Prince of Wales, hatched a plan to eliminate his father and open the throne for himself. He surreptitiously raised an army and enticed a few leftover Saxons to join him in Snowdonia to prepare for war.

When Arthur learned that enemy forces were gathering, he convinced his knights to dust off their armor and join him to defend their turf against the interlopers. Among the first to mount their steeds were Sir Bedivere the Wise, Sir Lancelot the Brave, and Sir Robin the Not-Quite-So-Brave-as-Sir-Lancelot. After this initial group had been mustered, others were allowed to catch up, and Arthur led them with relish into the Welsh mountains. There the king discovered that Mordred's army was staging in Cwm Llan, and he summoned his publicists to suggest a name for the upcoming campaign. After considering many alternatives, he settled on "The Battle of Cwm Llan—Operation Enduring Legend."

It was a vicious fight, with the two sides trading blow for blow, and yet the good knights succeeded in pushing Mordred's evil minions higher and higher up the valley. As the day wore on, Arthur was able to separate Mordred from his troops, and at the saddle between Snowdon and Lliwedd, the two men came face to face. As they fought, arrows from below rained around them, thus giving the place its name—Bwlch y Saethau, "Pass of the Arrows."

His strength waning, Mordred delivered a desperate but deadly thrust into Arthur's soft underbelly, but before falling, Arthur swung Excalibur hard into Mordred's helmet, piercing all the way to his hippocampus. The son collapsed at once onto the rocks. He had time for only a few last words, "Dad-dye, I hardly knew ye."

With Mordred gone, it was Arthur's turn to fall, and fall he did. Lying next to his son's corpse, the mortally wounded king peered into Cwm Dyli, where he saw Llyn Llydaw, the mile-long lake at the valley floor. When Sir Bedivere arrived, Arthur was just able to gesture toward the lake and whisper: "I feare I am kilt. Take me to the Lady." He then expired like a three-week old carton of Devonshire cream.

We all know what happened next. Bedivere carried Arthur's body down the mountain to the lake, where the Lady in White approached in a canoe that no one was paddling. Bedivere placed Arthur into the boat, and the lady sailed off, into the mists of Avalon. As his final act, Bedivere then hurled Excalibur into the lake, where a hand emerged from the water and caught the sword—luckily, on the hilt. The hand then sank beneath the surface. Arthur and Excalibur were gone forever, hidden in the depths of Snowdon's Llyn Llydaw.

Ever the solicitous guide, Jindra commented that it was an interesting tale. Yet it was obvious that she couldn't get excited about the Arthurian legend. As a Czech, she surely appreciated her own Charles IV, whose name is attached to the famous bridge in Prague, but it seemed that she didn't understand why the British, let alone an American visitor, would give a farthing about an ancient king whose actual existence is in doubt.

Perhaps in retaliation, Jindra nearly wasted me on the remaining portion of our walk. I kept up comfortably to the top of Lliwedd because I do well ascending, and the traverse across the summit ridge was exhilarating. But it was all downhill from there, and I am sluggish on any descent. It turned out that Jindra was not. As I fell behind, she would stop and wait, then sweetly ask if she should slow it down. "Oh, no," I would respond. "Keep it up." Then I would fall behind again. I blamed my leaden feet on the Blarney Stone and my sore throat, but I would not violate my rule never to ask for mercy on the trail. I would just push myself harder. And really, I had nothing in the world to complain about. I was hiking in the mountains with a delightful companion—what more could a person ask for?

Five hours after setting out, we returned to Pen y Pass in good spirits. For me it was especially satisfying—thirty years after starting it, I had completed the Snowdon Horseshoe.

24

Losing It

THE ITALIAN WOMAN AND I had an open day in north Wales, and we decided to spend it in Caernarfon, the town formerly known as Caernarvon, and before that Y Gaer yn Arfon. Our primary objective was to do laundry, and it turned out that two loads and the cost of parking came to thirty dollars. That spoiled the mood somewhat, but we did manage to enjoy ourselves for an hour at the castle. We then scored a fine lunch at a café called Y Gegin Fach, which means "the small kitchen" but sounds like an interjection, as in "Y gegin fach! Poochie just piddled on the carpet!" As we ate, we discovered that we were the only people conversing in English. Caernarfon, in fact, has the highest concentration of Welsh speakers anywhere, and when Prince Charles visited for his investiture as Prince of Wales, in 1969, he demonstrated his cultural savvy by proclaiming, "Y Gads!"

That evening I booked a room for the following night in Merthyr Tydfil, near the Brecon Beacons National Park. My plan was to check into the B&B and then drive into the park to climb a peak called Pen y Fan. The day after that we would travel to Pembrokeshire Coast National Park, where I would seek out its high point, Foel Cwmcerwyn. During the night, however, I was burning with fever, my throat was on fire, and my complement of over-the-counter medications was not helping. As I tossed and turned, barely getting any sleep, I wondered whether I could climb anything at all.

Every undertaking has its low point. Mine started with a drive south, through the heart of Wales. The trip was scenic enough, but I was flushed and sweating, and so I did not appreciate the villages we passed through, and their names gave me brain fatigue. From Llanberis we drove west through Brynrefail and Llanrug to Caernarfon, then south through Bontnewydd, Llanwinda, Groeslon, Penygroes, Llanllyfni, Pant Glas, Bryncir, and Dolbenmaento Porthmadog. That was just the first twenty miles. Then came Penrhyndeudraeth, Maentwrog, and Gellilydan. Then Trawsfynydd, Llanelltyd, Dolgellau, Ninllyn, and Mallwyd, where we left Snowdonia National Park. At that point were still less than halfway to Merthyr Tydfil. To maintain any semblance of control over this paragraph—which I will never attempt to read in public—I will mention just a few personal favorites among the ensuing towns: Llanbrynmair, Talerddig, Clatter, Llansantffraed Cwmdeuddwr (where we stopped for lunch—I am not kidding, we ate lunch in a place called Llansantffraed Cwmdeuddwr, something I'll wager you will never do), and Cwmbach Llechrhyd.

We eventually reached Brecon (also known as Aberhonddu), at the north edge of Brecon Beacons National Park. The Beacons are an east-west mountain range lying above the south coast of Wales and its major cities of Newport (Casnewydd), Cardiff (Caerydd), and Swansea (Abertawe). In ancient times the mountaintops were used for signal fires to warn of attacks by the Angles or Saxons, thus the "Brecon Beacons." The Welsh name, Bannau Brycheiniog, has the same meaning.

From the town of Brecon the A470 runs nineteen miles south to Merthyr Tydfil, through the heart of the mountain range and the national park. Near the midpoint of this stretch, we came to a pass at 1,427 feet, where a parking lot opposite a building called Storey Arms provides access to a developed path. From the trailhead it is a three-mile walk to the summit of the Beacons' highest mountain, 2,907-foot Pen y Fan. There were at least a hundred cars sitting in the lot, and I could see hikers on the first segment of the trail. I was tempted to stop and head up myself, but I knew the Italian Woman would object to sitting in the car, and I assumed it would be a short trip to our B&B. We could settle in, and then I would return to Pen y Fan.

The owners of the B&B were a married couple, and on the previous evening the husband had given me detailed directions on how to find the place. The key was to get to the roundabout junction of the A470 and the east-west A465 at the northwestern edge of Merthyr Tydfil, then continue south on the A470 to the fourth roundabout. I did this, and after exiting, I followed a side road, as instructed. After several miles I realized that nothing along the road resembled the remaining description, so I returned to the A470 and headed south again to the next roundabout. That didn't work, so south again to yet another roundabout, then another and another. After an hour of casting about, I was exhausted and frustrated. In exasperation I called the B&B, where the man informed me that I had not been listening very well and I was now closer to Cardiff than to Merthyr Tydfil. I was insulted by his tone. It turned out that when he had said the fourth roundabout from the A470/A465 junction, he was counting the junction itself, so it was really the third roundabout south of that.

The new directions were also wrong, and I called back to the B&B. This time the man's wife answered, and she gave different instructions. Those didn't work, and I rang again. In the middle of that call my phone minutes ran out. Eventually, after much improvisation, and nearly two hours after coming down from the Brecon Beacons, we found the B&B. It wasn't in Merthyr Tydfil at all but in a tiny village well outside the town. And the lodging appeared nothing like the cheery website photos—when we stepped inside, it struck us as run-down and musty. The husband greeted us with a rather cavalier, "So you're the lost wanderers." That was too much.

True to my Dutch heritage, I am not prone to outburst, but at that moment I let fly in a manner that my wife later described as "almost Italian." I began by saying that the man's driving directions were some form of malpractice, that I had a climb to do, and that his instructions had cost me two hours and had eaten up my phone minutes. I then told him that his website had led us to believe that we would be in the actual town of Merthyr Tydfil, where the Italian Woman would have things to do while I was in the mountains, but instead, it turned out that this was a cow pie of a hamlet with no establishments whatsoever. I said that I was sick and the past two hours had made me sicker—by way of proof of that last statement, my nose was running profusely, and my voice became so raspy that I could barely get the words out. On top of all of that, I couldn't remember the name Merthyr Tydfil, and every time I tried to say it, it came out differently: Mother Tidewell, Murderous Treadmill, Mirthless Tubfull, and finally, in complete surrender to the moment, Murky Turdville.

Once I was sitting in traffic in downtown Seattle, easing forward in the middle of a block, when one of those tattooed and nose-ringed bicycle messengers nearly ran into my car. He came to a lurching stop just inches from my door, dismounted, and started screaming at me. I rolled down my window, and he shouted, "You're supposed to yield!" I called back: "I'm in the middle of the block! You're supposed to cross at the corner!" He got a demented, cross-eyed look on his crimson face, then stammered, "Up your . . . up your . . . your . . . your . . . ." He couldn't remember the next word, which was the critical object of his prepositional phrase, so he just pursed his lips and spat some Lifesavers-infused saliva onto my windshield. Then he jumped back onto his bike and rode away. Baffled, I watched the red slime run slowly down the glass. Well, at the B & B in South Wales I was that sputtering bike messenger.

In response to my every complaint, the B & B owner defended his turf with increasing volume, telling me I didn't know how to follow directions, repeatedly correcting me on how to say *Merthyr Tydfil*, and generally treating me like a juvenile delinquent. At last the man's wife intervened, begged for a cease-fire, and offered to call a Travelodge that was actually in Merthyr Tydfil. We accepted, made a reservation at the hotel, and with a muted "thank you" made a hasty retreat. Once in the car, the Italian Woman started laughing and said, "You have no idea how ridiculous you looked back there." Then she thanked me for getting us out of that hellhole.

The Travelodge was a Spartan place, but at least it sat next to a complex of shops, restaurants, and a multiplex cinema. I toppled onto the bed, moaning that I needed to get back into the Beacons to climb Pen y Fan, but I could barely lift my head. The Italian Woman ordered me to take a nap. She insisted that I could climb two mountains the next day. Not believing that was possible, but nonetheless grateful for the suggestion, I fell asleep. A few hours later we walked to the theater and watched a movie, then ate a sandwich at a Subway. Back in our room I studied my maps to determine how, if I had the strength, I could organize a single day's trip to two national parks. I had hit rock bottom at the B & B, but I wasn't giving up.

IN THE FAR SOUTHWESTERN CORNER of Wales lies the county of Pembrokeshire, a peninsula that points westward toward Ireland. Its coast is a spectacular mix of beaches, cliffs, and off-shore islands. Covering its perimeter, the Pembrokeshire Coast National Park is the only one of Britain's fifteen national parks that is devoted primarily to coastal preservation. The 186-mile Pembrokeshire Coast Path offers endless days of recreational walking, and earlier in the summer I had envisioned us working our way around the peninsula by car, visiting towns like St. Dogmaels and Fishguard, and sampling the path here and there. Instead, with our time running out, I was forced to make a mad dash from Merthyr Tydfil to the high point in the Pembrokeshire park and then return to the Brecon Beacons on the same day.

The mountains in Pembrokeshire are really just hills, and that is what they are called—the Preseli Hills. They occupy the northeastern corner of the county, along its border with Carmarthen-shire. The Preselis are included in the coastal park because they offer scenic walking and significant prehistoric sites. An ancient quarry at Carn Menyn has been identified as the source of the spotted dolerite "bluestone" slabs that comprise the inner ring of Stonehenge. How and why the massive stones were transported 240 miles to the Salisbury Plain more than four thousand years ago is anybody's guess.

With a moan I dragged my sorry self out of bed at four forty-five the next morning. It was still dark outside and midnight in my soul. I hadn't slept well, and my throat ailment was now accompanied by sneezing and coughing. It would have been so easy to lie abed in the land of counterpane, but my ambitions overrode my circumstances. At five fifteen I was on the road, driving west on the A465. At Neath I joined the M4 to bypass Swansea. At one point the sky ahead—to the west—began to lighten, and I became convinced I had misread a roundabout and was going east, back toward Merthyr Tydfil. After pulling over to study my road atlas, I concluded that I was on course.

The M4 became the A48, and at Carmarthen it merged into the A40. A dozen miles west of St. Clears, I turned north onto the exceedingly narrow B4313. The night had turned into gray, so I could now see where I was going, and it was still early enough that mine was the only car on the road. After a construction detour that had me wending my way among sinister hedgerows, I lurched into the hamlet of Rosebush at 7:15 a.m. A heavy mist blanketed the countryside, but at least it wasn't raining. I parked near a sport field, finished a turkey sandwich that I had purchased the evening before, and at seven thirty-five started looking for my path. My goal was Foel Cwmcerwyn, which means the hill (foel) of the valley (cwm) of the vat (cer-wyn). Highest of the Preseli Hills, and second only to Elvis in the popular imagination, it rises to 1,759 feet in elevation but is a relatively modest hump on the landscape. From Rosebush the 889-foot rise to the top of the hill is spaced out over three miles.

I quickly determined that my directions from the internet would put me onto a strange and circuitous route. Rosebush lies south and west of Foel Cwmcerwym, and the description had me bypassing the hill to the west, looping around, and then approaching it from the north. On my map it looked as if I could cut through the Pant Mawr cheese farm next to the village and join a bridleway and path that leads directly to the hill. I walked into the farmyard, hoping to find artisans busy at work and ask them for directions, but they were apparently sleeping in, allowing their cheddars to age undisturbed. Trespassing boldly, I played through and entered a large cow pasture. At the far side I scrambled over a stone wall, across a ditch, and onto the bridleway—a bit unorthodox but nicely straightforward.

The bridleway eventually turned into a grassy trail, wet from the night's rain and often boggy. Except for the muck, it was an easy walk to the final, gently angled hill. I reached the summit trig point, three miles from the car, at eight twenty. The top of Foel Cwmcerwyn was in cloud, so I didn't linger more then ten minutes. On the way down I dropped below the mist and was able to see pasturelands and hills to the south. It was a pleasant vista, but I could not have cared less. I had reached the high point, and enjoyment was not part of the package.

To avoid repeating my route through the farm, I followed the path and bridleway all the way to the highway, south of Rosebush, then walked a third of a mile along the road into the village. It was a slightly greater distance than my ascent, but from summit to car took only forty minutes. I was back behind the wheel at 9:10 a.m. Two hours later I arrived at our hotel. The Italian Woman, meanwhile, had slept late and had just finished a large and highly satisfying breakfast. She was bemused that I had risen before five and driven four hours for a hike of ninety minutes. When I thought of how little of Pembrokeshire Coast National Park I had seen that day, I could not explain, even to myself, what I had actually accomplished. Truth be told, it had been a foel's errand.

THE ITALIAN WOMAN SAT WITH me as I ate a small pizza at a place called Frank and Benny's. Meanwhile, the sun had penetrated the gray skies, and my socks and boots were drying on the dashboard of the car. The combination of food, sunshine, and my wife's company energized me. I was able to ignore my ailments, and less than an hour after returning from Pembrokeshire, I was driving north on the A470 and into the Brecon Beacons. Improbable as it had seemed the evening before, I was going to Pen y Fan.

Twenty minutes after leaving Merthyr Tydfil, I arrived at the pass and the Storey Arms. At first glance the parking lot was full, but I managed to wedge my car into a narrow slot next to a trailer that served as a concession stand. The proprietor did not object, and we chatted briefly about the weather. There were more clouds in the mountains than in the city below, but they were scudding by in too much of a hurry to stop and release any rain. The snack man thought I had a good chance of doing my climb without getting wet, and he assured me that he would be waiting with hot coffee or a cold soda when I returned.

There are several trails to Pen y Fan, and I took the one most direct, a hike of three miles. At the far side of the highway a wooden gate beside a red phone booth ushered me onto the path. Its initial segment rose directly up a grassy slope, and much of the track consisted of flagstones laid to protect the earth from the thousands upon thousands of boots that tread this most popular of all walks in South Wales. After a gain of five hundred feet, I reached the top of a broad ridge with a commanding view of the area. One mile east stood a prominent, tabletop peak named Corn Du (Black Horn), 2,864 feet, which hid its slightly taller twin, Pen y Fan. Corn Du's shape reminded me of a mesa called Pilot Butte in southwestern Wyoming, and from where I stood, it seemed that I could extend my hand and run my fingers across Corn Du's velvety contours. Even though I was not feeling my best, I was struck by the beauty of the landscape.

From the ridge the path dropped 150 feet into a shallow valley, where it crossed a stream called Blaen Taf Fawr. The next mile rose 650 feet directly to the base of Corn Du. A steep, angling traverse gained an additional 400 feet, and soon I arrived at the top of the mountain. I located the summit marker at the northern edge of the tabletop, just above an escarpment and a slope that drops a thousand feet to a broad valley, Cwm Llwch. On the valley floor a glacial lake named Llyn Cwm Llych reflected the changing blue and gray of the sky.

It was a grand vista, but less than half a mile off stood the now-visible Pen y Fan, and I was on my way. When I had told the Italian Woman that the hike would be three miles, she had commented, "You should be able to do that in an hour." I had ten minutes left to meet her challenge, and I needed to drop seventy-five feet below Corn Du to a saddle and then gain it back and ascend an additional forty-three feet to get to the top of Pen y Fan. Unexpectedly, when I arrived at the col, my legs turned to stone. I needed food, and my general fatigue had caught up with me. I cannot remember a single instance in which my legs have felt so dead. I wanted to sit down, but I taunted myself: *Don't be a baby. If you just push a little harder, you can rest at the top of Pen y Fan.* So, I kept moving, using my two hiking poles like crutches to take weight off my feet and hoist myself up the final slope. I may have looked like a lurching Frankenstein, but I was successful, arriving at the high point of the Brecon Beacons exactly one hour after setting out.

Corn Du and Pen y Fan are truly twin peaks, with the same flat tops and small cliffs running along their north sides. If you visualize the saddle between them as the seat of a chair and the two mountaintops as its arms, you can understand why the pair were once known as "Arthur's Seat," not to be confused with the mountain of that name in the city of Edinburgh.

At the summit of Pen y Fan, I sat on a tussock of grass that had been trimmed short by a flock of sheep that were on the scene. As I ate a protein bar and apple, I felt a nudge from behind, just as our sheepdog, Lucy, does when she wants something. This prod came from an actual sheep, and it was obviously interested in my food. I took a final bite of the apple and set the core down on the grass. The animal took a sniff, then looked me in the eye and said: "Is thaaaat the best you've got? I was hoping for a ginger cream cookie." It turned and ambled away.

On the descent I skirted Corn Du but missed a turnoff back to my ascent path. When I realized what I had done, I had to head cross-country across the mountain's grassy west slope. Fortunately, I was feeling better, and my legs were functioning normally. I regained the trail, then crossed the stream, climbed the final ridge, and began dropping toward the highway. Near the bottom I caught up with a Nepalese couple who had just climbed Corn Du in flip-flops. She was smartly dressed and wore jewelry and perfect makeup. For them the Brecon Beacons weren't mountains at all—just a place to stretch their legs while on a driving tour.

WHEN I ARRIVED AT OUR hotel, I was ready to crawl into bed without bothering to wash up. The Italian Woman had other plans. She was bored after having spent the past few hours doing Sudoku in our room, and she wanted to go out. This presented a delicate situation that all climbers have faced at one time or another. You return home, having survived the most punishing day of your life, and you find yourself saying, "Of course, I'm happy to mow the lawn, cook dinner for the kids, and then take you to *Götterdämmerung*."

In Merthyr Tydfil I was directed to the shower, and then my partner ushered me to Frank and Benny's for seafood linguine and a bottle of pinot grigio. After that we paid a second visit to the cinema for a plotless comedy aimed at thirteen-year-olds, with special emphasis on farting and belching. The Italian Woman was disappointed, but I laughed and laughed. Actually, I was so rummy after my exceptional day and a half in South Wales that I would have laughed at *Götterdämmerung*.

25

Reunion

THE DAY AFTER MY MARATHON we escaped Merthyr Tydfil and made our way to the West Midlands. Our destination was the home of the late J. LeRoy Harrington-Pumphrey.

I had met the gentleman in 1980 on the Matterhorn in Switzerland. We had eaten dinner together in a climbers hostel high on the mountain, and the next morning each of us had gone on to the summit with our own Zermatt guide. Harrington-Pumphrey was an engineer and retired race car driver, then occupied with designing sleds for the luge run at St. Moritz. He spoke of fast times and alluded to even faster women. His appearance was striking—he had a sharp nose and piercing eyes, his face framed by silver sideburns grown long and swept back. Complementing his looks was an apparent obsession with his own uniqueness. He urged me to see myself that way—a man set apart from others—and at one point he suggested I have naked photographs taken of myself. At thirty-two I was in my prime, he said. I needed to record my physical beauty so that in later years I could remind myself of the man that lay within. He had posed for such pictures some years earlier, and at the age of forty-nine he treasured them as a source of reflection and pride. In his own way he had been a harbinger of today's Age of Selfies.

During the year after our Matterhorn encounter, Harrington-Pumphrey and I met once in London and had written each other several times, but then the connection was lost. I hadn't given much thought to the man until 2010, when I set about to write a memoir of my mountain travels. The first chapter described my climb of the Matterhorn, and the star of the show was the Englishman, the single most eccentric character I have ever met. His comments on his personal photographs also inspired the title of the book, *The Naked Mountaineer*. As I began assembling my notes, I thought it would be rewarding to talk once again with the Great One. Half an hour of internet research unearthed an email address for his engineering company, and I wrote to ask of his whereabouts. The next day I received a reply from his widow, Victoria.

Harrington-Pumphrey had died in 2003, but Victoria was delighted that I wanted to write about her husband, and she was keen to discuss him. We exchanged emails and spoke on the phone, and she sent photos (he was clothed) and a recording of him reading his poetry. The information was intriguing, and when Victoria and I concluded our business, we agreed that we would meet when circumstances allowed. That led to my contacting her just before our arrival in England, and it resulted in her assistance in finding a rental car. Later we scheduled the second weekend of August for a visit to her home.

THE HARRINGTON-PUMPHREY HOUSE WAS called "Meadowbrook Manor," an oddly cheerful name for the home of a man who bore the heavy burden of being extraordinary. It sat at the outskirts of Worcester in a small wood at the end of a dirt lane. It was near the city but yet completely tucked away, out of sight—a private retreat from common society.

As we stepped from the car, Victoria greeted us with a gracious welcome. She was an attractive woman, with long dark hair and a youthful figure. Before entering the house, she suggested we do a walkabout. The manor was constructed of stone, covered with ivy, and it stood in a sunny clearing surrounded by a lush garden. "Roy loved flowers, and he enjoyed sitting on that bench," Victoria explained. We then strolled to the outbuilding where Harrington-Pumphrey had spent many hours tinkering and inventing and where Victoria had often assisted. In the center of the barn stood a vintage Bentley, LeRoy's pride and joy. He loved taking long drives in it, often with Victoria at his side.

Inside the house we were shown the main floor with its entry hall, water closet, pantry and kitchen, dining room, and a comfortable parlor with fireplace. From the hallway that connected these rooms, a stair rose to the second-floor bedrooms. Overall, the home was English to the hilt—a bit dark, with old furniture, lovingly worn rugs, heavy curtains, and the smell of centuries-old fireplace smoke. There was one surprise, however. Everywhere we turned, there was a photograph of J. LeRoy Harrington-Pumphrey.

Family pictures are a requisite feature in every home. We want to be reminded of our children and other relatives, whether they live near or far. We treasure the memory of a deceased parent or grandparent. Even so, most people are content with a few photos, discreetly placed. That was not the case for Victoria. Every room—every single room—displayed one or more portraits of her late husband, so that it was impossible to move about without being subjected to his gaze. Moreover, Harrington-Pumphrey was not smiling in any of the pictures; he stared at the camera with intensity and gravitas. Even more peculiar was the fact that he was always alone. I didn't see a single picture of him with Victoria or anyone else.

On a table in the hallway lay a climbing rope, knapsack, boots, and crampons, along with trousers, plaid shirt, and wool sweater. I recognized them from a picture Harrington-Pumphrey had sent me, and I said to Victoria, "These are from LeRoy's climb of the Matterhorn, aren't they?" Yes, she replied, and she added that Roy had never climbed again, so everything was in the same condition as on the day he had returned home from Zermatt in 1980. From time to time in the remaining twenty-three years of his life, he would examine these mementos, deep in thought. I picked up one of the boots and discovered that a pebble was lodged in the lug sole.

Over sandwiches and tea on a second-floor balcony, Victoria told us that she had met Harrington-Pumphrey when she was eighteen and he was forty. She was overwhelmed by the dashing man who had risked death in auto racing and who was so sophisticated and self-assured. He had had many girlfriends, but in Victoria he found the love he had been missing. He settled down, and the two of them lived together for thirty-two years. A few months before his death, when he knew that he had lost his battle with cancer, he had made her his wife and given her his name. Interesting to me was the fact that when Harrington-Pumphrey had told me his life's story on the Matterhorn in 1980, he and Victoria had already been together for eight years, and he never mentioned her. I suppose it didn't fit with his "we are men set apart" narrative.

During their years together, Victoria had never known what to expect from Harrington-Pumphrey. He would go off from time to time, not telling her what he was doing. She had had no idea he was on the Matterhorn until she received a telegraph after the fact, with the news that "the mountain is ours." Then there was the matter of Meadowbrook Manor. One day Harrington-Pumphrey arrived at their earlier home with the news that he had a surprise for Victoria. He had bought the country home without consulting with her because he was sure she would love it. "He was right, of course," Victoria added. "He knew me so well."

It seemed that Harrington-Pumphrey had been a Svengali who dominated the much younger woman, but what did not fit that narrative was the fact that for most of their years together, Victoria had maintained a career as a social worker. She was devoted to Harrington-Pumphrey, but she had kept her own professional identity. Moreover, since LeRoy had died, Victoria had joined a senior women's soccer team and taken up ballroom dancing. She was living an active life, but still, as we talked, everything reminded her of something Roy had once said or done or an opinion he had held. At times she spoke of him in the present tense.

The bell rang downstairs, and Victoria excused herself. Moments later she returned with a man and introduced him as James. She explained that the two of them were ballroom partners. They danced three or four nights a week, and they often did other things together on the weekend. After my initial feeling that there were far too many reminders of Harrington-Pumphrey in Victoria's world, I was relieved to see that she had a boyfriend.

James was in his late sixties, tan and fit, with a twinkle in his eye. He said that he had had sixty jobs along the way to his current retirement. He had been a policeman, car dealer, and osteopathic doctor. Living in Australia at one point, he had owned a trucking firm. He had traveled the world and had lost some of his hearing due to an infection contracted while washing an elephant in a Sri Lankan river. And what a charmer he was, interested in everything and not the least self-centered. He clearly doted on Victoria, and the two of them seemed a perfect couple. Not surprisingly, he joined us at dinner and then stayed the night. What was unexpected was that he was relegated to a guest room next to ours. Did they think we would be uncomfortable if they slept together?

THE NEXT MORNING, OVER BREAKFAST, Victoria announced that all of us were going to visit her brother and his wife, who lived on the River Avon near the village of Wyre Piddle. Without thinking, I chuckled. When I was a boy, there had been a persistent rumor in my Iowa hometown that a fellow named Harold had peed on an electric fence, and the electrical current had flowed upstream and knocked him flat on his back, clutching his member. Whether the story was true or not, my friends and I had a little jingle in the cadence of the roadside Burma Shave signs: "If you piddle / on a wire / you'll sing soprano / in the choir." It was, shall we say, a jolt to have a town in England remind me of hapless Harold.

In fact, Wyre Piddle was idyllic, made more so by the colorful array of live-aboard boats lining the riverbank. Victoria led us to her brother and sister-in-law's barge, and after a relaxing lunch, we cruised through a set of self-tendered locks to Pershore and back. In the course of one private conversation, the Italian Woman learned that the family wanted Victoria to have a loving relationship, and they had become very fond of James, but they felt that they had to accept the fact that their sister was content with her widowhood and her platonic friendship with her dancing partner. As the Italian Woman described the situation to me, she commented that Victoria was engaged in what author Joan Didion called "magical thinking," a form of denial. At some point she might even become Miss Havisham from *Great Expectations*, allowing her loss to define her life. Yet we could not ignore the fact that Victoria was an accomplished person. We might feel bad for her, but she was entitled to make her own choices.

James, on the other hand, was not satisfied with the state of affairs. He and I returned to Worcester in his car, while the Italian Woman and Victoria rode with another family member. James was eager to talk about his relationship with Victoria. They had been dancing partners for three years, and he relished holding her in his arms on the dance floor. She was attractive, vivacious, and sexy, and he was in love with her, but he despaired that she was so fixated on Harrington-Pumphrey. He had never met LeRoy, and he was impressed that Victoria had been so devoted to her husband while he was alive. Yet enough was enough. Victoria should not waste her life this way. She had laid out Roy's climbing gear just for my visit, but the photos were always there. Moreover, Harrington-Pumphrey's rain jacket hung near the back door, while his muddy garden boots lay under the hallway bench. On Victoria's bedroom vanity sat a brush and comb with LeRoy's hair in them. James was weary of playing second fiddle to a ghost. He wanted to take his relationship with Victoria to a deeper level, to sleep with her and become her partner in every way. He wanted to liberate her from

Meadowbrook Manor. He couldn't last much longer. If she was not willing to change, he would have to walk away.

I offered my sympathies, and to my surprise James responded that he would be grateful if I could somehow point out to Victoria that she needed to move on. He understood that this was a long shot, but he desperately wanted her to come to her senses and love him back.

At dinner that evening, with James in attendance, we chatted about many things. Eventually, I told Victoria how much we had appreciated the weekend with her and the chance to meet her family and James. She had so much going for her, I said. I wondered, hypothetically, whether a widowed person in good health and with many years of life ahead should be open to a new relationship. She smiled and nodded. Of course, she said, that is the way it should be . . . normally. In her case, however, no one could ever replace Roy. He was the love of her life, there would never be anyone else, and that was that. She was looking at me as she said this, and she probably didn't notice that, to her right, James had shifted in his chair and his face had fallen.

Later, after we had shared the cleanup duties, James excused himself, saying, "Victoria must rise early tomorrow to go to work, so on Sunday evenings I return home when I am no longer useful." He said this cheerfully, but I knew of the great sadness in his heart. Later I peered into the second guest room and noticed that James had left clothing and personal items for the next weekend's sleepover. Elsewhere in the house, J. LeRoy Harrington-Pumphrey's things were also lying about, ready for his triumphal return.

THERE WAS A SECOND-FLOOR bathroom at the end of the hall, next to LeRoy and Victoria's bedroom. In the middle of the night I needed to use the facilities, but I didn't want to disturb Victoria. Instead, I decided to make my way to the WC downstairs. It was very dark in the house, so I was forced to grasp the banister and feel my way down the steps with my bare feet.

When I was halfway down, I was struck by two thoughts. The first was that I had no clothing on; if Victoria were to come out from her room and turn on the light, she would be nonplussed, to say the least. The second was that at the bottom of the stair hung a picture of Harrington-Pumphrey, and beneath it lay his climbing gear. I felt a cold wind float past me, and I trembled. I wanted to retreat to our room, but I had to carry on.

A few minutes later I was emerging from the WC. In the lower hallway my eyes had adjusted to the dark, and I realized that J. LeRoy Harrington-Pumphrey was staring at me. Then I heard a voice whisper: "Stephen, you are in my home at last. You were fortunate to have known me on that side of the divide, and now you will never forget me. Treasure this moment and this place . . . and there's one thing more, Old Bean. If you didn't have yourself photographed after the Matterhorn, I feel I must tell you that now it's too late."

26

Wandering in a Fog

AS THE ITALIAN WOMAN AND I left Worcester on August 12, we had three weeks left in the UK and six national parks to visit. At that point I should have been optimistic that I could achieve my highpointing goal, but there was one obstacle I couldn't seem to surmount: despite all my self-medicating, I couldn't shake the Blarney bug. I knew I needed to see a doctor, but then again, Britain's fine weather was continuing, and I wanted to capitalize on it. I would keep moving and seek a cure later.

We drove the M5 to Birmingham and then the M6 northward toward Manchester, as we had done on our trip to the Yorkshire Dales in late May. This time, however, we exited short of Manchester, turning east into the Peak District National Park. The name was tantalizing—the only one of the fifteen British parks labeled with the word *peaks* or *mountains*. I had visions of alpine vistas like those in Colorado's Rocky Mountain National Park, but of course this was England, and "peaks" is wishful thinking. A better name for the park would be the Derbyshire Dales because its topography is so much like the nearby Yorkshire Dales. The Peak District is actually less mountainous than the Lake District.

Even so, it was a beautiful drive through the western section of the park. The road climbed over green ridges and dipped into embracing valleys with tidy farms tucked here and there. I was happy to be entering this pastoral oasis in the heart of England's industrial Midlands—the park occupies the center of a kite-shaped region with Birmingham on the south, Stoke and

Manchester on the west, Leeds on the north, and Sheffield, Nottingham, and Derby on the east. With so many people nearby, the Peak District is the UK's most popular national park, and it is said to be one of the world's most visited. The high point of the Peak District is a 2,087-foot mountain named Kinder Scout, actually a tabletop plateau of several square miles without a prominent summit. Its western edge is a three-mile escarpment, along which runs the southernmost segment of the Pennine Way.

In a light rain we passed through the spa town of Buxton, home to annual music and opera festivals. From 1994 to 2013 it also hosted the prestigious International Gilbert and Sullivan Festival, but a dispute over local subsidies led festival managers to announce in a hissy fit that they would take their dear little Buttercup and relocate to Harrogate in Yorkshire. Despite its loss, Buxton is undoubtedly worth another look, but we had booked a room five miles down the road, in a village with a more musical name, Chapel-en-le-Frith. Chapel was founded by Normans, and its French name translates as "Chapel in the Forest." It is sometimes referred to as the "capital" of the Peak District, a boast not subscribed to in Buxton.

Our B&B was Forest Lodge, which sits not in a wood but in town along the highway. Its owner, a Singaporean Chinese woman named Noreen, welcomed us in from the drizzle and immediately plied us with tea and cakes. Later we followed her recommendation for dinner at a pub called the Hanging Gate and then hunkered down in our room. I was still feverish, and I wanted to conserve my strength for Kinder Scout the next day. Fortunately, the forecast was generally good—a clear morning, chance of a midday shower, and a dry afternoon. I assumed I would be fine. As it turned out, at eleven thirty the next morning I was a third of the way up Kinder Scout, soaked to the skin, and as cold and miserable as I have ever been in my life.

I HAD SEEN IT COMING. As I drove the five miles from Chapel to Hayfield, a light drizzle began. Then, at the Bowden Bridge parking lot along the River Kinder, a steady rain developed, so I stayed in the car and did the front seat limbo to get into my rain gear. It was the first time that summer that I had donned my rain pants. Then, as I stepped out and into a deep puddle and a downpour, I knew that Kinder Scout would test my mettle.

I started walking at ten thirty-five, gradually upward on Kinder Road. At a fork, signs indicated private property to both left and right. For no reason other than the need to choose one, I went to the right. I followed the road, now climbing a bit more steeply for another quarter-mile. There I came to a large gate with a prominent sign that said: "Not only are you soaking wet, but you have arrived at the entrance of these estate lands because you do not know how to read a map. You are not allowed to proceed unless you are one of us (you wish) or have the privilege of being in service to us. You are, however, on camera as you read this, and if you so much as touch this gate, we will send a pair of Pembroke corgis to bite your leg. Kindly return to the half-life that brought you here."

As I retreated to the river valley, I noticed people on the opposite side of the stream, walking uphill, and I realized that I should have gone left at the fork. Slightly wiser and thirty minutes older, I crossed over and followed the other hikers in the steady rain. We were now moving along the western, left-hand side of the Kinder Reservoir, along the slope of a hill called White Brow. At the northern extremity of the reservoir, where it filled the lower reaches of a narrow valley, my map showed two alternatives. Proceeding straight north, one path continued up the valley, which is called William Clough—*clough* rhymes with *tough* and is an ancient word for a gorge or ravine. At the upper end of the clough, the trail reaches the Kinder Scout plateau and swings southeastward along the Pennine Way.

The map also showed a less prominent path heading due east, directly up the flank of the plateau to the Pennine Way, saving nearly a mile of walking. As I was considering which way to go, a couple named David and Marie caught up with me and stopped to talk. They said that they had done the direct path once before and that it was easy to follow—a good shortcut. We decided to take it, and we started upward, with me in the lead. Five minutes later David called out: "The rain doesn't look like it's going to stop. We don't need this. We're turning back." I wanted to do the same but didn't feel I had that option.

I started moving more rapidly, up a grassy and occasionally rocky slope. Strangely, my climbing didn't feel like any effort at all, and I asked myself why. The answer came at once: I was so wretched in all other regards that I didn't notice the workout my legs were getting. It was raining hard, visibility was poor, my throat was raw, and my nose was running. I was sweating from the exertion and walking in a downpour, thus saturated through and through. Water was streaming down my legs, sneering at me and filling my boots.

This seems like the appropriate place to offer a word on the high-tech fabrics used in modern jackets and rain pants: they are an overpriced, overhyped crock. To be sure, the manufacturers offer laboratory demonstrations of how their membrane allows body vapor to pass through to the outside (it's breathable!) while holding off all forms of precipitation (it's waterproof!). Famous mountaineers and other professional athletes sing the praises of this magical substance, enticing you to spend obscene amounts to look just like them. Yet ask anyone you know who is not being paid to endorse these products, and they will tell you that it is simply impossible to hike in the rain without getting soaked twice, once on your body and once in your wallet.

The foregoing rant should not suggest that I was taken by surprise in the Peak District. I have spent most of my climbing years in the Pacific Northwest, where the Creator perfected the art of precipitation. I know firsthand that if a gully washer finds you when you are in the mountains, you are going to get wet. It's that simple, and that brings me back to Kinder Scout. An hour under way I felt as if I had stopped for a swim in the reservoir, fully clothed.

JUST BELOW THE SUMMIT PLATEAU, I met a man and woman coming down. The man was wearing glasses that were fogged up and had beads of water running down them. He did not look happy, but he stopped for a moment. He told me I was near the top, and when I found the Pennine Way along the escarpment, I should turn left. I told him I had been planning to go to the right. We went back and forth on that, and I finally produced my map, which fortunately was in a plastic sleeve. He studied it, sighed, and said that all along he had meant I should turn right.

At twelve ten, an hour and a half from the car, I reached the Kinder Scout plateau at 1,969 feet. There I found the Pennine Way, a much broader trail than the climbers' track I had just negotiated. Before continuing, I studied an unusual rock formation at the point where I had emerged from below. Visibility was poor, and I wanted to know where to turn down on my return.

The path was clear enough—running through sand and mud punctuated by slabs and boulders—but it was still raining, and now a cold wind swept up from the valley to my right. In less than a mile I came to a junction where the Pennine Way makes a ninety-degree turn to the south, continuing to follow the edge of the plateau. At that point I could hear, but not see, Kinder Downfall—such a lovely word, *downfall*—where the River Kinder pours over the gritstone escarpment and plunges ninety-nine feet, the longest drop of any waterfall in the Peak District. I crossed the river on stepping-stones and continued south.

Two-thirds of a mile later I forded another stream—this one called Red Brook—and again I could hear the water making its dive over the cliff. From there the path began to veer away from the edge, and I knew that I was not far from Kinder Scout's trig point, a place called Kinder Low, elevation 2,077 feet, or 633 meters. Most people reach the summit pillar, congratulate themselves, and return home. The problem for me was that my map also indicated that half a mile east of the path, somewhere in the soggy heart of the plateau, lay a spot simply identified as "636." So, Kinder Low is not the true high point, and anyway, why would you name a high point "Low"? Interestingly, the website walkingbritain.co.uk reports that there are actually three spots that reach 636 meters, or 2,088 feet. One of the three is apparently marked by a small pile of rocks with a protruding stake, while the others just sit there with no identifier.

I decided I had to find the true summit, and so I left the trail before getting to Kinder Low. Heading directly east, I was not more than twenty yards under way when I stopped myself. In the mist I couldn't see more than fifty feet, and the landscape was a confusing blur of black mud, humps of grass, and jumbled rocks. Also, there were many footprints in the mud, so I realized that I wouldn't be able to trace my own back to the trail. I thought I should turn around, but then I felt the cold wind coming at me from the west, from the valley where my car was parked. As long as the wind kept blowing, I would know which direction was west and I could return to the Pennine Way. So, I rambled eastward, looking intently into the gloom for any feature that appeared to be higher than the surrounding land. I knew that in the fog my chances of finding the cairn were not good, but I thought that if I climbed enough of the mounds east of the path, I just might stumble onto one of the high points.

Being cold and wet is a pretty strong disincentive to do what I was doing, and after twenty minutes I had climbed a dozen knolls and found nothing. I decided to retreat. I would go west, back to the Pennine Way. To my surprise, in ten minutes I practically stumbled into a boulder topped by a cement pillar—the trig point at Kinder Low. I was relieved to know my location, and I should have called it quits at that point, but my map showed a faint track heading northeast from that spot directly to the elusive 636. I started in that direction.

The path turned out to be no more than a scattering of footprints in the mud, and they wandered off in many directions. Once again, I was relegated to looking for hummocks, walking to their tops, and peering into the mist for the next one. *Stephen, this is idiotic.* But I need to find that summit cairn. *Look, you have already climbed fifteen or twenty mounds; one of them must have been a 636.* But how can I claim to have climbed Kinder Scout if I don't know for sure? I need to find that cairn. *You climbed from the valley to the plateau—so what if you don't locate a little pile of stones?* But I want to find the high point! *Oh, grow up. You climbed the mountain, and you have a fever. Think of what you are going through for a technicality. In the fog and rain and with no trail markers, you can't be expected to find one of three spots that look like everything else up here. You could climb fifty more humps and never know.*

Eventually, the "turn back" argument won. I somehow found Kinder Low again, with the Pennine Way just beyond. For the first time that day I took a rest break. Standing in the lee of the summit marker and sheltered from the wind, I drank some water. I also ate a few ginger cream cookies, which normally would have cheered me up, but they had no effect. Finally, I dug out my camera and took a photo of my trekking poles leaning against the pillar.

I had been on the plateau for an hour, and I was just about to start walking north on the path, to return the way I had come, when three very soggy teenage boys approached from the south. They said they were doing a counterclockwise loop across Kinder Scout. Looking at my map, I realized that their route up from the valley had been shorter than mine. The boys said it was straightforward, so I decided return by the southern portion of the loop. I left at one forty, and in less than half a mile I had dropped several hundred feet to an east-west track called Edale Road. This would take me a mile and a half west, dropping into the valley, and then north another mile to Bowden Bridge.

Edale Road was rough and rocky, but I had my walking sticks to steady myself. Then, just minutes after I reached the path, it stopped raining. Twenty minutes later the clouds began to lift, and the sun broke through. I paused to remove my rain gear. My clothes were still soaked, and my boots squished as I walked, but words can't describe how good the dry air and warming rays felt. A bit later I looked back and saw that the mist over Kinder Scout was breaking up, and for the first time I could see the plateau.

I returned to the car four and a half hours after leaving. The next morning my boots were still wet, but as I stepped outside the B&B, I was greeted by a sky of purest cobalt. There wasn't a cloud or even a hint that the mind of God had ever conceived of clouds. The Italian Woman and Noreen, who had spent the previous day bonding over coffee and sandwiches, teasingly asked if I wanted to put off our departure and return to Kinder Scout. I declined, but I have to admit that the number 636 was on my mind that morning and is nagging at me still.

27

No Beach Access

NOBODY TALKS MUCH ABOUT VISITING East Anglia. If you are a foreigner touring from a base in London, you are naturally drawn west to Stonehenge and Bath or northwest into the Cotswolds and beyond. You may join the hordes going south to Brighton and southeast to Canterbury—but northeast? True, you could travel the fifty miles to Cambridge to see its famous university, wander through King's College Chapel, and pick up a CD of the choir's *Nine Lessons and Carols*, but that's about the end of things. There's not much point going farther in that direction.

The problem is that East Anglia is generally described as lacking in scenery. Coming from the American Midwest, I can relate: very few Europeans look at a map of the United States and exclaim, "Let's take this summer's vacation in Iowa!" If you are going to England, you want to see stone villages nestled among green hills. I would have given no thought whatsoever to East Anglia, but then I discovered that it is home to a national park.

The Broads—that is the entire name—is a low-lying region of rivers and lakes just inland from East Anglia's North Sea coast. Most of us think of *broad* as a common adjective or possibly a crude term for an unrefined woman. In the United Kingdom it is also a very respectable noun referring to a shallow lake. The national park encompasses sixty-three such broads and seven rivers, which fan eastward from the city of Norwich toward the seashores of Norfolk and Suffolk. If you are into boating, marshes, and waterfowl, and if you prefer a country where they don't speak Dutch, then the Broads are for you. If you are a climber looking for elevation and commanding views, you have come to the wrong place. The high point of the Broads, an unnamed and unmarked bit of earth in a forest above the River Waveney, slouches into the record books at ninety-eight feet above sea level.

The Italian Woman and I allowed ourselves an entire day to travel from the Peak District to Norwich, and well that we did, because I was so exhausted from Kinder Scout that a drive of several hours was all I could possibly manage. From Chapel-en-le-Frith (do you suppose that the people there get tired of typing all those hyphens?) we returned to Buxton, then drove southeast through the heart of the national park. When we passed through the town of Bakewell, it was so overrun with tourists that it reminded us of Gatlinburg, Tennessee, at the entrance to the Great Smokey Mountains National Park. I want to apologize to Bakewell for that comparison. Nothing could possibly be as bad as Gatlinburg, whose cultural claim to fame is Dolly Parton's theme park, Dollywood. Still, seeing all the people milling about Bakewell, we were happy to be heading for anywhere else—even East Anglia.

East of Bakewell lay Darley Dale, worth mentioning only for its adorable name. I would like to have a granddaughter named Darley Dale.

Somewhere just past Ripley, believe it or not, we became entangled in the snarl of roads between Nottingham and Derby. When we popped out to the east, near Grantham, I got completely turned around, and instead of going east on the A52, I headed north on the A153. In my confusion I pulled over to study the road atlas, and that is when we found ourselves as quite possibly the first tourists ever to visit the village of Wilsford. That's certainly how it felt when we walked into the Plough Inn, where the seven other patrons went silent and just stared at us. Fortunately, our dialect of English was intelligible enough to garner two tuna sandwiches.

The final forty miles, east from King's Lynn, did indeed feel like Iowa. The farms were large, the tractors massive, and the land flat as a coffee table. A full five hours after leaving Chapel-en-le-Frith we finally reached our new home, a Best Western hotel at the suburban edge of Norwich. We paid an extra ten or twenty pounds for a premier room, which meant that although the air-conditioning didn't work, the extra size of the room was intended to make us feel less claustrophobic. By the time the maintenance man had given up trying to repair the cooling system, we had unpacked and lethargy had set in, so we declined the receptionist's offer of a different room. We accepted a portable fan instead. Then, violating a rather strict rule of ours, we ate dinner at the hotel's restaurant.

A DOZEN MILES SOUTH OF Norwich, over the county line and into Suffolk, the town of Bungay was beckoning. Its claim to fame is not that it is the namesake for a pain-relieving muscle cream, but that on August 4, 1577, as villagers knelt in St. Mary's Church beseeching the Almighty to spare them from a raging thunderstorm, the building was struck by lightning. From the ensuing flames a black Hound of Hell appeared and began attacking the supplicants.

> All down the church in midst of fire,
> The hellish monster flew
> And, passing onward to the quire,
> He many people slew.

When the blood was mopped up, the townspeople sought closure, and grief counselors from nearby Beccles urged them to "own" the event. In response, they incorporated the beast and a bolt of lightning into the Bungay coat of arms. Later they named the local football team the Black Dogs and organized an annual Black Dog Marathon.

The Italian Woman and I thought we would stop for lunch in Bungay and then find St. Mary's Church to experience the black dog vibe, but on that Thursday every parking space in the village center was filled. There may have been a farmers market or just an influx of devil worshippers, but we were rejected and driven out. With nothing else to do, we moved on, in search of the Bath Hills.

The River Waveney approaches Bungay from the southwest and then forms the letter omega—Ω—with the village at the bottom. At the west edge of town, the river turns north and then loops back to the town's east side, before meandering eastward to the North Sea. The interior of the omega is a miniature Holland, low and level, with pastures separated by water ditches and dikes. The outer edge of the loop is a raised bank rather fancifully called the Bath Hills. The western section of the bank is traversed by Bath Hills Road, the eastern by Free Lane. Each road dead-ends in a small wood, and a quarter-mile walking path connects the two. The Waveney loop, its interior, and the surrounding bank form the southwesternmost extremity of the national park. Somewhere along the wooded footpath lies the high point of the Broads.

Our conquest of the Bath Hills was thuswise: A quarter-mile east of Bungay we turned north on the B1332. Three-quarters of a mile later we turned left onto Free Lane, followed it for half a mile, and parked next to a farm at road's end. We passed through a gate and started along the grassy path into the trees. The track was nearly level, and it was not obvious which spot might be higher than the others. We kept walking until we saw a house ahead, and we knew that we were coming to Bath Hills Road at the far end of the path, so we turned back. Looking forward and back every fifty feet, I found a place where the trail seemed to drop just slightly in both directions. "This must be it," I said. "Can you take my picture?"

The Italian Woman obliged, then refused to be photographed herself, commenting, "Do you know how lame this is?"

Nonetheless, I congratulated her on her second national park high point—the first since Whernside ten weeks earlier. Exactly seventeen minutes after leaving the car, we climbed back in. Once we were seated, I turned to my intrepid companion and asked, "What would you like to do next?"

Without a moment's pause she responded, "Me needs me fish and chips."

Because Bungay didn't want us, we decided to drive to the coast, where we would surely find a nice seaside village, sit on a bench overlooking the water, and dive into a tasty, deep-fried lunch. Salivating, we made our way to the coastal town of Lowestoft, but once there, we couldn't find the waterfront. We knew it was somewhere to the east, but in one neighborhood after the next, we ran into dead ends. Finally, we found a sign that read BEACH ROAD, but half a block farther a second sign said NO BEACH ACCESS . We gave up and headed north out of town.

Near the hamlet of Corton, which also offered no seafront, we came upon the Broadland Sands Holiday Park, which surely deserves an entry in *Guinness World Records* in the category "Most Pennants in One Place." In the UK it is called a "static caravan" facility; in the United States it would be a "trailer park," albeit a fancy one with "crazy golf," water slides, and a casino. For the fortunate few, some of the trailers are available with "double glazing and central heating!" We stopped at the entrance, because one of the brightly colored signs promised "Fish and Chips!" Unfortunately, just next to the food stand was a betting service called "Bubbles the Bookmaker," and we couldn't bear the thought of food prepared by someone who was a friend of someone named Bubbles. Better, we thought, to press on to Great Yarmouth—a real town.

I am very sorry to tell you this, but Great Yarmouth is nothing more than a citified version of Broadland Sands. The Seaport area is a massive tourist trap with carnival rides, games, and water slides—everything except Bubbles the Bookmaker. We were pleased to see an endless array of fish stands, but as in Bungay, there wasn't a single parking spot open, and it occurred to us that a sunny day in the middle of August is a bad time to go anywhere near the coast of East Anglia. We lowered the car windows just to get a whiff of hot oil as we drove by the chippies, and then we left Great Yarmouth with the certainty that we would never again cast a shadow there.

We drove west into the heart of the Broads, hoping to find a national park headquarters or visitor center with a sandwich shop or tearoom. We found no such thing, and in desperation we broke out the apples we had bought somewhere in Wales. When we arrived at the outskirts of Norwich, we discussed taking the ring road around the city and returning to our hotel to watch television. To me, a return to bed sounded wonderful. Fortunately, the fruit had given us just enough energy to buck up and try something more ambitious, and so we followed signs to the city center.

After the requisite fits and starts, we drifted into St. Andrews Car Park and started exploring on foot. Not more than half a block away, we found the No. 33 Café Bar, a homey place run by several women. There we upped our game by ordering salade Niçoise garnished with anchovy. After that we were feeling so good that we sprung for walnut cake and cappuccinos. As we finished our lunch, we decided that notwithstanding the fact we had seen very little of Norwich, it was the nicest city in England.

Our search for fish and chips reminded us of one holiday weekend in Seattle when, with no advance arrangements, we decided to go camping in the mountains. North of the city we drove east to Stevens Pass on Highway 2, then down to the town of Leavenworth. Along the way we stopped at every campground and found them full. From Leavenworth we drove south on Highway 97 over Blewett Pass. There we did find one open campsite in the Okanogan-Wenatchee National Forest, but next door a trio of rough-looking fellows were cleaning their shotguns and drinking whiskey directly from large bottles. We moved on. Eventually, we arrived at Interstate 90 near Cle Elum, headed west past another series of NO VACANCY signs, and returned to

Seattle. Sullenly, we set up our tent in the living room, unrolled our sleeping bags, and opened the door to the balcony. We told ourselves that we were camping out. The point is that sometimes your persistence is rewarded with a salade Niçoise and walnut cake, and other times you go the extra mile but end up sleeping on the floor. In travel, as in life, there are no guarantees.

28

Mainly in the Plain

IN THE ELEVEN DAYS SINCE returning from Ireland, we had
been constantly on the move, staying in five different towns
and visiting five national parks. After our day in the Broads, the
Italian Woman announced that she was finished catering to my
nonsense. Any consideration she might have owed me for the
Irish bus tour had long since expired, and now we would spend
our final two weeks in Britain in one place. No more packing
and unpacking, no more pointless running around—we would
live the quiet country life, pure and simple. I asked if we could
at least set up camp to the west of London so that I would be in
position to visit the four national parks that lie in southwestern
England. She said she would consider it, and after unsuccess-
fully searching for a place on the English Channel, she found
us a self-catering cottage on the Salisbury Plain.

On the way to our new home we stopped in High Wycombe
to visit with my former sister-in-law, who had fled the United
States four decades earlier and had lived with a succession of
husbands in Greece and England. Barbara and I had not seen
each other for thirty years, and she had never met the Italian
Woman, so the three of us had many stories to tell over tea and
cakes. The encounter was pleasant all around but also productive, because Barbara directed us to a local medical clinic where
I could be attended to.

The doctor determined that I had strep throat. Had I recently
been on a long flight? No, but there was a twelve-day Irish bus
trip with a narcissistic guide. Was it Declan? Okay, I made that

up, but the woman did note that streptococcus bacteria are easily transmitted in close quarters with other people. I asked whether my ailment might have come by way of the Blarney Stone. Perhaps, she mused, but only if I had been foolish enough to make an open-mouth, full-on, French kiss . . . What she said next nearly floored me: "I'm going to prescribe a strong dosage of amoxicillin for the next seven days. Take it faithfully, and you will be fine. You can stop obsessing over that Irish castle." After the Italian Woman's experience in the north, I was stunned to find an English doctor who did not view antibiotics as the spawn of Satan.

We found Brambleberry Cottage on a tiny lane in Spittoon, a Wiltshire village so tiny that I dare not use its real name. Its only establishments were a pub and a church. The owner of the cottage, a man named Peter, was waiting to check us in. He told us that he and his partner Paul live in Kent, work in London, and use the cottage and its lush garden as a quiet retreat. The house was a cozy two-up, two-down, with an extension for the bathroom, and it was so filled with antiques and knickknacks that there was very little room to turn around. The furniture was draped in throws and doilies, and the overall feeling was of your grandmother's home—not exactly what you would expect from two men. They had also retained a certain authenticity by not installing a shower or even a shower hose in the tub. For the first time in many years, we were forced to bathe ourselves using a plastic pitcher to rinse off.

Following a trip to nearby Warminster to stock up on groceries, we unpacked and settled in. The next day was Sunday, and we walked to morning prayers at the village church. We were two of ten people in attendance, apparently not enough of a critical mass for an actual mass. The entire service was read and sung from a first edition of the Book of Common Prayer. The overall experience was of skillfully applied torture.

Afterward we visited with the locals, all of whom knew where we were staying because there were no other accommodations for rent in Spittoon. I was particularly intrigued by a fortyish woman in a long skirt and tidy hairdo. Her name was Cordelia, and she lived with her parents on a nearby estate. She apparently devoted herself to keeping a few sheep, chickens, and horses, and it was she who would ride clip-clopping past our cottage every morning and evening. In another setting she might have been a Royal, puttering around until Mum and Dad departed, leaving the palace and its responsibilities to her. She was a bit weatherworn, and her handshake was milkmaid firm, but she was not coarse. She reminded me of the farm girls of my youth, and I found her attractive. I wondered what had led her to stay in Spittoon or return there, where everyone else was old. She had to have a story, likely a good one and quite possibly sad. In any event, despite some difficulty making eye contact, Cordelia was friendly, and later, at her suggestion, we ate Sunday lunch at the village pub. She said we would enjoy the roast beef with Yorkshire pudding, and she was right.

We spent the next three days reading books, watching movies, and surfing the internet. My antibiotics were beginning to take effect, and for the first time in two weeks, I began to feel normal. One afternoon we took a two-mile walk in the countryside north of the village. The Salisbury Plain was a rolling, mostly treeless landscape, with vast fields of corn and barley extending in all directions. As we walked, the TANK CROSSING signs reminded us that we were in the middle of a military training area. People in church had told us that for several weeks every summer, there are fighter planes roaring overhead and hundreds of khaki green vehicles rumbling about. When that happens, many locals repair to the South of France.

By Wednesday evening I felt ready to climb again, and I wanted to take advantage of the still-excellent weather—the forecast for Thursday was for midseventies and little chance of rain. I printed route descriptions for the high points of the Dartmoor and Exmoor national parks in far southwestern England—they lay close enough to each other that I could visit them both in one day. I asked the Italian Woman whether she might want to join me, with the understanding that she would have to stand by while I was on the trail. I believed that the climb in Dartmoor would take two hours and the walk in Exmoor less than an hour. She reminded me that she had driven through Somerset and Devon twenty-five years earlier, but under the circumstances she would come along for the ride; despite all of its charms, Brambleberry Cottage was confining, and she needed some breathing room.

AS WE DROVE WEST THE next morning toward Exeter, my thoughts went back three decades to my previous visit to that region. It was 1983, and I was touring with my father. He was sixty-two, I was thirty-five, and we hadn't seen much of each other since I had begun my career in Seattle eight years earlier, far from my Iowa hometown. I would like to say that our week together was a wonderful bonding experience, but it was surprisingly awkward. We didn't argue—to the contrary, both of us struggled to make conversation. In addition, his snoring kept me awake, and by day he wanted me to make all the decisions—what to see, what to photograph, what to order from the menu. He was a friendly and easygoing man, but his passivity became irritating. He lived another twenty-eight years, and we remained on good terms, but neither of us ever suggested another trip together.

Dad and I had visited sister-in-law Barbara, who was then living in Windsor with a husband she later called "the biggest mistake of my life"—an Irishman who ultimately found his true calling as a bartender in Phuket, Thailand. From Windsor we drove to Bath, then Cornwall. We toured the castle ruins at Tintagel and worked our way out to Penzance and Land's End. We then followed the south coast eastward through Plymouth, Exeter, Lyme Regis, and Weymouth. At some point we must have come very close to Dartmoor and Exmoor national parks, but I don't recall driving into either one, and we did not do any hiking. Ten years later the Italian Woman was exploring the area, but she, too, seems to have stayed on main roads just outside the two parks.

The highest mountain in Dartmoor National Park is 2,037-foot High Willhays, which locals pronounce *Willis*. It sits in the northwestern corner of the park and is accessed from the A30 near the town of Okehampton. Actually, the closest highway exit is west of Okehampton, at the hamlet of Meldon, but it proved to be an eastbound exit only. As a result, we were forced to continue westward on what must be the single longest stretch of dual carriageway in the UK without a place to get off and turn around. That diversion added a half-hour to our drive, and by the time we found the parking lot at Meldon Reservoir, we had been traveling three hours—much longer than I had expected. The Italian Woman commented that she did hope for more than just a day in the car, and that put me under pressure to make good on my two-hour estimate for High Willhays.

We left the car at twelve thirty and walked together across the dam, at an elevation of 950 feet. From there the Italian Woman would amuse herself by ambling along the reservoir as I trotted up my mountain. The route description called for me to go westward above the reservoir and then angle back up the slope of Longstone Hill, but I saw a rough track going directly up the hillside, and I decided to take the shortcut. I worked my way upward through thick patches of fern that showed dark green against dry, straw-colored grass. At 1,352 feet I crossed the top of Longstone, and from there I could see my initial target, a rounded mountain one mile to the east, called Yes Tor. A nub of rock marked its 2,030-foot summit. I set out directly toward it, walking cross-country through grass that had been cropped by black cattle that were grazing about.

At one point I followed an old farm road for a quarter-mile, then returned to grass as I climbed up the western slope of Yes Tor. A sign just off the road reminded me that the area is occasionally used as a military firing range, and I recalled a warning in my Lonely Planet guide: "Some unexploded shells may lie beneath the surface, so use common sense if you need to relieve yourself in the open. While burying your excrement is recommended in most country areas, random digging around Dartmoor is not a good idea."

At the top of Yes Tor a small radio antenna and a cement pillar were positioned on an outcropping of rock, and from there I had to decide which of the distant mounds was High Willhays. My os map ended at Yes Tor, but I knew that High Willhays was directly to the south, so I started fishing for my compass to figure out where south was. One of the mountains, which I thought was in the right direction, looked discouragingly far off.

Just as I was opening a small gear bag, I was startled by a hearty voice saying, "Hello!" A man appeared from behind the pillar, and a few seconds later a woman followed. I returned the greeting and asked if they knew where High Willhays was. They pointed to a low hump half a mile off—seven feet higher than Yes Tor—and said that the true summit of Willhays was a prominent cairn on a flat rock at the south edge of the summit area. I thanked them, told them my wife was waiting at the car, and scurried off. It was one thirty, and I had an hour to complete the climb and get back to the Italian Woman.

It was sunny, probably seventy degrees, and a cooling breeze was blowing. Conditions for walking could not have been more perfect, and the wide path between Yes Tor and High Willhays was ridiculously easy, crossing a broad, grassy expanse. The plateau dipped slightly between the two summits—just enough to show that they were separate. It would have been nice to linger, lie in the grass, and watch the white clouds drifting overhead.

Ten minutes from Yes Tor, just before reaching the top of High Willhays, I picked up a stone, prompted to do so by an online source that said it is tradition to add to the mountain's summit cairn. The cairn was actually a six-foot-high pile of loose rocks, and I stepped carefully onto it to add my contribution to the very top of the heap. That afternoon my pebble became the highest point in Devon and, at 2,037 feet plus the height of the cairn, the loftiest bit of England south of my beloved Kinder Scout.

As I had done on other summits, I ate a few ginger cream cookies and drank some water. I took a photo of my backpack leaning against the cairn (it usually doesn't occur to me to take a selfie) and started down.

Rather than return by way of Yes Tor, I aimed directly toward Longstone Hill, ambling down the grassy northwest slopes of High Willhays. From time to time I had to walk around boggy areas or past cows that regarded me with suspicion. Along the way, and far from any path, I came across a circle of flat gray stones stacked three feet high. The enclosure had not been used for a very long time—the rocks were jumbled, and there was no litter or sign of a fire. Also, grass had grown in the center, and it was un-trampled. The ring had once been large enough for a few shepherds and their dogs to seek shelter from a howling storm. I wondered: Who were these people? What did they discuss as they huddled together, and in what language? What were they wearing? What did they eat? Were they afraid for their lives, begging their gods to protect them? Did they have loved ones waiting for them down in the valley? Had they chosen this life, or was it forced on them?

Approaching Longstone Hill, I reconnected with the farm road and followed it in a curve around the northeastern side of the hill. I was soon above the reservoir. I could see the Italian Woman standing on the dam, waving, and I scrambled down through the grass and ferns. We were reunited at two thirty, and her first words were: "Nice going. Right on time." As we strolled back to the car, she told me of an extended conversation she had had with a local couple. They were flattered that I would want to walk up a modest hill in Devon, but the idea of dashing about the UK seeking out high points was, to them, most peculiar. The Italian Woman agreed wholeheartedly, but she loved me nevertheless.

NEAR OKEHAMPTON WE FOUND A roadway restaurant that was modeled after an American Denny's, the sort of thing we normally try to avoid. On this occasion, however, we appreciated being able to order a large chicken salad—the perfect cold lunch on a warm day.

Returning to the A30, we drove as far as Exeter, where we turned north. Following the River Exe, we passed through Bickleigh, Tiverton, and finally Exbridge, where we entered the southern extremity of Exmoor National Park. Unlike Dartmoor, where we had barely encroached into the park, we would make a full south-to-north transit of Exmoor. The going was slow, and I became frazzled by the endless curves, narrow lanes, and oncoming trucks, but the reward was that Exmoor was a jewel. The Exe danced and sparkled beside us; the farms and hamlets were clean and comely.

At Wheddon Cross we turned left onto the B3224, where I pulled over to take a photo of a wide, gently pitched hill on the skyline three miles to the northwest. Even from that distance I could see a small bump at its top—likely the summit cairn. We had found Dunkery Beacon, or Dunkery Hill, whose 1,703-foot summit was the apex of Exmoor National Park. After a mile we left the B road and turned onto an unnumbered lane, still heading northwest. Inadvertently, I drove right past the Dunkery Bridge car park and trailhead, because I was looking for a bridge that never materialized. Instead, I followed the lane northeastward, and I soon noticed that the mountaintop was now to our left and then, a few minutes later, behind us.

When I saw a second car park, I pulled into it and stepped out, clutching my OS map. A man walked over, and he showed me that we were still on Dunkery Beacon but now northeast of its summit. The good news, he said, was that from Dunkery Bridge the road had climbed, and from this spot the walk to the summit was even easier. It was less than a mile on a well-developed trail, the Macmillan Way West, and the elevation gain was only 225 feet.

I explained the situation to the Italian Woman, and I asked whether she might want to walk with me. She said she was worried about her ankle, still tender from her fall in June, but she would give it a try. I offered her my arm, and like two aging sweethearts on a seaside *passeggiata*, we sauntered up the fine path. It was five thirty, and the late afternoon sun was bathing the landscape in shades of yellow and gold. We were hill walking across a slope of heather in Somerset, and we were doing it together.

Even at our leisurely pace, it took only thirty minutes to reach the massive summit cairn of Dunkery Beacon. This one was not just a pile of rocks but had been professionally laid and cemented together into a perfect cone eight feet high. This was the skyline nub we had seen from Wheddon Cross. From that spot we looked down on endless miles of green fields separated by hedgerows, punctuated here and there by dark forest preserves. On the earlier trip with my father, it had been October, and when we crossed the Bodmin Moor in Cornwall, it was gray and bleak. I was happy to find that Devon and Somerset in August were verdant and alive.

To the north we could make out the blue of Bristol Channel, our next destination. The salads of Okehampton had worn off, and the Italian Woman had another craving for fish and chips. This time her wish was granted. After an achingly scenic descent to the coast, we wound our way to Minehead, and there we located the waterfront and discovered it to be free of the carnival atmosphere of Great Yarmouth. Many people walked about, but the commercial establishments were mostly restaurants and small hotels. We found a parking spot near the beach, directly across from a food stand. While in line, we talked to a local couple who lived twenty miles away and had come for the evening to give their two spaniels a romp. The man said he had been to Seattle once, and he wanted us to know that he liked it better than San Francisco. He had never heard of Omaha.

We ate on a bench overlooking the sand and water. In such a setting, after such a delightful day, any food would taste good, and this meal truly did. We lingered, relaxed, and watched people enjoying themselves on what was surely one of the warmest evenings of the year.

The drive back, initially on hills overlooking Bristol Channel, was eye-catching, but at Bridgwater we lost our daylight, and the remainder of the trip was a succession of small roads in pitch-dark. Now then, England does have a first-rate health system, but it apparently has no funds left to spend on highway lighting. A perfectly sensible rule for night driving is: Just Don't Do It.

We passed through Glastonbury, Shepton Mallet, and Frome before returning to familiar ground in Warminster. By the time we reached Spittoon, it was ten o'clock, and we had just spent eight of the past twelve hours in the car. That was more than we had expected, but in the process we had accomplished so much. Two more high points, lovely vistas, and the Italian Woman's return to the mountains. And for the first time in a month, she had gotten her fish and chips.

29

It Ends in a Car Park

THE ONLY HIGH POINTS THAT remained were South Downs
National Park, between London and the English Channel, and
New Forest National Park, directly west of South Downs. The
crown of South Downs—a 919-foot hill called Black Down—
was only fifty miles as the crow flies from Spittoon. From there
it was another fifty miles west to Telegraph Hill, at 417 feet the
highest elevation in New Forest. On the map it appeared that
we could travel to Black Down in an hour and then drop farther south to Bognor Regis on the English Channel. Following
the coast westward, we could drive through Portsmouth and
Southampton as far as Bournemouth, before turning north and
stopping in New Forest on our way back to Brambleberry Cottage. The Italian Woman had wanted to spend our final two
weeks on the sea, but at the height of the school holidays she
hadn't been able to find a vacancy. Now, on a leisurely day trip,
we would see what we were missing.

But of course, English crows don't fly in a straight line, and
despite ten weeks of having driven in the UK, I was just as
naive as when I arrived. The fifty air miles from Spittoon to
Black Down were actually seventy-two road miles, and the trip
took two and a half hours. First, we were caught in a backup
near Stonehenge, which, incidentally, we had managed to avoid
during our two weeks in Spittoon, under the theory that if you
have seen it once—which we had, many years earlier—there's
not much point in going back. Then we somehow got lost in
Basingstoke, but that was child's play compared with Farnham,

where road repairs had brought traffic to a standstill. It took forty-five minutes to navigate two miles through the town, population 39,488, and we escaped only by taking the wrong highway south, which forced us onto unmarked country lanes to get to Haslemere, the village nearest Black Down.

So, here is my advice for anyone planning to use a car in England: If your destination looks close enough to drive in an hour, add a little extra time to allow for slower going through the villages, then multiply the total by two or three. Even then, never ever make a time-sensitive appointment without a half-day cushion, especially if you are going anywhere near Farnham, county of Surrey.

WE HAD HOPED TO MAKE a brief stop at Black Down and then enjoy a seaside lunch in Bognor Regis, but by the time we reached Haslemere, breakfast had worn off. More to the point, the Italian Woman was in her food-deprived state of grumpiness, so we had no choice but to present ourselves at a sandwich shop and ask the owner for the most tasteless meat he could slap between two slices of white bread and take twenty minutes doing so. And if the sodas could be room temperature, so much the better.

Two women at the Haslemere public library cheerfully gave us directions to the Black Down car park, two miles out of town along Tennyson Lane. Near the Down, they told us, Alfred Tennyson had built Aldworth House in 1869 as his summer retreat. Fourteen years later he accepted a peerage (when I was a boy playing Authors, I had always thought that Lord was his middle name). His cottage had running hot water—the poet was known to bathe three times a day—and the home's stone and woodwork inspired his description of King Arthur's castle in *Idylls of the King*. Tennyson loved walking on Black Down, and in fact he owned sixty acres of it.

Black Down is a long, forested ridge, a dark-green peninsula above the surrounding countryside; it projects to the south from a wood named Black Dog Copse. *Down* is a curious word. It usually refers to a low position or direction, but in England sometimes down is up. In the case of Black Down, the word means "hill," and it relates to *dune* or the Old English *dun* and the suffix found in *Snowdon*.

When we parked just off the lane, we were near the northwest corner of Black Down and only slightly below its flat top. Our walk of three-quarters of a mile to the high point would gain only 140 feet.

The path was wide and flat, similar to the trail on Dunkery Beacon, but this one was wooded. A short distance from the car, just before setting foot on the down proper, we came to an opening in the trees. From that vantage point we could see the ridge extending to the south. Due to intervening hills or perhaps as a result of clouds on the horizon, we could not make out the English Channel twenty miles off. Tennyson, however, once wrote to a friend: "You came, and looked and loved the view / Long-known and loved by me / Green Sussex fading into blue / With one gray glimpse of sea."

The Italian Woman and I strolled along, using the midday sun for navigation wherever paths branched off to the left or right. When we met people, most of them locals walking their dogs, they confirmed that we were moving south. The main trail ran directly to a viewpoint on the southern prow of Black Down, but along the way we needed to leave the path to find the summit monument. As best I could tell, it stood fifty yards off the trail, somewhere in the trees. When I thought we were in the vicinity, we turned right along a faint track, perpendicular to the main path. In something like fifty yards we found another track parallel to the main one. There I suggested that the Italian Woman go north, while I turned south. The forest was not thick at that point, and there was no danger that we would lose each other.

We hadn't been separated for more than a minute when I heard my partner calling, "Here it is!" I turned back and joined her at the cement column, which stood at the edge of a clearing, partially in shade. It had taken only twenty-five minutes to get there. We took pictures of each other, and the Italian Woman flashed that enormous smile of hers that everyone finds so inviting.

Rather pleased that she was the one who had discovered the monument, my mate readily agreed to return to the main path and walk to the end of the down. That took only ten minutes more, and at a point called Temple of the Winds we were rewarded with a sweeping view of the countryside rolling south. Twenty miles distant, beyond a set of low-lying hills, lay Chichester and Bognor Regis. Twenty miles east was Gatwick Airport, whose air traffic was visible. And directly below us lay the spot where, on November 4, 1967, a Heathrow-bound Iberian airliner plunged to the ground, killing all thirty-seven people on board. With that sober thought we decided we had seen enough of Black Down.

IT WAS THREE THIRTY WHEN we left Tennyson Lane. We knew that not only had we missed lunch on the coast, but there would not even be enough time to do a quick drive-by. Resigned to another excursion with far more driving than sightseeing, we returned to Haslemere and made our way to Winchester. From there we followed the M3/M27 around Southampton, and west of the city we planned to leave the motorway at Brook Hill and head northwest on the B3078. It should be no surprise if I report that it was not as easy as it looked on the map, and we found ourselves south of the motorway, passing through tiny hamlets called Minstead, Bartley, Netley Marsh, and Cadnam. All was not lost, however, because the New Forest countryside was pastoral and soothing. The region had been set aside in 1079 as a royal hunting ground, and much of its unfenced pastureland has been preserved for nearly a millennium. The area is protected by a tangle of ancient laws, finally being designated a national park in 2005. The park has no hills or mountains, but its grasslands, wetlands, and woods are scenic and even a little wild. Lying only eighty miles (and probably five hours driving) from London, New Forest is a jewel of rural preservation in a densely populated country.

Once we found the B3078, only five miles lay between us and Telegraph Hill. We soon discovered that *hill* was as serious a misnomer as ever made its way onto a map. To the naked eye the land was flat in all directions, but at the junction of the B3078 and the B3080 sat a dirt parking lot whose entrance was marked with a green monument sign proclaiming FORESTRY COMMISSION—TELEGRAPH HILL. Unfenced horses grazed nearby, and I asked one of them: "Is this it? Could this really be the high point of a national park?" She just ignored me.

The Italian Woman, on the other hand, sensed the importance of the moment. She happily took a picture of me at the monument sign and even posed for one herself. She smiled and held up five fingers—her fifth and final high point. "Stevie, I'm proud of you," she said affectionately. Then she added, "Can we leave now?"

SO, THERE WE WERE, AT 5:20 p.m., the twenty-seventh of August. Over the course of ninety days we had crisscrossed the British Isles, and I had reached the high points of four countries and fifteen national parks. At the beginning of June those dots on the map—places with names like Ben MacDui and Kinder Scout—had sounded remote and daunting. Now that the journey was over, I realized that the summits of Britain were not remote at all, but accessible to anyone with a car and a pair of boots. Not rugged or savage, but green and gentle. The primary challenge of the national parks had been internal to me, about my own attitudes and my flexibility as a traveler.

I was not the first to ascend any of the ancient heights of Albion or even the whole lot of them, and I had set no records other than being the first person in my family to do so. There, in a car park at the edge of New Forest, I knew that my walking accomplishments were far less important than spending three months in the occasionally confounding but utterly endearing British Isles. Best of all, I had done it with the Italian Woman. She had tolerated my peculiar desire to complete a personal checklist. In fact, she had recognized that this was important to me, and at times she was the one to urge me onward. In return, I had done my best to be a good companion to her and to spend as much time as possible doing the things she wanted to do. And so, the two of us, two people with quite different ideas on how to spend a holiday, managed to share a peripatetic existence, a summer of pleasure, pain, and quiet moments, and we came out of it happy to be together. Through our misadventures in the land of low mountains and high tea we had found each other, still in love and still in one piece.

Epilogue

High Point Tally

AFTER THREE MONTHS OFF THE Continent, we had restored our visa-worthiness, and we were able to enter Italy as tourists. So we did, and we settled in Perugia for two months, followed by three weeks in Rome. But this time we kept an eye on the calendar, and as a new ninety-day deadline approached, we knew that we again had to make for the exit. We considered returning to the United Kingdom, but December there is dark and damp, and our fondness for British life yielded to our common sense—we diverted to Puerto Vallarta. I should add that in Italy and Mexico I never so much as gazed at a mountain, let alone set foot on one. The Italian Woman—truly in her element in the urban environment—was in charge, and most of the time we knew exactly where we were.

I must also recognize that, more recently, Britain itself has been on the move, the result of a 2016 public referendum approving withdrawal from the European Union. As this book was going into publication, it was still uncertain how that decision would play out, but one possibility may be the eventual secession of Scotland from the United Kingdom. If that happens, the two Scottish national parks will no longer sit on the UK list, and the trip described in this book may prove to have been one of the last grand tours of Britain's fifteen national parks.

Now, in order to remain true to my climbing sensibilities, I would like to offer a chronological tally of my United Kingdom high points, all of them reached in the summer of 2013:

Sequence	Name of high point	Height	National park and country	Date climbed
1	Whernside*	736 m (2,415 ft)	Yorkshire Dales NP, England	June 4
2	Round Hill (Urra Moor)	454 m (1,490 ft)	North York Moors NP, England	June 7
3	The Cheviot	815 m (2,674ft)	Northumberland NP, England	June 11
4	Scafell Pike	978m (3,209 ft)	Lake District NP, high point of England	June 17
5	Ben More	1,174 m (3,852 ft)	Loch Lomond and the Trossachs NP, Scotland	July 6
6	Ben Nevis	1,344 m (4,409 ft)	*Not in a national park*, high point of Scotland	July 8
7	Ben Macdui	1,309 m (4,295ft)	Cairngorms NP, Scotland	July 10
8	Slieve Donard	852 m (2,795 ft)	*Not in a national park*, high point of Northern Ireland	July 27
9	Snowdon	1,085 m (3,560 ft)	Snowdonia NP, high point of Wales	August 6
10	Foel Cwmcerwyn	536 m (1,759 ft)	Pembrokeshire Coast NP, Wales	August 9
11	Pen y Fan	886 m (2,907 ft)	Brecon Beacons NP, Wales	August 9
12	Kinder Scout	636 m (2,087 ft)	Peak District NP, England	August 13
13	Bath Hills*	30 m (98 ft)	The Broads NP, England	August 15
14	High Willhays	621 m (2,037 ft)	Dartmoor NP, England	August 22
15	Dunkery Beacon*	519 m (1,703 ft)	Exmoor NP, England	August 22

| 16 | Black Down* | 280 m (919 ft) | South Downs NP, England | August 27 |
| 17 | Telegraph Hill* | 127 m (417 ft) | New Forest NP, England | August 27 |

*With the Italian Woman

Finally, let me note that in this book I have included a fair amount of information on the roads we traveled and the paths we walked. I have done so to satisfy my own penchant for detail and to assist anyone who might be interested in replicating any portion of our journeys. There is, of course, the distinct possibility that I have left something out and that you will find yourself in the wrong town or on the wrong hill. Rather than rue the day, please embrace the experience as your own British adventure.

Study Guide

Did You Read the Whole Book?

WITH THE EXPECTATION THAT THIS book will become mandatory reading in secondary schools throughout the civilized world, this study guide is provided for the benefit of our overworked and underpaid educators. Note to teachers: These thematically arranged exercises should provide hours of intellectual stimulation for your students. Reward them by continuing your practice of grade inflation.

With Regard to the Author's Experiences

1. Comment on the level of intelligence involved in taking a reluctant, non-climbing individual up a mountain shortly after spending five months in Spain eating tapas.

2. How would you celebrate arriving at the highest point in the British Isles?

3. What would you recommend to avoid the illness that eventually drove the author to seek medical attention in High Wycombe?

4. Create a list of adjectives (those are words that describe other words) that apply to your cellular phone service.

With Regard to Everything Italian

5. Will you ever marry an Italian woman? Explain your enthusiastically affirmative answer.

6. Analyze this hypothetical: While traveling with an Italian woman, you wish to suggest that she do something differ-

ently. What approach should you take? What should you avoid?

7. For extra credit: study the Republic of Italy's visa system and write a five hundred–word essay explaining how an intelligent person might obtain permission to enter the country.

Matter of Britain

8. If you had built a colonial empire on which the sun never set and then lost it, what adjective, other than *great*, might you use to describe your nation? Be creative.

9. If you were next in line for the British throne,

   a. How would you spend seventy years waiting?

   b. Which common personal chores would you assign to a fawning assistant?

10. Should they just let go of Wales? In the alternative shouldn't they at least prohibit namesconsistingofphrasesthatlookexoticbutareactuallyrathermundane? Discuss.

11. Recalling the author's pleasant flashback in the village of Wyre Piddle, find a list of UK towns, select one, and write a paragraph describing why you love its name.

12. In the same vein, identify which of the following is not an actual British town:

   a. Upper Crust

   b. Dressing Down

   c. Tory Bottoms

   d. Spanking Proper

   e. Tassett under Standing

English Language and Literature

13. With your study partner, create your own list of things that should be included in the definition of *pudding*.

14. Define *Eton mess* as it relates to your own choices in life.

15. Write a sonnet extolling the virtues of single malt scotch whiskey and ginger cream cookies.

16. Multiple choice: To which of the following classic English works would you favorably compare this book?

   a. *Withering Heights*

   b. *Tristram Loves Shandy*

   c. *How Green Was My Pudding*

Recipe—Authentic British Ginger Cream Cookies

1 cup ginger cream

24 cookie halves

1 knife

Using knife, gently spread cream on one cookie half. Apply second half. Yields twelve.

Pair with: Talisker, Laphroaig

Suggestions for Further Reading

The Naked Mountaineer: Misadventures of an Alpine Traveler (University of Nebraska Press, 2014, ISBN 978-0-8032-4879-3)

The Book of Common Prayer (Church of England)

Acknowledgments

TO THE FORCES IN THE universe who conspired to plant us in the British Isles for an entire summer, *grazie*. Without your good offices, we would never have met the agreeable people described in this book, including Roger and Margaret Purkiss, Les and Veronica Grant, Jendra Kaplicka, Olivia Harrington-Pumphrey, Barbara Ewing, Kevin Johnson, Billie Prue, and Manisha and Vivek Malhotra. Thanks also to Jen Sutton and her colleagues at Collett's Mountain Holidays.

Special gratitude goes to Debbie and Nigel Hunter and to the members of the Cave Rescue Organisation in Clapham. Without their help we might still be sitting on that mountainside in Yorkshire. In the same vein we thank the National Health Service for opening its doors to us.

It has been a real pleasure to work with the dedicated staff at the University of Nebraska Press, including Rob Taylor, Courtney Ochsner, Elizabeth Zaleski, and Elizabeth Gratch. Thank you for taking me on for the second time. During the past several years, as I have conducted readings of *The Naked Mountaineer*, I have heard again and again how well respected UNP is in the literary world. And that leads me to the independent bookstores and libraries who have hosted me. I urge everyone to do their shopping at the The Bookworm (Omaha), Elliott Bay Book Company and Third Place Books (Seattle), Tattered Cover Book Store (Denver), The Traveler (Bainbridge Island), or a bookshop near you. Then pop into your public library and give the librarian a hug.

Thanks to Brent Spencer and Susan Yirak, and to Rod Wagner of the Nebraska Library Commission, for their ongoing advice and encouragement.

Thanks, Carmelicia. Let's do it again.

Finally, I am grateful to you for picking up this book. Your enthusiasm for reading makes it worthwhile for people like me to chain ourselves to our keyboards until the stories emerge.

Praise for *The Naked Mountaineer: Misadventures of an Alpine Traveler* by Steve Sieberson

Named by *Booklist* as one of 2015's Top Ten Sports Books

"Take a walk on the weirder side of mountain life with Sieberson, whose alpine misadventures include bizarre local cuisine, insistent music fans, and oh yes, the Englishman who revels in taking naked selfies. . . . This delightfully anecdotal memoir hops from Norway to Japan to Greece, among other high altitude locales."

—BACKPACKER.COM

"For climbing and travel enthusiasts, this will be a treasured read."

—JAY FREEMAN, *Booklist* starred review

"Author and lawyer Sieberson enjoys his hobby, which has taken him around the globe and to the top of many of the world's mountains. His mountaineering trials and tribulations provide ample fodder for this informative and amusing book."

—SARA MILLER ROHAN, *Library Journal*

"It is Sieberson's unabashed enthusiasm for climbing that is exposed here, and his bare appraisal of it all is engagingly straightforward. *The Naked Mountaineer* guides us up mountains—including his beloved Matterhorn—and offers an insightful travelogue. The observations are fresh and yet familiar, as welcome as clean socks from a well-worn rucksack at the end of a long day's hike."

—KYLE WAGNER, travel and fitness editor for the *Denver Post*

"A delightful commentary on Sieberson's global travels and opportunities to climb many of the world's highest and most challenging mountains."

—ROD WAGNER, *The NCB News*

"From Western Washington to Italy to Indonesia, this is a fun and delightful book. For anyone who has traveled or wished to travel to remote places, Steve Sieberson's *The Naked Mountaineer* gives an entertaining and humorous account of his mountain adventures and the characters he met along the way."

—MIKE MAHANAY, president of the Washington Alpine Club